The Weight of Violence

The Weight of Violence

Religion, Language, Politics

edited by
Saitya Brata Das
and
Soumyabrata Choudhury

OXFORD
UNIVERSITY PRESS

Oxford University Press is a department of the University of Oxford.
It furthers the University's objective of excellence in research, scholarship,
and education by publishing worldwide. Oxford is a registered trademark of
Oxford University Press in the UK and in certain other countries

Published in India by
Oxford University Press
YMCA Library Building, 1 Jai Singh Road, New Delhi 110 001, India

First Edition published in 2015

ISBN-13: 978-0-19-945372-6
ISBN-10: 0-19-945372-1

Typeset in Adobe Garamond 10.5/13
by Zaza Eunice, Hosur, India
Printed in India by Rakmo Press, New Delhi 110 020

Contents

Part II

Acknowledgements

We would like to express our gratitude to Indian Institute of Advanced Study (IIAS), Shimla, and Indian Council of Philosophical Research (ICPR) for sponsoring the international conference on 'Religion, Violence, Language' that was held at the IIAS in April 2012. We thank Professor Peter Ronald deSouza, the then Director of IIAS, for his indispensable encouragement and tireless support. The editors have profited from an anonymous reviewer; we wish to acknowledge our gratitude to him/her. We also thank Ashok Sharma and Debarshi Sen from IIAS who were indispensable in making possible the conference and the publication of this collection. Siba Barkataki took out her precious time to translate Gérard Bensussan's difficult text into English; 'thanks' to her for the good work. And 'thanks' to Gérard Bensussan from the University of Strasbourg, and Mike Grimshaw from Canterbury, New Zealand, for contributing their thoughtful essays to this collection. Their contributions have decisively enriched this collection. Soumyabrata Choudhury wishes to acknowledge IIAS for permission granted to republish his article titled 'St. Paul, Gabriel Naudé, Antonin Artaud: Three Violent and Delicate Exceptions to Law and Liturgy', which was previously published in his book *Theatre, Number, Event: Three Studies on the Relationship between Sovereignty, Power and Truth* (Shimla: IIAS, 2013), pp. 275–290.

At the end, but most importantly, the editors would like to express their deepest gratitude to Professor Franson Manjali from Jawaharlal Nehru University, New Delhi, and Professor Eric Jacobson of Roehampton University of London for making the conference possible. The idea of the conference on violence, basically, came from Eric Jacobson. It was *his* 'messianic' idea! Unfortunately, they could neither attend the conference nor contribute their papers to this volume. If something of a sort of regret or sadness remains with us today, it is their irreducible absences.

Saitya Brata Das
Soumyabrata Choudhury

Introduction
The Weight of Violence

Saitya Brata Das

DESTRUCTION OF SENSE

This is a collection of the papers read in the international conference on 'Religion, Violence, Language' that was held at Indian Institute of Advanced Study (IIAS), Shimla, on 9–11 April, 2012. The conference was jointly sponsored by ICPR, and IIAS. The essays by Gérard Bensussan and Mike Grimshaw, however, are especially written for this volume. The conference was attended by scholars from diverse parts of the intellectual world, such as USA, Portugal, Chile, Australia, Israel as well as with some of the most promising young scholars from India. From the experience of the conference, we hope to say that it was an intellectual event in true cosmopolitan spirit; in other words, it fulfils the idea of an *international* dialogue or exchanges of ideas that help enriching each of us, while allowing us to put to test each of our assumptions, presuppositions, or even prejudices. It is in this sense, and not in the most prevalent sense of an academic-scholarly discipline, that the conference may perhaps be called 'philosophical', if philosophy in a very profound sense is none other than a passion, or, 'the passion for the universal' par excellence. Especially because of the overwhelming importance of a topic like this that poses profound problems for the world at large and the world today which is so affected and wounded by both religious and linguistic violence, it is all the more imperative for the scholarly-philosophical community to come together from all parts of the world to debate, to think, to question, to critique and to find solutions—at a 'philosophical' level, with its own limitations as well as in its fecundity—to the problems posed by the phenomenon of violence to our very *existence* itself.

How do we now make *sense of existence* in a world that is constantly threatened by destruction of sense, for is it not that violence none other than destruction of sense itself which always is the very *sense of existence* as such? This question—so profound and urgent in our time—that finds such searching inquiry in the works of Jean-Luc Nancy, a prominent philosopher of our time, is a question that demands responses that are existentially engaging at all levels of thinking and questioning, acting and living, demanding responses from us that go beyond the national-communitarian-religious boundaries as well as disciplinary closures that often determine to a great extent the space called 'university' as it exists today. Therefore it is necessary, more than ever before, for a collection of essays from scholars and philosophers from different parts of the world, dealing with different concerns in their singular modes of inquiries, to come together so as to think again and to think together the simple and yet so difficult and intriguing questions like: Why violence exists in the world? What are the modes of its manifestation? What are the ways that violence derives legitimacy in the world, and why at all we give, unknowingly or knowingly, legitimacy to violence that threatens to destroy our very sense of existence? In the face of the undeniable fact of countless events of violence in today's world, should we develop some form of pacifism as counter-movement, as counter-discourse? Will that alone be enough? What are the conditions of possibility of a discourse of a radical pacifism, let's say 'a pacifism beyond pacifism', an unconditional pacifism, should such a thing to be able to exist at all; and if, supposedly such a thing should exist, what would it look like? Should not the posing of a question to violence articulate itself in the form of 'a critique of violence'? Is not any critique, one that is historically conditioned—and whatever impurity and contingency the 'historical' brings with it—already an act of violence?

These are difficult questions, difficult because of their aporetic character with which they persist without satisfying us with any short-termed, conditioned form of resolution and strategic negotiations. They are difficult because we brush them aside as being mere 'philosophical', 'abstract', and 'jargons' that do not fit comfortably to our familiar modes of questionings, our habitual disciplinary-methodologically dogmatic mode of formulating our 'academic-scholarly' question-answer and because these questions often exceed our 'good' faith in the intelligibility of the world. They are, therefore, not anyway harmless, value-neutral adjectives that we use but they actively take up, negatively, the role of not allowing certain disturbing questions to be posed in a fundamental manner. In fact, they inhabit or resist, better to say foreclose, any possibility of posing some disturbing questions in the nakedness of their apparition. What we refuse to accept is that the world is often so unintelligible, and that in the face of such unintelligibility of the world, our academic disciplines, in their dogmatically fixed contents and methods that stake their faith in the intelligibility of the world, often appear to be superficial or inadequate. It is such dogmatic understanding that is to be called 'jargon' or 'abstract' thinking, to put it correctly, to which our academic world often succumbs. It blindly believes that the world is intelligible enough, corresponding to our neatly arrived categories or methodologically sophisticated scientific concepts, and that if we do not understand anything, that has to do with the *hubris* of arrogant scholars who make everything so unintelligible by their strange language which no one understands, while everything is in fact 'homely' today, familiar and harmless, and that events like violence or evil are mere privation or minor aberration of our otherwise 'the good old world'.

It will be a necessary task to unmask the blindness of this faith in the intelligibility of the world, and to show, beneath this lucidity, a negative 'jargon' that violently legitimize various closures of the world. If, however, one takes a 'step back' from the habitual assumptions and modes of inquiries, one can't help being assailed by a fundamental problematic: What is the phenomenon of violence if not that which in its manifestation, or in its inexhaustible *potentia* of manifestation, puts into question the idea of intelligibility of the world itself? This demands, first of all, that we acknowledge the measurelessness and nakedness of the apparition of violence in today's geo-political reality which is referred as 'the globalized world', the world brought together and pulled apart by the immeasurable accumulation of the capital and consequently, the unconditional spreading of the culture of mass consumption, and the dilapidation and impoverishment of the world at the same time, the damage to 'life' and utter destruction of the 'spiritual'. In the face of such a condition, or rather, un-condition, responses need to be unconditional as well and not just strategic, conditioned politics of negotiations on the part of the technocratic-bureaucratic apparatus of state or multi-national company sponsored rationality. The unconditional critique of violence must be accompanied by an infinite vigilance over this self-proclaimed 'neutrality', over the technologically-bureaucratically perfected rationality that offers 'peace' in the name of 'democracy' from which, however, totalitarianism of an unheard shape will never be far from. This is a violent democracy that never has ceased utilizing the power of the exceptions for routine violence at everyday level in the most imperceptible corners of life. Nothing of life must now remain sacred from the touch of this 'violence' (let's say: from the 'benevolent' culture of consumption, which is, in fact, a tautology. All modes of consumption in the neo-liberal economy can only be culturally mediated which, while differentiating and multiplying itself only escalates the tendency of the homogenization of the 'demand and supply'). This is now the most a-theological theology of violence, the 'ethics' and 'metaphysics' of the culturally-economically mediated 'globalized' world where theology means accumulation of wealth at the costs of others. In such an *atheologically theological* age in which all critiques of religion have now exhausted itself, where is religion now? What happened to it? In what language do we now speak of these terms, concepts, events, realities like 'religion', 'politics', 'ethics'? What is happening to language itself? Would it not lament in this burden of over-determination and over-signification? Is not this demand of signification and determination, which is the demand on language as such, inseparable from the rationality of the technological-bureaucratic-economical apparatus, itself an act of violence: violence on language, and linguistic violence? Does the 'essence' of language primarily reside in the act of signification and over-determination of reality which we are forced to recognize as 'ours', or does it reside elsewhere? How would we now point toward, in what language and in what trembling speech, in what mode and in what gestures, this 'elsewhere', this 'utopia' (in true sense of not yet having a *topos* or a 'place')–the utopia of redemptive happiness which is increasingly replaced and eroded by the illusion of pleasures which mass media and entertainment industries daily feed us with? How to point towards or to hint, in a non-signifying gesture, to that which has *not yet* a place, which does *not yet* have a 'habitation and a name', and yet which alone will redeem us from the violence of over-signification and over-determination? The critiques of violence may not ignore such questions. It will be illuminating here to quote the concept-note of the conference.

While manifestations of violence are quickly dismissed as exceptional, the difficulty of understanding the character of violence and thus the task of a critique of violence persists, for violence assumes a mode of existence that is not merely manifested and actualized (having the character of 'figure' or 'form') but also carries the sign of its *potentia*, of a not yet. Therefore a possible critique of violence can only be an infinite interrogation of the historical world at any given moment where violence is seen not as one particular question amongst others but in a more fundamental and in a more originary manner, an interrogation which seeks to disclose the grounds of its appeal to legitimacy and ultimately its justification. Hence the problem of violence is not only sociological or historical in any particular, localizable events or sites of violence, but is also a metaphysical question, or rather, the very question of metaphysics. The task of the critique of violence is not to see it as 'religious' violence in one instance or as 'linguistic' violence in another (where 'religious' or 'linguistic' may appear merely as qualifying, or adjectival terms) as two particular questions, but to interrogate the very place of religion and language in relation to existence itself. Its aim is to render apparent the immanent claims of violence, to demonstrate its regulating principle, its legitimacy, and hegemonic standing. This would demand the deconstruction of the violence of the dominant metaphysics itself: its claim to totality whether in the name of a transcendental principle, or without any such transcendental principle but rather in the name of immanence constitutive of historical reason.

Such a critique of violence may assume a certain political theology that seeks to challenge the violence of historical reason, a political theology that takes as its task the delegitimization of any violence that justifies its action under the guise of divine sovereignty or a task that assumes the critical-immanent demand of reason, the infinite questioning of any justification in the name of an exceptionality contained within the power or force from which every 'law-positing' and 'law preserving' violence can be said to emerge. Religion and language may appear redemptive or suspect, both dangerous and promising, and for this reason, one is justified in asking whether the primacy upon which philosophy stands, the discursive grounds of reason, can offer an alternative to the manifestation of violence. Or is it necessary to open up a far more radical critique that would demand the old notions of religion and language to be thought anew? If the justification of violence on religious/linguistic grounds is to be understood not merely in an accidental manner, we require an explanation of religion and language as inherent and originary locations from where the question of the power of violence positing itself is inseparable. Religion and language would be revealed in their originality as promises in the name of which a negative gesture, a critique of violence, can be carried out.

What remains of religion and language without the force of violence? Can religion and language be thematized as self-enclosed entities governed by their pure essences, or without attributing to them essential and inherently governing principles? Should they be seen as that which wounds us because their promises are negated, erased, forgotten by 'originary violence'? Where does this 'originary violence' stem from? The urgency of these questions cannot be denied, and for this very reason, demands a more rigorous examination of the metaphysics of potentia that underlie the empirical-historical investigations of violence once it has taken place. We wish to question the apriori status of violence, not merely its manifestation. What may be at stake are commonly held notions of the secular and the theological, the end of metaphysics and ethical self-certainty, eschatological politics, and the irremissible claims of historical Reason.

This book hopes to address the Aporias that the phenomenon of violence presents to us in the hope of working toward a new critique. From the very etymological meanings of religion (*religio, re-ligare*), we refer to at once its binding and communal, de-linking and fractural characteristics, a generosity of being and a violence of existing. Its absolute homogeneity and absolute heterogeneity may disrupt any possibility of what Jean Luc Nancy calls 'being-in-common'. How to address, without minimizing them, such aporias that the phenomenon of violence on religious and linguistic grounds presents to us today? How to make sense of the logic of exceptionality when such logic appears to govern most ethico-political decisions and determines the very sense, or senselessness of existence for us? What remains of the ethical or political in the face of such unspeakable violence that presents itself to us every day?

THE WEIGHT OF VIOLENCE

One may infer from above that a collection of essays of this nature would consist of essays that will address the question of violence from different perspectives and would have irreducibly varied modes of inquiries, questioning and addressing the problematic at stake. This poses, however, serious problems for the editors since a collection of this sort demands a certain thematic unity which it apparently lacks. The editors, on the one hand, must respect the singularity and multiplicity of the approaches of these essays, each essay bearing its unique and irreducible signature; and on the other hand, they must also be brought under certain thematic unity in order for the 'collection' to manifest itself as 'collection' at all. The editors must confess that they still don't have a 'solution' to this problem. As such, the 'decision' to divide the book into two parts lacks a strict criterion of division at hand. What is at all taken into account is the possibility of finding certain 'affinity' or 'resonance' among the essays that belong to a specific division, and the possibility that the essays reciprocally illuminate each other. This attempt is more a 'mosaic' of ideas or a 'constellation' of stars—two most fascinating metaphors that Walter Benjamin uses: as in a mosaic of ideas or constellation of stars, when these discontinuities are brought together, they suddenly disclose their affinities to each other without being absorbed into a homogeneous unity imposed by a violent power from outside. In this sudden occurrence of resemblance among discontinuous events, there arises for us recognition of their truth-content which lies immanent in the sheer nakedness of their apparition but is not yet explicit as the element of their 'truth'. In the task of editing itself, the editors must, thus, constantly encounter the power of violence that lies in imposition of unity and in the idea of 'collecting' and 'editing' itself. In such cases, they must find such 'affinities' without doing violence, as much as possible, without guarantee and without any given, calculable, workable and programmatic solution at hand. This is, one can say at best, the 'gesture' or 'style' of arranging these essays rather than any well-defined or strict method.

The volume opens with the essay by Gérard Bensussan, titled 'On Violence: Mimesis, Death Instinct, and Alterity'. In this beautiful and thoughtful essay, Bensussan brings together three thinkers of violence– Réne Girard (the notion of 'mimesis'), Sigmund Freud (his notion of 'death instinct') and Emmanuel Lévinas (his 'phenomenological'—ethical notion of the face of the other)—to argue that the radical movement beyond violence is inseparable from such a weakness that is irreducible to power or mastery. Opening to the infinity or transcendence of other from the very heart of finitude exposes us to that which can't be grasped in the 'violence of the concept': the utter vulnerability and fragility of the unique and singular other. Violence, going by this way, can neither be grasped with any empirical criterion that distinguishes 'good' (legitimate) from 'bad' (illegitimate) violence or by any anthropological method (that deduces the cause of violence from the nexus of historically given conditions that give rise to violence) or even conceptual movement of thinking (that thinks that to stop violence, it may be necessary to use violence). Violence (*bia*) in its profound connection with life (*bios*) is that which binds us with the possibility or impossibility of speech, speech that responds to the face of the other in responsibility. This response, this speech that responds and wherein lies our responsibility, this response puts us in a double bind: the face that prohibits my act of destruction or annihilation is the very face that I would want to annihilate. Further from minimizing this aporia of violence, Bensussan suggests via Lévinas that an ethical response to violence may be elicited via this aporia or double bind or alternation: between 'talk' or 'kill' (between 'speech' and 'murder'), between the power having at our disposal to annihilate and the resistance to this power, arising from this utter weakness and fragility of the other, un-assimilable to the conceptual language of philosophy.

Andrea Potesta's essay 'The Experience of Silence: Derrida and the Language of Negative Theology' attempts to show that the question of violence is at the very heart of Jacques Derrida's thought. It is a fundamental challenge of deconstruction to open the *spacing* where the movement of *differance* takes place between speech and power. This leads Potesta to link or de-link the distance and proximity of Derrida's deconstruction to negative theology, and his attempts not to reduce the language of 'no' (as well as 'yes') saying to any unitary principle of negativity. What arises, then, in this challenge of deconstruction is the very challenge of violence in and through and beyond language that links and de-links us to violence at the same time as *differential*, non-homogenous, and non-unitary saying. The task and the challenge of deconstruction of violence must traverse through this *passage* fraught with ineluctable aporias: to say 'no' without having to reduce to a mere negativity by subsuming it under the fold of a conceptual violence. In the highly erudite and complex essay that follows Potesta's essays—and I can't do justice here to this un-introducible essay in these few words—Jason Wirth argues that the question of 'stupidity' constitutes as a 'critical element in any possible critique of violence'. Reading such diverse thinkers and writers together such as Schelling, Deleuze, Nietzsche, Whitehead and Musil, Wirth argues that philosophy must constantly negotiate the two-fold violence that link or de-link philosophy (or thinking) to violence: 'metaphysical dogmatism' and 'melancholic paralysis', without being consumed in it. At stake here is not only the kind of 'thinking' which is called 'philosophical' in its intimate connection with madness and stu-pidity but the very ontological status of 'the human' as such which is exposed to the animality and divinity at the one and same movement of opening of being itself. This is difficult problem where at stake is not so much determining which violent act is legitimate or illegitimate but rather the ontological question per se concerning the ontological status of 'humanity' as such in (non)relation to the divine and animals.

Aïcha Liviana Messina's essay ' "No Eye has Seen It": The Renewal of the Human Condition in Marx and Lévinas' brings together, in a manner that surprises us, the historical materialism of Marx and the messianism of Emmanuel Lévinas. A reading of Marx purified of eco-nomic determinism ('human beings do not recover their humanity through distributive justice', says Aïcha in this essay) is brought closer to the eschatology or messianic intensity of hope of a Lévinas but without the 'form' assumed in dialectical movement of the former. The result is a transformative reading of Marx whose profound messianic promise of a world renews Marx himself in relation to us, we who are the bearer of this messianic promise. She hereby follows, extends, and renews the line of thinking opened up by Jacques Derrida's deconstructive reading of Marx where Marx is thought, not as an apologist of a definitively estab-lished worldly regime, but as a messianic thinker who conceives an infi-nite task of opening up the world to an unconditional justice to come. Such messianic justice, promised but not yet fulfilled, can neither be reduced to the conditioned order of law nor to be reduced to any polit-ico-economic determinism.

This essay is followed by the illuminating reading of Walter Benjamin by Maria João Cantinho. Benjamin's critique of the ideology of 'homogenous empty time' opens us to the radical re-thinking of the question of history, and the place of violence, a messianic vision of his-tory that is discontinuous and interruptive. This vision of history, mes-sianic in resonance, is not a political projection and one that is teleological conceived, on the level of the profane, worldly politics but has merely 'religious', that means, messianic sense. Task of the historian is to read the dialectical image that momentarily advents like a lightning flash. In a nuanced reading, Maria shows that the germ of Benjamin's idea of messianic justice can be seen in his very early essays. My own essay follows somewhat the same movement of thought, opened up in Maria Cantinho's essay. Reading Franz Rosenzweig, especially his *The Star of Redemption*, I suggest that the innermost movement of the messianism of Rosenzweig lies in his radical critique of violence that accompanies certain speculative-dialectical determination of history and that lies in the very philosophical notion of 'concept' itself as such: 'the violence of the concept', so to say. The following essay by Mike Grimshaw discusses Walter Benjamin again, raising the question of violence in the framework of political theology. Relating to the famous debate between Carl Schmitt and Jacob Taubes, Mike Grimshaw argues that while liberalism is an attempt to escape from history, the events of violence remind us in the most concrete manner 'the abandonment of humanity within history'. Our ethico-political responses to the undeniable phenomenon of violence must arise from this very abandoned (non)condition of humanity which is always already opened by the historicity that makes possible, if not in a determinate manner, these very responses. Herein lies, according to Mike, the distance and proximity between political theology of Schmitt and the negative political theology of Jacob Taubes: how to think the notion of 'abandonment' in historical terms without reducing this historicity to a determinate form of historical reason. This is a task which, as Mike shows, still ours, difficult as it is.

John Frow's highly argumentative-polemical essay 'Kingdom-Come: Eschatology and Apocalypse' reads a popular series of Christian novels that posits an end of history and he discusses the problematics associated with politics of such eschatological notions of the 'end of history'. The essay ends with contrasting such transcendental violence of Apocalypse (that brings together Benjamin and Carl Schmitt, Réne Girard and Sorel) with the possibility of a critique of violence that understands violence primarily in terms of *dispositif* without positing violence as unitary category in immediate connection with law and sacred as it is seen in the case of the former. One can see here a *polemos* raging within this collection itself: against the messianic approaches of some other essays, Frow attempts to think the question of violence as the question that can properly be addressed only if *dispositif* of certain historical condition is taken into account. Frow here follows, without making it explicit in his text itself, the approaches of Giorgio Agamben and Michel Foucault who differ, in this respect, from that of Levinasian and Derridian thinking on such questions.

Clayton Crockett's essay 'Capital Violence' argues from certain 'post-secularist' perspective that the phenomenon of violence in the age of neo-liberal globalized world can't be separated from spreading of the unrestricted capitalism all around the globe that increasingly produces and reproduces the polarization of accumulated wealth and consumer products. It is only in relation to such overspreading of unrestricted capitalism that the rise of neo-conservative violence of a reactionary type can at all be understood. He thereby situates the problematic of violence in the historical condition of our 'post-secular' age and envisages the possibility of a radical political theology that must be able to think together and separately 'capitalism' and 'religion'. For him, such radical political theology must envisage delegitimation as its fundamental task which will put into question the violence that arises when religion is use used and abused in certain manner by a certain politico-economic world-order. Soumyabrata Choudhury brings together the materials of (apparently) disparate character such as the letters of St. Paul, the political writings of Gabriel Naudé of 17th century and Antonin Artaud's texts in an attempt to reveal the juristic and liturgical obligations that underline the politico-theological question of the occidental history. Here thereby discloses what is essentially at stake in such obligations which determines in such a complicated manner the very destiny of our historical existence.

Part II of the volume opens with Rustam Singh's deeply poetic text. In this beautiful essay, Singh shows that the human beings draw justification of their violence against animals by their alleged 'superior' 'power to think'. Reading through some of the seminar philosophical works, Singh argues that such justification does not earn much merit insofar as using such a 'power' to think, human beings have been able to deploy such irresistible mechanism of repression and such technology of violence turning against themselves, against nature and animal kingdom. Asha Sarangi's highly erudite essay on linguistic violence takes a close look at the *nation-form* as one specific form of violence, and thereby arguing that it is necessary to take into account the historical locatedness of the phenomenon of violence in order to understand the logic or reason of violence as such. She thus understands the question of violence in terms of 'social categories of community and national identity formation', arguing thereby that 'there is some kind of relationship between onto-logical and social violence, one defining the other in a democratic politi-cal society'. She illustrates her essay by undertaking a historical-social analysis of South Asian, especially Indian social context where an intri-cate nexus is to be found between religion and language. This essay is followed by the article of Selma K. Sonntag who argues that the linguis-tic cosmopolitanism of certain sort, in their privileging of instrumental (which she associates with the universal) over the affective (which she associates with the particular), fails to radically address the phenomenon of violence. Situating the linguistic cosmopolitanism played out in India, she shows that we need to have a more political understanding of lan-guage than that has been offered by the linguistic cosmopolitans. In a thoughtful re-examination of the violent event of India-Pakistan parti-tion through Partition literature, Prachi Gurjarpadhye relates phenome-non of violence to language and speech as such. The powerlessness of language—powerlessness that lies in its very structural finitude—to sig-nify such traumatic events and experiences in the given mode of cogni-tion does not, however, leads to the abandonment of language on our part and to relapse in absolute silence; rather, it is the very self-transcen-dence of language that resonates in the creative works of art and litera-ture which can have 'cathartic' effect, a new mode of cognition that offers redemptive possibilities for us. The concluding essay by Veena Sharma is a re-examination of the role of conflict in traditional as well as in post-colonial African society. What emerges from her essay is the role that is played out by resources of traditional religion that, instead of fol-lowing the strictly punitive measures of exclusion, prefers to arrive at reconciliation and forgiveness which alone may heal the wounds left by violence. In that sense, even conflicts may have, indirectly though, posi-tive roles to play in the constitution of the social fabric. This recognition comes from the traditional wisdom of African society that any rigorous or strict exclusion of dissonance or adamant insistence on the unitary principle of society and on consensus as the only mode of political exis-tence itself can have violent consequences for us.

***

It thus appears that the essays collected here are of very diverse concerns. Each essay appears like a highly individual and irreducibly singular contribution to the problems of religion, violence, and language. Yet they touch each other in varying degrees and intensities, in their distance and proximity, and through this touching and withdrawing, pose the fundamental question of this collection of essays: how to make sense of existence—*existence as sense*—when such a possibility is constantly threatened by this destruction of sense? Each of these essays is a unique response to this difficult question. Perhaps the decisive answer was not arrived at, but it is hoped that at least the question was raised in a decisive manner.

Part I

1 On Violence
Mimesis, Death Instinct, and Alterity

Gérard Bensussan

One does not have to be an expert to observe that philosophy and violence share an eternal relationship. The former is known to have questioned the latter's grounds right since its Socratic constitution and presumably even before that. We can even go to the extent of considering that the secret of the philosopher—a secret much out of proportions—would be to want, by all means and mostly by convoluted ways, a world without violence. Besides, a philosopher is perceived in a rather ironical manner. 'Ah, so you are a philosopher!' otherwise means: you live in your own world, on the clouds, whereas the world 'the real one', the one that you ignore so arrogantly, is full of tears and blood. This persistent insinuation brings forth an obvious fact which merits some consideration.

But one must start by observing the situation in its complexity. It is to be noted, to begin with, that there are philosophies of violence and violent philosophies. These can be more or less linked to philosophies of life: life and violence, in Latin, just as *bios* and *bia* in Greek, confirm a common and clearly problematic etymological origin. These philosophies could also stem from grand superstructures of ontology which, in order to help reflect upon and understand violence, in other words to determine its meaning, assign it a place and a function in history so as to discover its rationale and even its legitimacy. There could also be a form of violence which is characteristic of philosophy itself, the 'Violence of Concept', which seizes all that lies outside it in multiple, diverse and complex forms only to categorically reduce them to a familiar uniformity and unity, in order to justify it. 'To be justified' astonishingly means to legitimately commit an act of violence—either on a rearing horse or on a reality that offers some resistance, thus domesticating it and proclaiming oneself its master with the intention of making sense out of chaos, both of which boil down almost to the same thing.

The word 'violence' takes one who tries to define it, a philosopher or otherwise, in very different directions with extremely contrasting definitions, right from violence that is 'symbolic' to the most barbarous extermination of the masses. We could perhaps, while keeping in mind the common etymological foundation of life and violence, *vita* and *vis*, begin by attempting to temporarily distinguish between good and bad violence. The first would stand for a fighting spirit, a vital aggression, a spirit of competition characteristic of all human action which is required to construct and develop; the second, on the other hand, would embody all that threatens human constructions, individual or social, the danger of a destruction that cannot be undone, i.e., annihilation. 'Good' violence would thus signify a function which is shared by all living beings, that is entirely mobilized for the phylogenetic service of the species and its survival, through the ontogenetic individualization of *zôè*. I attack and make use of violence when my vital interests are at risk, I defend them, I defend myself and this defence is legitimate. This 'good' and 'just' violence is nothing but the realisation of my capability to act and to live. It could even stand for life itself in the sense that the latter is always engulfed in conflict and self-preservation. The other form of violence, the 'bad' and the wild, excessive, uncontrollable violence, would be, on the contrary, the sinister ally to the destruction of mankind, which as a result is condemned as it spells out all that stands for bad or even for insanity. The analytical distinction between 'good' and 'bad' violence, useful in describing or classifying a number of phenomena is limiting in its approach. In reality, the entire problem begins when one is faced with specific and singular cases where it is required to differentiate between different types of violence. All 'bad' violence present and represent themselves as 'good', in other words as rational, understandable, justifiable, based on an indefinite variety of reasons and motives. All violence is categorized as *ubris*, i.e., hybrid: it asks itself the question of its necessity or its pseudo-necessity which is supposed to anticipate other forms violence which is more serious. All forms of violence, whether individual or historical, without exception, must indicate what they aim to achieve in order to legitimize their existence. Therein lies the first node of complication, i.e., in the discourse, often silent, which accompanies an act of violence: if I resort to violence, it would mean that I fought back against violence, my violent intervention is only to restore a state of harmony which was disturbed. It is when they justify thus, that all forms of violence fall under one explicative and argumentative category, that is, violence takes place only to suppress violence. As a general ruling, the violent person speaks in the aftermath of his violence, once the act is accomplished. This is the very reason why, as we all know and very often state, that violence gives birth only to more violence. The moral dilemma is displayed around this very problematic node. It is important to tell the difference between different forms of violence. However, it is practically impossible to come to a consensus regarding the modalities and the criteria of such a judgement. Inquiring on the nature and the essence of violence inevitably brings us to a point where we question ourselves on what we are as moral subjects. I will come back to this point later.

For the moment, we have pointed out the inextricability of the two faces of violence, the good and the bad, the difficulty that lies in clearly distinguishing them, and the profound ambiguity that follows, the paradoxically evasive character of violence that presents itself as an enigmatic constant feature: it has always existed and it will always exist, it represents the permanence of disorder, of brutality, of oppression, not only in the history of man but also in his individual behaviour. Its ineradicable nature leads to an anthropologic pessimism which sometimes seems to be insurmountable. One must also observe that when the nature of violence is taken into account within the domain of violence and is evaluated with regards to its consequences, then, it orients itself towards a general rule of conduct which unconditionally justifies its vitality. There has to be a limit to the movements that provoke an outrage as soon as a border is crossed: *yesh gvoul* (there is a limit!) is the name of an Israeli pacifist wing, *basta*, that's enough; this cannot go on further, etc. Without the imposition of a limit, the overflow and the spontaneity of energy can endanger life itself, as pushing the limits to the extreme can put life in peril. However, nothing is less assured than finding this limit that needs to be defined. But how does one understand this violence which is implanted in the living and yet carries the danger of death? This lack of distinction troubles the possibility and the efficiency of the divide that categorically separates the human from the inhuman, the will to live from the desire to kill. Herewithin lies the underlying reasons as to why violence can never suppress violence, contrary to what it establishes while trying to prove its legitimacy. What does that signify? That the difficulty we face in arriving at a *definition* for violence which is more or less stable is in no way logical. It is the indicator of the fragility, the finitude of man. Fragility, that takes us further to the question of bad and the impossible or improbable moral progress of humanity. It is perhaps required at this point to approach the difficulty from a pragmatic point of view: we can very well speculatively consider that human violence is radical, in the Kantian sense, that it is unfathomable and baseless, created only to fight against itself, to eliminate or partially limit its own boundaries. Relief aid given to victims of human-to-human violence, of wars, for instance, which is a measure that preserves our dignity, in the Kantian sense, constitutes the pragmatic interface between theory and practical. I would now like to reflect upon this problematic axiom: What is this inscrutable nature of violence? Who is the morally uncertain and fragile subject that can at any given time be either the victim or the author of violence? Who is a victim in such unpredictable conditions?

FIGURES OF WEAKNESS

I will start by determining what we might generically call *figures of weakness* (Abel, Isaac, Iphigenia), in a (counter-)Nietzschean sense, that is to say in an effort to re-evaluate the radical evaluation of values or 'transvaluation' proposed by the author of *Zarathustra*. These figures are both similar and different from that of the victim of violence whose condition would require taking into account the social, psychological and other such conditions that led to the act of violence. The situation of the victim, without considering that of his violent aggressor, does not sufficiently leave any information on the circumstances that could more or less help us to understand the act of violence, even though one can detect the factors that could have led to it. If an act of violence could be reduced simply to the factors that led to it, we could almost certainly foresee the source of a violent act and predetermine the conditions of its possibility and its apparition; just like in the famous film, *Minority Report*, where a 'precognitive' determination of its agents was done in advance. This means that I would globally accept violence of a certain 'profile'. I would therefore start by predetermining, classifying, and foreseeing with the help of the expertise that I claim to possess (which is, however, not portrayed intelligently and precisely in the film.) However, no one is capable enough to retire from the weight of violence, nobody is rightly preconditioned to bear its weight and nobody can escape from it. One can undoubtedly consider that certain situations (urban for instance), certain configurations (socio-economic), and certain frustrations are the carriers of violence. But one must always pay attention to the considerable margins of error attached to them, which are so significant that they hardly remain as marginal. Such causal explanations are based on a resigned tautology, which becomes evident owing to its poor 'explanation', according to which all imposed violence inevitably produces a reactionary violence. One must try to put together two diverse and heterogeneous elements: 1. All forms of violence are not equally legitimate, 2. All violence is violent. Violence caused by a revolt that is carried out to reaffirm one's dignity, which is the result of 'that is enough', is obviously not of the same nature, degree, or context as the calculated and premeditated violence which pursues a more rational motive (the economy, a revolution, development, logic, a superior interest) and considers violence as a necessary process that can be overcome, a good in the form of bad, a bad in search of the good. At the same time, how does one neglect the harsh effects of the radical constant which states that all violence used against violence in order to put an end to it is categorized as 'good intention'. The road to hell is paved with it and the aforementioned violence will continue to prevail uninterrupted forever. One will recall Lévinas' last words in *Otherwise than Being*: 'For the little humanity that adorns the earth [...] in the just war waged against war to tremble are shudder at every instant because of this very justice. This weakness in needed. This relaxation of virility without cowardice is needed for the little cruelty our hands repudiate' (Lévinas 2004, p. 283; 1994, p. 185). Justice and the shudder that it entails: not refusing to listen to the cries caused by violence that is just; it is legitimate to surrender oneself to violence but not without trembling at the sight of the same. The disproportion pointed out by Lévinas between 'the little humanity', i.e., the multitude of violence of all sorts that 'adorns the earth', and the 'little cruelty' that we manage to curb in our finite existence, allows us to question well beyond the limits of the bad infinite which advocates that violence suffered leads to violence that is more or less justified, thus causing more violence in return and so on.

According to a line of thought which does not belong to the social sciences or to philosophy, the great narratives which lay the foundation of the history of the western civilization since the Biblical-Hebraic tradition or the Greek tragedy, offer exemplary and fundamental narratives of the origins and the consequences of violence.

The first incident of murder in the history of humanity, emphatically speaking, is that of Cain. The biblical text talks of the latter as an honest cultivator who believed in offering God what he produced. Cain's younger brother Abel was fearful, modest, virtuous and generous. Both the brothers, sons of Adam and Eve, were the first children of this world. It just so happened, for reasons we do not know, that God agreed to accept the offering made by Abel and refused that made by Cain. Cain murdered Abel out of resentment and frustration. This paradigmatic murder holds the first fundamental significance: all murders are a fratricide, violence against a humanity of brothers. Moreover, it signifies that we are descendants of the murderer and not of the murdered, i.e., of Cain and not of Abel. The path of humanity paved by the latter, which is radically non-violent, is forever closed by his physical elimination. After having committed the murder, Cain is expelled to the 'East of Eden', left to wander and to work on unwanted infertile lands. However, God protects him with a 'sign' that scares away all those who intend to kill him and become murderers of the murderer. It is as if the survival of humanity itself (according to the biblical text, Cain does not delay in taking a wife and having a son) was not possible until the violence of murder was not interrupted by God. And this interruption itself is not possible unless it is nonfatal, with a divine protection and deterrent which saves the assassin and gives him a long line of descendants. Thus, an inherent violence, deeply rooted in the desire, the urge and the sentiment of injustice forms the basis of the history of humanity. Cain is the unloved older child, the younger being preferred to the elder. Cain's desire to murder and the accomplishment of his desire can be understood as his irresponsibility and his lack of accountability 'Am I my brother's guardian?' We understand and share his opinion to a certain extent, being descendants of Cain we have inherited a reactive violence and wish to see the same reactive power of Cain in Abel. In this way, the Cainaic gesture of fratricide, might threaten to *repeat itself* in an abyssal manner—as a matter of fact, it is repeating itself in many forms and many modalities. God wishes to curb this fatal repetition and he does it with a 'sign' which protects the violator. Men, the sons of Cain, and not those of Abel, alas can imitate and reproduce this divine interruption. Born murderers and not victims, who nevertheless are nostalgic of Abel, are capable of putting an end to the chain of violence. The victims, right from the beginning, represent the younger brother who was sacrificed as he was too weak to stand up against the murderer and was reduced to nothingness, to a mist or a breadth of air (*hevel*) quickly removed from the surface of the earth.

In Isaac's story of 'sacrifice'—from what the Jewish tradition rightly calls his 'binding'—the victim, here also, is a child, a being completely left to our mercy. Isaac's innocence is proved by the kinds of questions he asks his father while they walk up Mount Moriah. All Abraham could give as a reply to his son's questions was a deafening silence as a way of contradicting God, the same God who protects Cain and demands the death of his son who he loved more than his own life. But the 'sacrifice' is annulled, as opposed to that of Abel. The task was not accomplished, and it seems like the objective of the narrative is to recount Abraham's endurance when he was put to the test and faced the absurdity of violence and the death of his son. He did not utter a word of retaliation, and especially not the question: 'Am I the guardian of my son?' The death demanded by god was *Abraham's responsibility*.

In Euripides's play as well, Iphigenia's sacrifice is not accomplished. The high priest had asked for her sacrifice to appease the gods so that the Greek fleet could take advantage of the favourable winds and easily make their way towards Troy. Iphigenia incarnates the exemplary figure of visible weakness. Pure and chaste, she was still a child when she learnt, to her terror, that she was going to be immolated and then discarded. However, at the time of sacrifice, a doe is sacrificed instead, just like the battering ram in the biblical text. This tragedy is also a tale of sacrifice of the innocent. It speaks of the urgent interruption of atrocity without ever removing the terrible violence in whose clutches human existence is trapped. The law of blood and the offering of blood positions man in a radical inhumanity. This foundation needs to be reformed and the position has to be reaffirmed. The narrative communities of these three stories which expose defenceless weakness have fundamentally different styles. They do not raise the same questions when faced with sacrifice or an unjust death. Abraham confronts a commandant that is irreducible to principles of humanity, his act is therefore of an obvious absurdity and immorality, and is possible only when there is unconditional obedience. The murder committed by Cain leads us to the question of the responsibility of a brother towards another brother. In both the cases, and despite the differences (I have noted one), the perspectives outlined lead us to a direction that we can call in strict contemporary terms, *ethics*.

Agamemnon's dilemma as Iphigenia's father was that he had to choose between the welfare of his kingdom and the life of his daughter, between the interest of the state and filial love—a choice very Cornelian in nature. The injustice of the violence to be committed is balanced with a perspective of a *political* order. Even today when we reflect upon the question of violence and think of ways to contain it, we see that these two dimensions are inextricably linked. The last figure that I would like to evoke is that of Antigone. It confirms the political orientation of violence perpetrated by the Greeks. Sophocles' famous play recounts the story of a heroic young virgin whose brother is killed in the war against Thebes. Creon, the King of Thebes, refuses to allow his remains to be entombed using the pretext of it being against the law of his city. Antigone, however, gives a burial to her brother. She breaks the law of the city in the name of an 'unwritten' law, a humane law which, in some way, is superior to any other man-made law. Sentenced to death, she, however, hangs herself before they could execute her. The violence in this case is perpetrated by the State which refuses to acknowledge any other external authority, even if it is superior or worthier. The victim is a very young girl (Sophocles mentions that she had not yet known the love of her fiancé Hemon) once again a symbol of innocence. However, this time round, innocence wages a rebellion against the inhuman laws of man. As opposed to Abel, Isaac or Iphigenia, Antigone is as much a figure of insubordination as she is of weakness. Hers was a heated violence against the cold violence of the State; one may call it a resistance against the illegitimacy of law. She is no less than a sacrificial victim, she cried before killing herself, she knew that by burying her brother she was renouncing her own life. Four stories, four figures of death and of disobedience (Abraham against God and Antigone against the State), four sacrifices, accomplished or unaccomplished, that were governed by the double perspective of ethics and politics, of Jerusalem and Athens.

CRITICAL MODELS

Are these four figures mere 'scapegoats' in the sense developed by René Girard (2007/1979; 1978/1987; 1982/1989), substitute victims? According to the major hypothesis developed by the latter, the killing of a scapegoat (Abel, Isaac, Iphigenia, Antigone, and many others) is the only way by which a community in crisis restores peace, provided the expiatory victim undergoes a process of divinization. The sacrifice repeats the original violence of the beginning of mankind in a ritualistic manner while trying to overcome it at the same time, since it is carried out on an arbitrary member of the community, in a sort of auto-vendetta. In *Totem and Taboo* (1913), criticized by Girard, Freud talked of his intuition of the profoundly formative dimension of the murder of the father by horde. The sacrificial victim serves as the middle-man, the medium and the means at the same time, while communicating with a superior being. Therefore religions are a result of—more precisely what Girard calls the 'sacred'—which is meant to curb violence with the help of an initial sacrificial violence. The sacred functions like a system. It gives birth to myths, to rituals and codes of interdictions and obligations. A myth recalls the first instance of sacrifice by transforming the sacrificed into a 'mythical' and supernatural being. The ritual consists of imitating the violence before the sacrifice and its interruption by substituting it with a scapegoat. The restrictions and the obligations help to preserve the sanctity of the interruption itself, i.e., to make sure that the murderous violence before the sacrifice never takes place again. The Girardian explanatory model helps to understand at least one thing, or a part of it: that is, sacrifices that recount and inform us of ancient rituals unveil a universal dimension that we can immediately perceive. The four examples (it is also important to add the stories of Noah and the Great Floods) from where I had taken off, signify in various unequal degrees, the birth and the rebirth of the history of humanity, the 'sacrificial crisis', whose function is to re-inaugurate or to re-start and to re-enact the beginning.

How does one understand Girard's take on the present statement?

The origin of the sacred or the religious is the exteriorization of violence or at the very least, it is the worried quest of man to understand his own violence and the attempt to control its manifestations since the first violence and the first sacrifice.

It is appropriate to add the notion of mimesis to the key notions of sacrifice and scapegoat. For Girard, who is very Hegelian on this point, inter-human relations and the desire which constitutes this relationship is of the mimetic order. This affinity, therefore, flows less from a subject to an object, than from a subject to an object that is already possessed by another subject. When I take control of the object of my desire, I actually lose control of it. This dispossession is a deception. For what I desired was to imaginarily take the identity of my rival who held the object of my desire. This mimesis which can take all kinds of forms and can even have a number of avatars is the matrix of all violence and also the curtailment of all violence in man's world. The desire to imitate the other gives birth to the desire of possessing the same object or objects and therefore to a method of violence and of vengeance which knows no limits. One cannot escape this violence, going by Girard, if not by using a diversion such as a scapegoat which will establish the sacred and the social. The notion of mimesis therefore suggests that the violence of a subject, from the very outset, is in relation to another subject. It further allows—it is certainly a point which needs to be discussed—to envision the possibility of having a successful relationship with another, i.e., the possibility or even the probability to triumph over mimesis.

At this point emerges a difference with Freud. I will raise only one essential element of his thought in order to avoid any digression and to stay focussed on the question of violence. This point, which is particular to the economy of the entire psychoanalytical theory and is disputed even among Freudians is called the 'death instinct', *Thanatos,* as opposed to *Eros,* the 'life instinct'. I started with the tendency—which can be called 'psychologizing'—of considering various mechanisms of violence according to the rigid dynamic of intra-personal conflicts: a reaction to an unbearable situation, the consequence of a frustration, a legitimate defence, and a reactive violence. To understand this perspective, the violence of the subject can be analysed from the point of view of his incapability to distinguish between the 'unsound'—the bad violence which I talked about above—and the 'sound' in him—transforming natural violence by channelling it into law and behaviour. The basis of a Freudian reading lies in its radicalism. According to Freud, in any case for the Freud who talks of the death instinct that is 'beyond the principle of pleasure', violence as an instinct of destruction precedes every other conflict. This is the reason why it is, to an extent, linked with angst, since both violence and anguish are constitutive elements of the death instinct. The latter represents the original and fundamental tendency of all living beings, right from cellular organisms to man, to auto-disintegrate and to return to the inorganic state. The libido therefore has the role of overcoming this destructive instinct by reorienting itself towards other worldly objects; it converts itself into an elementary aggressiveness which is useful in sexual functions, and also in a number of other libidinal combinations which account for the development of the individual and even that of major civilizations' 'cultures of the death instinct' as Freud calls it. We would therefore be dealing with a vital duel between Eros and Thanatos grafted on an archaic anguish, i.e., the fear of being disintegrated, a fear brought alive by the possibility of murder. This duel between the two instincts gives rise to more or less satisfying configurations for the subject, which only causes destruction of the self or of the external object. This has been the case since the beginning of the neolithic period or even possibly right since its own birth (it is based on this that Mélanie Klein, for instance explained the bites inflicted by the breast-feeding baby on the mother.) In the Freudian scheme roughly outlined here, violence precedes all mimetic rivalry and the presence of the other perceived as an object to be destroyed or to be relied upon. Thanatos exists inside the subject even before the subject knows it. With the death instinct we can find the position of a hypothesis which represents the impenetrable reverse of all thought, which further explains the impossibility to explain and to derive its causes and sources.

The Greeks considered that the frontier, i.e., the passage between *bios* and *zoê*, between human life and animal or vegetal life, established itself from *logos*, speech or thought. It is in this unique place that violence, *bia*, remains suspended between the question about its objectives and its destination. This anthropological and gnoseologic 'optimism' is opposed to what Freud calls the cultural 'pessimism'. According to Freud, all 'reasonable' solutions proposed to solve the problem of violence that of murder or of war, are at a great risk of being naïve and are therefore doomed to failure. All logos uttered by 'the animal of speech' and of the 'State' on violence will repeat itself indefinitely and for as long as the instinct repeats itself—its characteristic is to repeat itself forever.

Freud does not ignore the fact that man too has a history and he tries to articulate the genesis of this constant structural instinct. He goes on to explain its persistence with the help of religion, as the invention of a purely repressive mechanism which aims at limiting the full expansion without any instinctive obstacles, of Thanatos as well of *Eros*. If Thanatos is not repressed, then the destruction will spread to the extent of the potential extinction of the human race: hence the commandment 'you shall not kill' of the Biblical-Hebraic tradition. If Eros is not controlled, the chaos caused by the flow of impulses can threaten social relationships and human memory since at the whim of any vague desire, anyone, who desires the first object he fancies, can be responsible for an act of violence: this is the reason why incest is forbidden ('you shall not uncover the nudity of your father' which we can read in the episode on the children of Noah) and so is child infanticide (Isaac). Along with the desire for an object '*that*', in the form of repeated killing and sexual domination, comes also the recognition of '*me*', i.e., the consciousness of the person. This recall, Freud's *Werden* does not signify that the chaotic flow of impulses can be stopped or be definitively stabilized, which would ensure the permanence of the religious dimension that gives the illusion of its abolition. Violence, according to this model of reason, constantly gives rise to the conflict between the Self and Culture or History, as the latter by way of obligations and restrictions allows man to live together despite their different impulses. In this conflict, the Self, contained by the cultural constraint on impulses, will look for all kinds of tricks to escape the constraints. Freud calls these tricks 'defence mechanisms'. He analyses a few. I will name three, which concern the subject of violence.

The first being *negation* following which violence would be the opposite of love. The discourse on negation is very close to the discourse on legitimization in hindsight: the violent person would be a loving person who ignores the latter aspect; violence according to negation would signify a love that does not recognize itself. We could say that psychological negations like sociological legitimization, confuses everything. It removes the unsolvable and considerable difficulties caused by the problems of violence for those who have to deal with it. How does one treat forgiveness or reconciliation, in their enigmatic profundity, if love and violence are nothing but two sides of the same coin? What would it mean to resolve if at the root of every solution there exists an unsolvable absolute? What would one do with the hate of the victim who seeks justice against the one who has inflicted violence upon him? How would one perceive the devastation without any remedy caused relentlessly by violence? In order to deal with these questions it would require analysing violence, i.e., death, directly, keeping aside negation and denial.

The second 'defence mechanism of the Self', of the violent Self, is *projection*: when a repressed violence is not acknowledged, it causes further anxiety at the very idea that such violence could repeatedly manifest itself. I would throw or project it outwards so as to expulse it out of my system. Curiously, I would look at myself as the victim, or even as the martyr, but not as the tormentor. However, this projection does not diminish the anguish of the violent person when he is faced with violence and the outbreak of his extreme vengeance that could affect even those he does not intend to.

Finally *reactive formations:* They stand for what the psychoanalysts call counter-investment, or the return of that which is opposite to the repressed desire ('dirtiness' of the one who is obsessed with cleanliness, hate hidden in 'acts' of politeness, the sadism of a judge who wears the mask of virtue, etc.). Herewithin lies the infinite plasticity of the instinct. In the words of Freud, the reactive formation lays down the foundation on which the auto-legitimizing discourse of violence is constructed, whose forms and avatars, as I mentioned in the beginning, are numerous and sometimes are very difficult to be undone.

Therefore the Self, according to Freud, defined by civilization and monotheism, does not easily renounce the possibilities of his 'defence' out of self-concern. The conflicts which he takes part in, implicate various strategies of diversion such as appropriation, exteriorization and alterity, to produce the same violence. In reality, conflicts between the Self and the various societal constraints, the Superego, holds no significance in the Freudian explanation except the intra-subjective dimension, i.e., conflicts between the Self and the Superego, even though one has to deal with heterogeneous levels of the psychic structure of the subject. Here lies a notable difference with Girard. As far as mimesis and rivalry are concerned, violence cannot take place unless one is put against another, or many others that are mimetically generalized and its uncertainty takes place when the sacrificial victim is involved, which gives birth to the sacred and the social. These two lines of thought, that of Girard and of Freud which strongly oppose each other at this vital point, are both anthropological in nature. Both attempt to objectively explain the sources and the mechanisms of human and inter-human violence. The Freudian anthropological pessimism does not annul the rise of logos. We can now come back to our introductory question: in the absence of a satisfying *definition* of violence, can we find one or many *practices* that allow us to more or less adequately understand it? We can begin by highlighting one point that Freud and Girard both take into account. One of the differences between the biblical narratives on the one hand and the Greek tragedies or the Roman myths on the other is that the first seem to articulate itself from the point of view of the victim or at least from the perspective of the 'figures of weakness', Abel, Joseph, and the assassinated prophets—whereas Romulus for instance, in the Tite-Live version, who kills his twin brother, is not deprived of qualities that allow him to form a State. Freud is rather attentive to the process of sublimation which takes place in various episodes of the biblical narratives, of the many modalities involved in the conversion of hostility to hospitability, of violence into softness, of the principle of pleasure into the principle of reality. Girard pays attention to the state of the victim, who is sacrificed, Jesus par excellence, and also Oedipus, who is considered to be guilty by the entire community. These anthropologies of violence highlight the extent to which the religious dimension or religion per se forms the basic principle of culture because in the larger sense they reduce the effect of violence and show how social relationships transcend the world of man, to attain the level of the sacred or the saintly, and are thus functional means to soften, appease, pacify, and polish. The question of practicality remains intact. What does one do with the violence of the humiliated and the offended? How does one comprehend, that violence can be legitimate, either by its monopolization by the State, or by that which distinguishes it from all legalities? These questions open the ethical dimension of all interrogation on violence, starting with responsibility.

That Which I Would Want to Kill

Based on the thought of a third 'intervener', Lévinas, I would understand this responsibility in its strict sense as a reply to a question. It therefore does not stand for a reply in the legal sense, in the sense where I am responsible for myself, for my violent acts and where I am answerable in a court of law according to the law. This responsibility of imputation is of decisive importance often in the management and the regulation of violence and it does not mean that they are in any way negligible. The other responsibility—we will call it 'ethical'—forces me to reply *to*. With the Freudian idea of death instinct, the relation between self and self is established, via culture. For Girard, a relation begins from the self to the other, through the mimetic desire. In the ethical responsibility, the relationship which is very particular starts entirely from the other who makes the call. I could or could not respond but I cannot ignore the call. Talking of the subject here leads us to a difficult paradox since the 'subject' acquires a meaning only through the other, through the otherness, even (and perhaps especially) when the other is not empirically present. This otherness of the other makes the 'subject' a subjugated subject. This is the first pole, that is constitutive and which will precede me and will always do. The idea of the other's call—which could manifest itself in multiple forms—torments me and prevents me from having a relationship with anyone but myself, with my desires, my pleasures, which are not in any way dull or subsided; they appear on the contrary in their 'responsible' extreme exacerbation. The first aspect of violence and the manner in which a subject handles it lies there, either in my desiring and overpowering violence, in this banal mine-hood of the desire to kill. The experience of the call and of self violence which can always accompany the former as a denial is very normal and quite frequent: a man who is beaten before my eyes, a raised hand who demands, or worse commands for food, a manifest distress begins and so on.

Lévinas made a theme out of it under the meta-concept of the face. The face is nothing but a sensitive form, whether beautiful or ugly, an aesthetic figure or an ensemble of physical features. It presents itself as an obligation-to-respond and exposes itself in a way that is extremely nude, fragile, and vulnerable in its expression which speaks to 'me', in its utmost weakness and says 'you will not kill.' This face which is so vulnerable and weak would be the easiest thing to destroy, yet this face stops me and puts forward a strange resistance. The face, according to Lévinas, does just that. It offers itself to my violence but at the same time it resists it and commands me. Its imploration, its misery, and its call enigmatically arrest my power and my violence, as it troubles me and stops me. However, unlike in the case of pity or compassion, it comforts and reassures me. The face stares at me and, in this confrontation, I am constantly constrained. All that I can do is accept it, submit to it or refuse it. Violence is dismissed. I do not have the choice, says Blanchot (2003), between talking and killing, between replying to a call, sharing a talk, saying, or rather destroying silently. Violence, arrested by the face, is like its double. There is the murderous violence of refusal which I put forth against the face until I remove it from the face of this earth. There is also, without a doubt, the violence that the face inflicts on me, which makes me submit to its command of not fighting against its weakness, of not surrendering to the force that I might use against it, of not acting at all. This soft violence of the face inflicts a kind of violence on the extreme violence to which it exposes itself and to which, in a certain manner, I too am exposed through it. It makes me get in touch with the murderous violence in me. It is important to add another dimension of violence which takes shape in the Levinasian thought on the face. This confrontation can in fact lead to a terrible violence which affects everyone, even those who are not involved in it. Lévinas calls it 'the wild barbarian character of alterity' (Lévinas 1994, p. 187; 1986, p. 345) which signifies a third stratum of violence, that which can be a product of ethics as soon as it excludes itself from the community of equals. Only politics and justice can correct this form of 'barbarity' that is a product of ethics and love. I will not elaborate this point. I would only like to briefly highlight it in order to underline the immense richness of the solicitations of thoughts, around violence, which support the Levinasian deliberation on the face. Why? Essentially because, the face is the only thing I would want to kill. In the *Human Races*, Robert Antelme (1998) shows that the experience of the concentration camps taught the prisoners that in order to hope to survive, it was imperative to form a face-less mass, in order to save oneself from the executioner. If even the slightest sign, a gesture, a headgear or a pair of spectacles, reminded him of the face among the usual anonymous forms to which he is subjugated, it would mean the end of one's life. One might suspect that I would never want to kill a thing, for the most trivial reason that I know I can have complete control of the thing. However, the others radically escape this empowering knowledge that the Girardien mimesis establishes as the core of all relationships with the thing. What the face tells me is what it really tries to express. It is evidently ontologically possible and very simple for me to kill it. However, this simplicity and this 'banality of murder', according to the Levinasian expression, lead to a withdrawal and thus make it even more problematic. On the one hand, the face makes a 'phenomenological' escape from my power and on the other hand, it ethically resists me. It is this ambivalence and this ambiguity which figures in the murder itself and also in the murderer. Murder in fact constitutes an attempt to radically and completely annihilate the other, like a definitive domination. However, as soon as it is over, the attempt is disclaimed. By killing, the murderer destroys that which he wanted to subjugate, to dominate and to reduce to his mercy. The violence of murder is thus different in this respect from the hate violence and sadistic violence. The hater wants to make his victim suffer. He therefore keeps intact the subjectivity of his victims; so that they know why they are suffering and thus suffer even more from this knowledge. We can say, in Freudian terms, that the hater belongs to the oedipal stage and the murderer to the pre-genital stage.

Thus, the face expresses the weakness of a unique being, the former being the reason why the latter faces death as well as asylum from death—mortality, finitude and transcendence, at every instant and in the most insignificant circumstances, become possible from a singular call. The face's injunction, the commandment that it 'utters', 'you shall not kill', is evidently not of the order of a necessity or a law. Nothing is simpler than to disobey it, to rebel against it and to refuse the place in which it places me. Cain kills Abel, who, due to his mist-like fragility is the Face itself. The former 'rationally' explains, that he has the right not to respond ('am I my brother's guardian?'). Ethics, in the sense explained by Lévinas, completely involves itself through an examination of violence, of extreme violence, that which took place with the extermination of the European Jews. It thus seems to me to be imperative for all reflections on the question. It articulates in a singular and defining manner the 'banality of murder' and reflects upon the 'shall not kill' until it substitutes the former by the latter. 'Kill me instead of my child!' exclaims the mother, the real mother of the child, in front of the king. Solomon's judgement has the power to authorize such a substitution which is considered to be the most certain and ultimate criteria. The thought of the face, by shifting the questions towards the other, without withdrawing from my responsibilities, allows the interrogation of violence outside the more or less sophisticated scheme of causality that most explanatory and objective theorizations propose. I will recall three points which do not have the ambition of holding any universal value but which can nevertheless be indicative elements.

Violence and speech: Violence governs itself often on the possibility or the impossibility of speech, 'talk or kill' according to the Blanchotian alternative. Violence causes a breakdown of speech. The violent person, for reasons that the social sciences or psychoanalysis could perhaps partially explain, is not able to speak, as though he is not able to gain access, at least momentarily, to *phone* that the Greeks identified as a trenchant human specificity. But the face's thoughts tell a whole new thing: the violent person does not listen, he is not bound by any speech and as a result, he is removed from all responsibility, he is not responsible for any 'speech', in the sense of the 'ten speeches' of the Jewish tradition.

Violence and mastery: Violence aims at appropriating, controlling, and dominating. The violent person tends to make himself the master of an unbearable difference, the difference of the face, sexual difference, and the simple singularity of a person. Since he cannot speak, his violence aims to destroy all language which is the living vector of all these differences. All language constructions based on the articulation of the difference therefore needs to be violated or destroyed. Philosophically, one could say that violence is the refusal of the truth (of the difference). Under this aspect, the true opposite of truth is not uniquely the mistake which is embedded in a speech and leads to its own rectification, but its violent outcome. The mistake can in fact go against what is considered as the shared sense, that is, the endurance of a speech or the patience of language. Therefore it resorts to an act, to violence that negates the other, i.e., speech. When violence is exercised, there is very often a painful incoherence associated to the radical denial of the otherness of its position, of a hypothesis, of a call, of an engagement that awaits a reply.

Violence and its rectification: Every time that one inflicts violence in a logical chain of events, every time that one connects the contents of violence to its origins, causes and circumstances, it causes or threatens to produce a certain kind of catastrophic obliteration of the victim, and this has individual and historic significance. The violent person, according to a general rule, is not the one who has not heard the call (for Lévinas, the acknowledgement of the call constitutes the basis of all subjectivity). It is the one who having heard it not only refuses to respond, but goes on to silence the stridence of the call. In a certain way, the violent person hears the unbearable call more intensely than the others. This non-reception and this irresponsibility evokes in him an afterthought, like in the case of Cain—which is a proof, that comes too late, of the impossibility of withdrawing from the act. It is at this point that speech comes back and brings back the figure of the victim: the words of the victim on the violence suffered and also the words of the violent person on his violence. It is through this speech which is not interrupted by violence that the process of pardon, reconciliation and repair can be attained. In the political front, the South African Commission on Truth and Reconciliation sets a good and unique example of such cases of correction and repair, which do not exclude, at any moment, repression as a reminder of reality.

Violence, fear and the other: A word to define the end of the question with which I had started—that of the empirical criterion. One could say that all violence committed on a face can be considered to be violent, that is in the strict sense the violence inflicted on the victim even before the act that leads to it (we can well see the difference between the 'ethical' and the legal domain). The face, the victim, and the vulnerability signify neither specific people nor specific positions. Anybody can find himself in such a situation at anytime and anywhere. The fluidity is permanent, trans-individual, and trans-historic. The question of weakness is not as much about physical strength, than the force that could put a person in a bad situation. One can fathom violence only from one's own murderous potential. This is the final word on the question, on the thought of the face. One often talks about the fear of the other. One should invert its sign to understand it better and then reverse this inversion. This fear of the other that we invoke so often to talk about instances of 'lack of civility', of violence, of murder, is the fear felt when in front of the other, in front of the face, we experience fear from the knowledge that we could kill the other—it is thus a fear for the other, but a fear which starts from me commissioning the violence. This double mechanism which needs to be elaborately formulated can help to indicate a certain origin of violence with the help of which most of its numerous and diverse forms can be *situated*.

Translated by Siba Barkataki

References

Antelme, Robert, *The Human Race,* trans. Jeffrey Haight and Annie Mahler (The Marlboro Press, 1998).

Blanchot, Maurice, 'The Limit Experience' in *The Infinite Conversation*, trans. Susan Hanson (Minneapolis and London: Minnesota University Press, 2003), pp. 85–284.

Girard, Réne, *La Violence et le Sacré* (Hachette, 2007); *Violence and the Sacred*, trans. Patrick Gregory (The Johns Hopkins University Press, 1979).

Girard, Réne, *Des Choses Cachées Depuis la Fondation du Monde* (B. Grasset, 1978); *Things Hidden Since the Foundation of the World*, trans. Michael Metter and Stephen Bann (Stanford: Stanford University Press, 1987).

Girard, Réne, *Le Bouc* émissaire (Livre de Poche, 1982); *The Scapegoat*, trans. Yvonne Freccero (The John Hopkins University Press, 1989).

Lévinas, Emmanuel, *Autrement Qu'etre Ou Au-Della de L'Essence* (Livre de Poche, 2004); *Otherwise than Being or Beyond Essence*, trans. Alphonso Lingis (Springer, 2010).

Lévinas, Emmanuel, *En Découvrant L'existence avec Husserl et Heidegger* (Paris: Vrin, 1994); 'The Trace of the Other', trans. A. Lingis in *Deconstruction in Context*, ed. Mark C. Taylor (Chicago: Chicago University Press, 1986), pp. 345–359.

2   The Experience of Silence
Derrida and the Language of Negative Theology

Andrea Potestà

> Peace, like silence, is the strange vocation of a language called outside itself by itself. But since finite silence is also the medium of violence, language can only indefinitely tend toward justice by acknowledging and practicing the violence within it.
> —Jacques Derrida (1967, p. 172; 1978, p. 145)

WEAKENING THE MEANING

A correct and, I think, fairly comprehensive way to understand the character of deconstruction as a gesture towards the origin of a new philosophical sensibility is to situate it as a question of language that can topple the discursive *strength of metaphysics* and the dominating *violence* of the originary. Derrida's gesture lies mainly in his prescription of a limit of saying, of an order of un-transcendability in every word that seeks to direct the meaning to a unitary principle. Derrida tries to create via his thinking an experience of language and of thought that goes through a 'trembling voice,' as he likes to say; that is, a philosophical disposition that obliges the experience of a radical uncertainty or ambiguity and an arrest that is finely anti-speculative and can destabilize the power of language.

Especially by distinguishing his gesture from the 'fundamental question' of Heideggerian philosophy, understood as the exhaustive formulation of 'the question of the meaning of Being in general', does Derrida breach the question of language as Heidegger is always looking, at any given moment in his oeuvre (although in varying ways), to create a questioning of the meaning of Being in order to produce its 'conceivability' and to solve the chronic forgetfulness of philosophy, Derrida suggests the need to abandon the 'hope' (Derrida 1972, p. 29; 1982, p. 27) of joining the original, to relinquish the search for the unique origin of thought. Derrida calls 'logocentrism' the intent to find the ultimate formulation of meaning by means of a gesture of resolution: the intrinsic binding of the philosophical gesture to the *logos*' principle of domination and the orientation to see through to the ultimate principle of thought. As he says in *Violence and Metaphysics*, 'Metaphysic is *economy*: violence against violence, light against light: philosophy (in general) [...]. The becoming is war. This polemic is language itself. Its inscription' (Derrida 1967, p. 173; 1978, p. 146). Against this violence 'embedded in the root of meaning and *logos*', (Derrida 1967, p. 184; 1978, p. 156) deconstruction is meant to be a *movement of infinite weakening of meaning*. As such it can remove from philosophy the search for the 'last' or 'final word' that would direct everything to a principle, as does the Heideggerian ontological difference, which wants to find the exhaustive strength of a thought capable of reaching the *Abgrund*, the abyss of the meaning of Being.

Derrida attributes to the philosophy aimed at solving the problem of the origin of meaning 'the intractable traits of an impossibility, an impossibility so impossible and intractable that it is not far from calling an interdiction to mind' (1996, pp. 24–5; 1998, p. 9). He thus finds in the *impossibility*, as a barrier against any appropriation, a point of force (the force of interdiction) against any *force* (in a metaphysical sense): the impossible then comes to achieve a diversion from the domination of language that can no longer be solved via the positivity of the sayable, but must be deeply bound to the negativity of interdiction. The 'law of the deconstructive interdiction' requires removing the force of the affirmation in front of the infinite *power* of the negative. This law, presented exemplarily as having the dynamics of a 'double bind,' requires, in effect, an interdiction, a deadlock: the impossibility is seen as a principle of un-transcendability, as a frontier, in the sense of an insuperable limit, that is, as a *negation* of all possible access. The notion of 'double bind' indicates situations in which we are at once obliged to say a thing and its opposite; it is, then, a double contradictory affirmation that, because of its contradictory nature and inability to resolve itself, *produces an interruption of thought* (and thus a suspension of its discursive violence).

One example of double bind is the thematic of gift. When I offer a gift to a friend, what does this in fact mean? I give to that friend something (there is therefore an exchange), and yet, if I am offering this thing as a gift, I must do so without asking for anything in return—otherwise it would not be a gift but a trade. So, what is a gift? What are its *conditions of possibility*? That there occurs a 'transition' that should not be an economic transaction, because the gift is unrelated to any quantification. So, making a gift means not wanting anything in return; to receive a gift is to accept the free act of the other.

However, Derrida observes that when a person makes a gift to another, immediately a distance is created between the two people, a 'potential difference,' which means that the giver occupies, even if he does not want to, a position of superiority, as he awaits feedback from the other person, at least a 'thank you.' Likewise the gift's recipient most likely feels indebted to the giver and at the very least wishes to thank him, and perhaps reciprocate by giving him, at the first opportunity, another gift.

Thus, Derrida concludes that if, on the one hand, the condition of possibility of a gift is to occur in a non-economic context, on the other, once a gift is given, it is again included within an economy of debt. The donor, even if hardly aware that he is giving, is, despite himself and inevitably, bound by expectation vis-à-vis the receiver, which is what makes him so immediately disappear as a 'real donor'; the receiver, too, if he is aware of the gift, does not meet, despite himself, the imperative of gratitude and debt, and therefore he disappears as the 'real receiver' and is forced in turn to be a donor. Therefore, the given gift ends up as something, as remainder or transferable-exchange substance, that occupies the consciousness of both donor and receiver, and therefore, as a concrete, tangible entity, cancels the free nature of the gift.

Therefore, as Derrida observes, the gift is always a trade; it becomes *impossible* at the same time that it takes effect. In other words, *the conditions of possibility of the gift are at the same time its conditions of impossibility*. What only can make it possible also makes it impossible. The gift is an *impossible possibility*. (A true gift could exist only if the donor is not aware of giving it and the receiver is not aware of receiving it. But in this case, is it still a gift? It has most probably happened that one has lost something that another has found and appropriated. Clearly this is not a gift in any sense!) Thus, the gift can be thought of *as such* only if it is considered as a *double movement*. As a gift it is simultaneously given and withdrawn. Giving is twofold; it produces a double contradictory bond: it is the act of generosity capable of suspending the economic context, and yet this act is already included, from the beginning, in an economic trade.

So, the 'logic of double bind,' or of 'possible-impossible' or 'indeterminable,' is more precisely an *aporia*, that is to say a figure of meaning—fundamental in Derrida's thought—which requires an interruption of thought, left unresolved and with no way out of this impasse. The thought of the gift requires that we consider it as having a 'bifid structure' (Derrida 2003, p. 43; 2006, p. 33) that allows no phenomenological point of view that would solve the problem inherent in its effectiveness. The double bind is thus an aporia, in the sense that it forces us to stop in front of the 'neither this nor that.' And yet, the 'neither this nor that' does not entail the resigned abandonment of the two terms, does not allow us to get by via a third way: it matters that we consider strongly the 'this' as well as the 'that' in the same curvature of the indeterminable; or, rather, we should rely on them, on their 'bifid' instances, without looking for a dialectical solution or an imposition of meaning that would force a resolution.

The primary aim of this Derridean argumentative process consists of observing the dialectical ease of any logocentric posture, which, in an aim contrary to that of this process, would like to find a solution to the aporia by the use of an ultimate meaning of meaning. We should, inversely, according to Derrida, oppose the history of metaphysics and denounce the violence of any hierarchical construction of meaning that seeks to solve or cancel this impossible phenomenal effectiveness; we must deconstruct any use of language leading to the domination of a final meaning, and call into question philosophy as a provision of resolutory force.

PERFORMING THE IMPOSSIBLE

However, we must now say that what has just been said is not the whole of the matter. The aporia for Derrida is not merely an instance of interruption of thought, of the refusal of conceivability, of the suspension of violence. Rather, it interests Derrida insofar as we can *experience* it. It is clear that the aporia cannot be overcome, even with an experience. But, by expounding the aporia through effectiveness, we can realize, according to Derrida, *the experience of the possibility of the impossible*, or *the proof of the 'no-way out'*. Speaking of the 'experience of the aporia', says Derrida,[1] is an oxymoron: *experior*, in Latin, is the passage, a transit towards an outside (*ex-*), while the *aporia* is, in Greek, the no-passage (*a-poros*), the path that leads nowhere, that interrupts the step.

Speaking of an 'experience of the aporia' indicates, then, the requirement of not finding, via the interdiction, a balance between the opposing affirmations, playing one force against the other and so suspending the violence of the opposition. Rather to experience the aporia means to show the un-transcendability of violence: the Derridean aporetic instance does not *neutralize violence*, but it irreversibly shows that *every work of thought presupposes an irresolvable conflict of non-hierarchical forces*. In other words, Derrida's analyses are intended not to release the thought of a supposed error (otherwise it would reproduce the logocentric argument, as a search toward an authentic originary of meaning), but, if one may say so, to embody this error with consciousness. Not only does deconstruction realize the interdiction as a goal, but it looks deeper into meaning in order to *create the experience of its aporia*. Thus it is, more than anything else, the exercise of being in this passage without crossing or without transit through the aporia. But, as we have to experience it, we cannot consider the aporia as a simple impossibility or mere affirmation of the impossible. The aporia in Derrida is rather *the negative dynamic that allows the consideration of the possibility of the possible as impossible*.

I'll try to explain this with another well-known example of a Derridian double bind: the issue of responsibility. How is one to make a responsible decision? We can imagine a difficult situation: I do not know which of two options to choose. There are two ways, according to Derrida, to make a decision. First, I can decide at the end of the most detailed consideration possible; that is, through a calculation as perfect as possible, in which I seek to anticipate all the consequences of a possible solution to weigh the best course of action. In this case, I analyse responsibly the options and, by means of this review, I *decide*. However, Derrida observes, this way doesn't lead me to a 'responsible decision' (it is not at all a 'decision'), because it is, rather, a weighing, partaking of an economy which, by my perfect calculation of the risks and decision regarding the best thing to do, puts the decision back in this calculation: It is the calculation that will tell me what is better and, in this sense, somehow, I have 'washed my hands' after my deliberative process. If I'm wrong, or if I regret the decision made at the end of a series of calculations, then I can always say I did what seemed best, and that, for this reason, these consequences are not my fault, because what I decided seemed the most rational thing to do (I made the rational calculation responsible for my decision). And if 'it's not my fault,' well, I am not responsible for that decision. Therefore, concludes Derrida, if one decides through a responsible evaluation, one actually does not decide at all.

On the contrary—the second alternative that we should consider— a decision can be deemed responsible only if it is taken against a background of in-determinability: only when I cannot really make a decision, because I lack the elements to weigh or to evaluate the impact of my choosing, is it a real decision. Thus, a decision is an invention without rules that goes beyond the prerequisites of its possibility, until an 'irresponsible' rupture occurs in the moment of in-determinability, without any consideration of consequences. In other words, to decide is always to *decide without knowing* and without the force of a thought 'well founded' where anticipation and responsibility are impossible. A decision is made only to the extent that it breaks with calculating and weighing. But this means, therefore, that we decide only when we cannot decide. (And in fact we don't commend a person for doing what the statistics suggest, but only a person who decides something that seems a priori incomprehensible and irrational and afterwards proves to be correct).

So, *deciding responsibly is always an irresponsible act*, realized by the breaking in of in-determinability. Here, again, as in the case of the gift, we can observe Derrida's movement: *the conditions of possibility of a decision are its conditions of impossibility*. However, this example clearly shows us something that was not explicit before: Derrida does not want to *affirm the impossibility*, to come to the conclusion that, ultimately, *we cannot decide*, but more precisely he wants to show that *the only possibility of a decision consists in the inability to decide*. The point now becomes clear: the challenge of deconstruction is not only to recognize an opposition and surrender to his impossible solution, but to show that *the impossible is the very event of the possibility* (and, as well, that the indeterminable is the very event of the decision). The decision is not only impossible; more precisely, it is *possible* under a radical *contamination with the impossible*. We can decide only if we go through the *experience of not being able to decide* (only if we have the experience of the aporia of the decision).

In the same way, the deconstructive interdiction of aporia indicates not that one cannot say anything, nor that the language of philosophy is blocked, but that we can experience the *power of language* only through the showing of its contamination with the *powerlessness*. The logic of 'double bind' is thus not limited to the interdiction, and is required to extend beyond the inadequate solutions–*it orders the doing of the impossible*. 'The sole decision possible passes through the madness of the undecidable and the impossible', writes Derrida (1993, p. 63; 1995, p. 55–8).

Thus, deconstruction is not a simple affirmation of the impossible or of powerlessness, in order to realize the inevitability of deadlock. Rather, it is a negative experience that can *performatively* destabilize language *in order to open it to what exceeds it*. This gives rise, at any time during the experience of meaning, to that dismissal (aporia), not to transform or dialectically think positively about the truth of the aporia, but to place a performative crack that exceeds any theoretical or demonstrative resolution. Alternatives are never put in the position of rational comfort capable of finding an ultimate meaning of the decision, but they place us into an experience of language that frees the performative force of excess. It is in this sense, then, that Derrida wants to articulate the *impossibility as possibility*: by thinking meaning and thought through the contamination of *strength and weakness*, and to do so in order to exceed such an opposition.

If we then refer the movement generated by deconstruction to the question of violence, we must recognize that Derrida does not simply oppose violence, as if one could find a non-violent or 'pure' posture in front of metaphysics, but, more accurately, he wants to recognize violence as *a condition for the practice of philosophy* and, at the same time, as a limit we have to pass through. He wants *to test the suspension of its practice*, in order to prove philosophically the violence of philosophical language. Here is where deconstruction's project takes place. If metaphysics is the mere practice of the violence of language, deconstruction is not intended as its suspension or an effort to find peace ahead of the domination of speech (which also would imply a violent solution, as a 'last word' or 'first meaning' of language). Deconstruction, by destabilizing the violence, posits its enforcement via a self-referential and performative *negativity*.

Derrida essentially asks: Is there a language that directs the destabilization of the negative and yet does not stop there? Is there the possibility of thinking the negative simultaneously in its twofold role, as a sign of deadlock and of performative enforcement? How to think this other language? In *Of Grammatology*, Derrida asked himself: 'If it is true, as I in fact believe, that writing cannot be thought outside of the horizon of intersubjective violence, is there anything, even science, that radically escapes it? Is there a knowledge, and, above all, a language, scientific or not, that one can call alien at once to writing and to violence?' (Derrida 1967, p. 195; 1976, p. 127). The answer, in a sense, to this requirement of rotating metaphysics through 'another negativity' is found by Derrida in a link made, and many times repeated, with negative theology.

PRESERVING THE NAME

Negative theology and deconstruction exist in a very intimate relationship (see Taylor 1990; Coward 1992; Caputo and Scanlon 1999; Almond 1999; Vries 2000; Marion 2001; Bensussan 2004; Lotz 2005). Certainly, Derrida is not interested in the merely theological aspect. In the lecture *On Différance*, Derrida observes that he thinks *différance* to be 'not theological, not even in the order of the most negative of negative theologies' (Derrida 1972, p. 6). And in *How Not To Speak*, his 1986 lecture (published later in *Psyche*), when he recalls the 'strange affinity' between deconstruction and negative theology, he adds immediately that, contrary to deconstruction, negative theology 'seems to reserve, beyond all positive predication, beyond all negation, even beyond being, some super-essentiality, a being beyond being' (Derrida 2003, p. 540; 2008, p. 142). Derrida thinks that there is still, in negative theology, as long as it remains theology, a small residue extracted from the silence, an imperceptible residue (that allows it in fact to be called 'theology') that haunts it with the search of an ultimate 'name' of God. But the rapprochement with deconstruction, considered from the point of view of the simple language dynamic, without taking into account the attempt to recover metaphysics, is continually replayed by Derrida himself. If, on one hand, Derrida opposes the fact that, being *transformed into a mechanism of production of meaning*, negative theology finds, in the silence, a way to affirm God (as a negation), it is nevertheless possible, on the other hand, to affirm that deconstruction realizes a kind of 'secularization' of the language of negative theology. But in what sense?

The language of negative theology is that which creates, more so than do other theological languages, the experience of the difference between speech and power. Negative theology *thinks* from the inequality between the expressible and what is to be expressed. It is a not-dialectical experience of speech, consisting of a word that speaks without joining the object of its speech, without identifying and producing the identity of the agreement made between speech and its meaning (which is the nature of the dialectic). In this sense, Derrida finds in negative theology the requirement of a word that says the essential difference, and that says it without saying it, because otherwise the difference would be filled.

In *On the Name*, Derrida provides a description of the experience of two simultaneous and contradictory voices (which thus act in accord with the double bind, but also given a further 'effectiveness'): one voice belongs to the power of the word, and says 'no, we cannot *say*, we cannot say God'—and thus imposes the law of the unspeakable, finding the truth of the negation as an imposition of silence, of *aphasia*. The other voice, synchronous and opposite, is inserted into silence with a word that shows the possibility of affirming, thanks to the denial, beyond the force of interdiction: this other voice then comes to destabilize the law of the negative, prohibiting the interdiction by showing its dialectical simplicity. Negative theology then reaches a point beyond the affirmative, and also beyond the negative, indicating the infinite demand of what is beyond any power to deny or affirm. The duplicity of voices is due to the fact that when a voice immobilizes its power of speech and interrupts the appropriative violence of onto-theology, the other voice shows that precisely in this interruption, there resurfaces the greatest opportunity of an appropriation. And, at the same time, this opportunity also carries the risk of making the silence a principle of absolute domination, stronger than any onto-theological appropriation.

In this essential round, negative theology is the evidence of misuse of power and not of its suspension. Negative theology plays with the question: 'Is silence God?' That is where it arrives at its 'performative' principle: on the one hand, there is a voice which, in the pure name of the concept of God, denies God, touching the terms of an absolute atheism, in order to devote to it the *respectful* silence due to a God, more authentic than any word or name; on the other hand, the other voice continues this gesture into its contrary, asserting that no God can ever be found, even in absolute silence, for otherwise we should deny him again. The first voice finds a theological comfort in silence and, within the *same silence*, the other voice must start to deny the comfort found via a new act of *aphasia*. And so on to infinity. But the infinity of the two voices, the aporetic and performative infinity, is neither violent nor non-violent. The voices make neither a duality nor a unity: the voices of negative theology go on *ad infinitum*, interrupting each other uninterruptedly, without producing a crack that could impose a final word and arrest the ceaseless interruption of interwoven voices.

Negative theology, like deconstruction, then finds by its own performative praxis a set silence-speech, a structured *aphasia*-language. Is this a denial? Yes and no: on the one hand, silence imposes itself as an unsurpassable law. On the other hand, the performative principle forces the collection of an absolute 'excess.' The more I deny, the more I admit and vice versa (according to the double bind). The essence of the language of negative theology is therefore an experience of 'eloquent silence' that is at the same time 'a silence that cannot mean anything.' This lack of distinction, or this inseparability of the *intention of saying*, replete and projecting directly beyond words, and the *impossibility of saying*, given over to silence and vacuum, thus offers the infinite terms of an opposition, in which each term is marked on the other side.

Derrida asks: is negative theology moved by a *desire* for God? And answers: yes and no. Yes, because negative theology looks for God beyond the names, giving God a place in the beyond-language; but no, because God can never be an object of desire—or, whenever he is an *object*, we must necessarily repeat his negation:

'God' 'is' the name of this bottomless collapse, of this endless desertification of language. But the trace of this negative operation is inscribed *in* and *on* and *as the event* [...]. *There is* this event, which remains, even if this remnant is not more substantial, more essential than this God, more ontologically determinable than this name of God of whom it is said that he names nothing that is, neither this nor that. [...] The event remains at once *in* and *on* language, then within and at the surface (a surface open, exposed, immediately overflowed, outside of itself). The event remains in and on the mouth, on the tip [*bout*] of the tongue, as is said in English and French, or on the edge of the lips passed over by words that *carry* themselves toward God. They are *carried*, both exported and deported, by a movement of 'ference' (transference, reference, difference) toward God. They name God, speak of him, speak *him*, speak *to him, let him speak in them*, let themselves be carried by him, make (themselves) a reference to just what the name supposes to name beyond itself, the nameable beyond the name, the nameable not-nameable. As if it was necessary both to save the name and to save everything except the name, *save the name* [*sauf le nom*], as if it was necessary to lose the name in order to save what bears the name, or that toward which one goes through the name. But to lose the name is not to attack it, to destroy it or wound it. On the contrary, to lose the name is quite simply to respect it: as name. That is to say, to pronounce it, which comes down to traversing it toward the other, the other whom it names and who bears it. To pronounce it without pronouncing it. To forget it by calling it, by recalling it (to oneself). (Derrida 1993, p. 56–60; 1995, p. 55–8)

So—here Derrida makes clear the principle of *apophasis*—we cannot even make a *right use of the negative dialectic*, as we would in a mechanism of positive infinity. We cannot rest in the interdiction. If we do not say the name of God, *because* we know that he is beyond names, then we admit him and we have to start again.

The negation here does not preserve any preservation, but falls performatively by the play of language beyond it (therefore *nowhere*). The performative element implies the suspension of knowledge and the interruption of all 'wink logic' gesturing towards an absent meaning (as in Heideggerian ontological difference). We cannot even make a sign to God as to that wink that would be on the other side of my affirmation or negation. Derrida then concludes: 'We have to leave everything, to leave every "something" for God's love, and certainly to leave God himself, to abandon him, that is, at once to leave him and (but) let him (be beyond being-something). Save his name—which must be kept silent there where it itself goes to *arrive* there, that is, to arrive at its own effacement' (Derrida 1993, p. 100–1; 1995, 78–9). *The 'not' said by negative theology does not save almost nothing.* It just lets exist a *performative movement* which exceeds the excess of negative meaning.

RESPONSIBILITY OF THE SILENCE

Now, as we have said, this principle of 'powerful powerlessness' or (what comes to the same thing), this principle of 'performative power infinitized' corresponds to the movement sought by Derrida via deconstruction. The language spoken by Derrida, according to the logocentrical opposition, achieves the same result: it exceeds and does not exceed metaphysics, it suspends and shows the un-suspendable violence. In this point of absolute in-discernibility of a *logos* which wants to dominate meaning by its word, and of a *logos* that empties itself of all power and that suspends all affirmation. This is how Derrida wants to face the originary experience of violence (and of metaphysics): the silence is only the illusion of non-violence, which actually has an even stronger force. A word that remains silent—maybe even more so than an explicit word—doesn't escape from the economy of violence. But in this point of radical contamination of power and powerlessness, the *performative principle* comes to show that it is neither a question of *making silence*, in a nihilistic transparency supposedly having been found, nor to speak or affirm, to say God or meaning. But it is more essentially a question of *experiencing* this dual voice that tears out the speech that goes through a 'trembling voice.' This doesn't resolve language, neither in the nihilistic violence that affirms the negative (because nihilism is too radically linked to the epiphany of the 'said' and to the exteriority of the 'not' or of the '*nihil*'), nor in the violence of a word who wants to cross into the said. It is more essentially the proof of a saying that fails to say, that feels its violence and that, exercising it, goes astray. Suspending the presumption to not apply force, we get to the point where the force in its own exercise threatens to not make its benefit and breaks fatally the language in its own power. The absence of God's name, Derrida observes, leads to a lack of strength and to exhaustion. 'Negative theology means (to say) very little, almost nothing, perhaps something other than something. Whence it's inexhaustible exhaustion....' (Derrida 1993, p. 45; 1995, p. 50).

In conclusion, we can ask: what happens in the *experience of silence*? The *apophasis*, the negative statement, whether theological or deconstructive, radically defies the notion of rational power and the force of language; it diverts any valid principle and abandons the thought in a constitutive state of powerlessness. But if we perceive the performative challenge of this negative declaration, or of such abandonment, we also can distinguish the new emerging philosophical task: resisting the language, foiling its original violence inscribed in the very phenomenon of the speech (in the naming of God as well as in the potential irradiation of the ultimate meaning of logos) involves a new *philosophical responsibility*: a responsibility to fight against any sovereignty of meaning, which neither atheism as such nor speculative nihilism can ever succeed in doing, finding themselves condemned to play one sovereignty against the other, the nihil against meaning, or the emptiness against God. Taking seriously the negative performativity involves the need to use the power of language in order to turn off the power of any ultimate speech, and to fulfil the requirement to practice the power of speech so as to produce a drastic *weakening of knowledge*. This involves changing the very *question of power*—or *power as a question*.

Derrida says, commenting on Nietzsche, that this is necessary; it is

[A]responsibility which, following the more or less latent—and thus silent—logic of the argument, can be exercised only in silence—indeed, in secret—in a sort of counterculture of knowing-how-to-keep-silent. As though the sage were speaking silently to himself about silence, answering himself saying nothing—in order to appeal to responsibility. One must know how to reach such silence (Derrida 1994, p. 71; 2005, p. 52).

We must then learn to access a responsibility that does not have the benefit of meaning and does not derive from a certain *power* of knowledge, and which knows then how to make a jump that is essentially irresponsible, because it must be done with awareness that knowledge is interrupted, and that we are beyond assurance of sovereign affirmation, left with a thought that has not yet been reassured of its own possibility. It is the responsibility to transform philosophical practice, which is now intended to be able to bring affirmatively to the experience what in the experience of philosophical language can pass as a pure negative form.

Note

1. 'When I say that they require the very experience of aporia, I mean two things. (1) As its name indicates, an experience is a traversal, something that traverses and travels toward a destination for which it finds the appropriate passage. The experience finds its way, its passage, it is possible. And in this sense it is impossible to have a full experience of aporia, that is, of something that does not allow passage. An aporia is a non-road. From this point of view, justice would be the experience that we are not able to experience. We shall soon encounter more than one aporia that we shall not be able to pass. But (2) I think that there is no justice without this experience, however impossible it may be, of aporia. Justice is an experience of the impossible' (Derrida 1994, pp. 37–8).

References

Almond, I., 'Negative Theology, Derrida and the Critique of Presence: A Poststructuralist Reading of Meister Eckhart', *The Heythrop Journal*, XL (1999), pp. 150–65.

Bensussan, G., 'Oui, la survie… Note sur le carré affirmatif de la déconstruction' in *Corpus* (n. 52, 2004.), pp. 53–62.

Caputo, J. D., Scanlon, M., *God, the Gift, and Postmodernism*, (Bloomington: Indiana University Press, 1999).

Coward, H., Foshay, T., Eds. *Derrida and Negative Theology*, (Albany: State University of New York Press, 1992).

Derrida, J., 'Violence et métaphysique', in *L'écriture et la Différence* (Paris: Éditions du Seuil, 1967); *Writing and Difference*, trans. A. Bass (Chicago: University of Chicago Press, 1978), pp. 97–192.

————, 'La differance', in *Marges – de la Philosophie* (Paris: Les Éditions de Minuit, 1972); *Margins of Philosophy*, trans. A. Bass (Chicago: University of Chicago Press, 1982), pp. 1–28.

————, *Monolinguisme de L'autre* (Paris: Galilée, 1996); *Monolingualism of the Other*, trans. P. Mensah (Stanford: Stanford University Press, 1998).

————, *Genèses, Généalogies, Genres et le Génie. Les Secrets de L'archive* (Paris: Galilée, 2003); *Geneses, Genealogies, Genres, and Genius: The Secrets of the Archive*, trans. B. B. Brahic (New York: Columbia University Press, 2006; *Sauf le Nom* (Paris: Galilée, 1993).

————, *On the Name*, trans. T. Dutoit (Stanford: Stanford University Press, 1995.

————, *De la Grammatologie* (Paris: Les Éditions de Minuit, 1967), *Of Grammatology*, trans. G. C. Spivak (Baltimore: The John Hopkins University Press, 1997), 2.

————, *Psyché, Inventions de L'autre* (Paris: Galilée, 2003), *Psyche: Inventions of the Other*, Volume II, trans. P. Kamuf, E. Rottenberg (Stanford: Stanford University Press, 2008).

————, *Politiques de L'amitié* (Paris: Galilée, 1994), *The Politics of Friendship*, trans. G. Collins (London/New York: Verso, 2005).

Lotz, C., *L'assoluto Postmoderno. Heidegger, Derrida e i Limiti Interni del Linguaggio*, in Limnatis, N., Pastore, L., Eds. *Prospettive sul Postmoderno* (Milano: Mimesis, 2005), pp. 149–74.

Marion, J.-L., 'Au Nom ou Comment le Taire', in *De Surcroît* (Paris: PUF, 2001), pp. 155–196.

Taylor, M. C., 'Non-Negative Negative Theology', in *Diacritics* (n. 4, 1990), pp. 2–16.

Vries de, H., 'The Theology of the Sign and the Sign of Theology: The Apophantics of Decosnstruction', in Bulhoff, I., Laurens, K., (eds) *Flight of the Gods: Philosophical Perspectives on Negative Theology* (New York: Fordham University Press, 2000), pp. 165–93.

3 Stupidity, Madness, and Malevolence
Schelling, Deleuze, Flaubert, and Musil and the Problem of Violence

Jason M. Wirth

> In the preface to the *Phenomenology*, Hegel chastised Schelling for placing stupidity at the origin of being. Hegel, for once, was unnerved. Clearly, the imputation of originary stupidity to human *Dasein* was an 'issue' for Hegel, tripping him up, effecting a phenomenal misreading. Schelling posits a primitive, permanent chaos, an absence of intelligence that gives rise to intelligence. Presumptuous man has refused to admit the possibility of such abyssal origins and is seen defending himself with moral reason.
>
> —Avital Ronell, *Stupidity* (2002, p. 37).

In *Difference and Repetition* (1968), Gilles Deleuze asks us to take up the problem of stupidity as a properly transcendental question: 'How is *bêtise* (and not error) possible' (Deleuze 1994, p. 151; Deleuze 1968, p. 197)? This chapter proposes to make a contribution to this transcendental problem, a problem that cannot be separated from the problem of violence.

In the rare moments when we are honest with ourselves, if such moments ever chance to transpire, what other kinds of words evoke more anxiety and incite, or perhaps unleash, more violence, than a phrase like *Mutter, ich bin dumm*; *Maman, je suis bête*; Mother, I am stupid? Although I will attempt not to carelessly conflate *die Dummheit*, *la bêtise*, and stupidity, I would like to follow a thread that can be first found in Schelling's 1809 *Freedom* essay and trace it primarily through the thinking of Deleuze and Flaubert by way of Nietzsche and Musil.

How does stupidity expose the violence and madness incipient but repressed within dogmatic thinking? How does stupidity expose a monstrous—and monstrously violent—valence of thinking?

In the opening monologue of Béla Tarr's film, *The Turin Horse* (*A Torinói ló*, Hungary, 2011), a cinematic meditation on what happened to the horse that Nietzsche embraced that fateful January morning in 1889, we hear that:

[i]n Turin on 3rd January, 1889, Friedrich Nietzsche steps out of the doorway of number six, via Carlo Alberto. Not far from him, the driver of a hansom cab is having trouble with a stubborn horse. Despite all his urging, the horse refuses to move, whereupon the driver loses his patience and takes his whip to it. Nietzsche comes up to the throng and puts an end to the brutal scene, throwing his arms around the horse's neck, sobbing. His landlord takes him home, he lies motionless and silent for two days on a divan until he mutters the obligatory last words, 'Mutter, ich bin dumm' and lives for another ten years, silent and demented, cared for by his mother and sister.

Far worse than death for a thinker as brilliant as Nietzsche: *Mutter, ich bin dumm*. *Maman, je suis bête* (Mother, I am stupid), Nietzsche, the prophet of the *Übermensch*, is now utterly infantilized, unable to understand even the most basic and trivial ideas. As Rustam Singh poignantly articulates it: 'For twelve long years Nietzsche could not think. He could neither think nor remember, nor remember to think, remember to go back to his thought, the only thing that he would have liked to remember' (Singh 2011, p. 164). The disaster had struck and Nietzsche was numb. The source of Tarr's anecdote is not clear to me. Although I do not want to deny him the use of poetic license, I am guessing that it comes from an unsettling report recorded in 1893 by Heinrich Lec, who collected some anecdotes from Nietzsche's mother, Franziska, while her son was under her care in Naumburg. The report, which appeared in a newspaper (the *Berliner Tageblatt*), itself no goldmine of philosophical athleticism, is rife with Franziska's insipid observations (she makes her son stick to a diet—'milk and honey, he likes to eat that'—the house where Nietzsche now stays is 'off the beaten track,' she recites him poems that she knows that he cannot understand, etc.). Franziska also recounts the following, quite striking conversation that seems to have inspired Béla Tarr's opening monologue:

'My mother,' he said to me, 'I am not stupid.' 'No, my dear son,' I say to him, 'you are not stupid, your books are now world shaking.' 'No, my mother, I am stupid.' (Gilman 1987, p. 230)

This is a rich interchange. Franziska's incessant clichés, including, as the *pièce de résistance*, that her son is not stupid because his books are 'now world-shaking,' are in their own way quite stupid. So what if the books are world-shaking? Has not our poor world been shaken again and again by stupid thoughts? To assume that a book is a good book because everyone reads it commits an *ad populum* fallacy at the level of taste and it does not address the more fundamental value question: is the book *worth* reading? At this point we come to the first paradoxical feature of stupidity: If you know that you are stupid, you are not so stupid, because you are wise enough to know that you are stupid. The stupid, on the other hand, are too stupid to know that they are stupid. Full throttle stupidity is impenetrable. The books that Franziska could never comprehend, let alone affirm, are celebrated as world-shaking.

The irony is completely lost on her when she recounts that her son told her, upon the appearance of a new edition of one of his works, 'My mother, don't read it, that can't give you any joy' (Gilman 1987, p. 231). Of course this is true. Although she is clearly not the sharpest knife in the drawer, I suspect that she is intelligent enough to understand that she has no idea what her son's books are about and that therefore she is in no position to offer an assessment of them. The fact that she esteems them nonetheless, has little to do with a meager cognitive capacity that somehow dooms her to such mistakes. Stupidity should not be confused with being dimwitted. Her assessment is not a mistake, but rather something much more difficult to ferret out: a commitment to judgements and convictions whose veracity or lack thereof is not at all an issue for her. In this vein, Franziska soon recounted that the 'preacher from the cathedral came to see me. No one folded his hands like Fritz, he said, so sincerely and piously and devoutly. All our friends called him: the little pastor' (Gilman 1987, p. 231). Nietzsche, the little pastor!

On the other hand, Nietzsche is right. *Meine mutter, ich bin dumm.* In his madness he is somehow not so stupid because he has some glimpse that he has collapsed into an immense, relentless, and punishing stupidity. This is already part of the poignancy that Béla Tarr's opening monologue evokes. Although Nietzsche had at best an ambiguous relationship to Socrates and his legacy, he nonetheless praised these Greek philosophers for taking on the happy and good conscience of those who take refuge in 'thoughtlessness and stupidity [*Gedanklosigkeit und Dummheit*]'. 'These philosophers did damage to stupidity' (Nietzsche 1988, p. 555). Although Nietzsche will not here decide if this 'sermon' against stupidity has better reasons to support it than those that gave rise to the alleged selflessness that bolsters and reinforces 'the herd instincts,' it is clear that the Greek refusal of the happy-go-lucky character of stupidity hints at an alternative to the illusion that ignorance is bliss and that joy is found in the selfless devotion to group think. It is worth noting, however, that although Nietzsche clearly embraces the Socratic refusal of stupidity's good conscience, he is ambivalent about philosophy's capacity to provide a better alternative ('We will not here decide if this sermon against stupidity had better reasons for it than the sermon against egomania [*Selbstsucht*]'). If Nietzsche is against stupidity and yet if philosophy's argument against stupidity is inadequate, does this not suggest that there can be ironically *stupid arguments against stupidity*? Such arguments would not be unintelligent arguments against stupidity, but rather the paradoxical stupidity of a certain kind of intelligence, what the great Robert Musil called 'intelligent stupidity' (Musil 1990, p. 284). The fundamental problem is not that a lack of intelligence makes us prone to errors. We can rather think perfectly true things that are utterly stupid, but not therefore somehow false.

Gilles Deleuze eloquently argued this point in *Nietzsche and Philosophy* (1962) in a chapter appropriately called 'The New Image of Thought':

Stupidity [*la bêtise*] is not error or a tissue of errors. There are imbecile thoughts, imbecile discourses, that are made up entirely of truths; but these truths are base, they are those of a base, heavy and laden soul. The state of mind dominated by reactive forces, *by right*, expresses *stupidity* [*la bêtise*] *and, more profoundly, that which it is a symptom of: a base way of thinking*. In truth, as in error, stupid thought [*la pensée stupide*] only discovers the most base—base errors and base truths that translate the triumph of the slave, the reign of petty values or the power of an established order (Deleuze 1983, p. 105; 1962, p. 120).

As we can see from Deleuze's lexicon above, he is not, despite their lack of metaphorical equivalence, proposing as a large a wedge between *la bêtise* and stupidity (*la pensée stupide*) as Derrida suggests. There is a univocity of stupidity—one clamorous stupidity, with so many different ways to think it! It was the endless multiplicity of stupidity's manifestations that drove two of the greatest novelistic thinkers of stupidity, Flaubert and Musil, to write unfinished and perhaps unfinishable novels about the problem of la bêtise and die Dummheit, respectively. They did not finish these novels, but these novels finished them. (Musil thought that the description of stupidity was 'an almost infinite task'; see Musil 1990, pp. 283–84.) These two masterpieces do not support Schopenhauer's claim that laughter emerges in the gap between what we think and what is the case, for that is merely to laugh at our endless errors. I note here that most errors are laughter neutral and that the comedy of stupidity must be tackled not among the dimwitted and the cognitively sluggish, but rather among intellectuals, self-proclaimed philosophers, self-congratulatory experts, and pompous professors.

This constituency was key for Musil. Planning for the Parallel Campaign, which would take place in 1914, only months before the outbreak of the First World War, the central characters in Musil's *Der Mann ohne Eigenschaften* plan to commemorate the coincidence that in 1918 Franz Joseph would have overseen the Austro-Hungarian Empire for 70 years and Emperor Wilhelm II would have ruled Germany for 30 years. Such a coincidence called for a world-historic event, although no one could say what it should be, and so endless committees are organized to come up with a totally game-changing idea. Diotima, whose 'soul' feels trapped in a loveless marriage as well as a hopelessly materialistic age, longs for something truly earth shaking. 'We must bring to life a truly great idea. We have the opportunity, and we must not fail to use it' (Musil 1996, p. 95). When Ulrich asks her what she has in mind, he learns that she 'did not have anything specific in mind. How could she? No one who speaks of the greatest and most important thing in the world means anything that really exists' (Musil 1996, p. 95). Such incredible, world-shaking ideas 'exist in a kind of molten state through which the self enters an infinite expanse and, inversely, the expanse of the universe enters the self, so that it becomes impossible to differentiate between what belongs to the self and what belongs to the infinite' (Musil 1996, p. 114). Only by tossing Austria into the dark night when all cows are black can we mark an occasion like the Parallel Campaign in its proper greatness! But how do we do that?

All this leads to committees, endless committees. In soliciting 'great ideas' the Parallel Campaign receives countless entries. This allows Diotima to fawn over Arnheim, the wealthy German businessman and author 'who possessed the gift of never being superior in any specific, provable respect but, owing to some fluid, perpetually self-renewing equilibrium, of still coming out on top of every situation.' Arnheim called this 'the Mystery of the Whole': 'in this life, in some mysterious fashion, the whole always takes precedence over the parts' and hence, everything is somehow saturated in mystery so that the 'profound goodness and love, the dignity and greatness, of a person are almost independent of what he does,' but they still magically ennoble them anyway Musil 1996, p. 207). Among the many characters in the background of these endless conversations and committee meetings is Moosbrugger, who sits in jail awaiting execution after murdering a prostitute, all the time in a psychotic stupor, extravagantly hallucinating. He was, however, 'pleased that he had this knack for hallucination that others lacked; it enabled him to see all sorts of things others didn't, such as lovely landscapes and hellish monsters' (Musil 1996, p. 258). When Moosbrugger had a handle on his hallucinations, he would engage 'in thinking,' although he had no idea what that really was. 'He called it thinking because he had always been impressed with the word' (Musil 1996). It described something that happened to him against his will, as if thinking 'were planted in him.' And what kind of 'thoughts' came to him when he was 'thinking'? 'A squirrel in these parts is called a tree kitten … but just let somebody try to talk about a tree cat with a straight face!' Moosbrugger was, however, convinced that in Hesse a tree kitten was 'called a tree fox. Any man who has traveled around knows such things' (Musil 1996, p. 259). Deep down, however, Moosbrugger's 'experience and conviction were that no thing could be singled out by itself, because things hang together.' It usually took 'his enormous strength to hold the world together' (Musil 1996, p. 259). Moosbrugger, lost in the madness of the dark night when all cows are black, struggled to hold the world together before it shattered into pure continuity.

Meanwhile, the search for a world-shaking idea continued as everyone attempted to invoke their powers of genius. The committee members are all fairly bright, but they are subject to Musil's intelligent stupidity, a stupidity that may deprive the thoughtless life of its good conscience, but which in its own way understands the problem of stupidity to run deeper than the mere abdication of thinking. 'For if stupidity, seen from within, did not so much resemble talent as posses the ability to be mistaken for it, and if did not outwardly resemble progress, hope, and improvement, the chances are that no one would want to be stupid, and so there would be no stupidity' (Musil 1996, p. 57). Stupidity's power to become a kind of profligate *Doppelgänger* for thinking means that there is 'no great idea that stupidity could not put to its own uses; it can move in all directions, and put on all the guises of truth. The truth, by comparison, has only one appearance and only one path, and is always at a disadvantage' (Musil 1996, p. 259). Such stupidity, Musil argued, is not merely 'a deficiency of the understanding' (Musil 1990, p. 276): 'The higher, pretentious form of stupidity ... is not so much lack of intelligence as failure of intelligence, for the reason that it presumes to accomplishments to which it has no right' (Musil 1990, p. 283). This produces a catastrophic 'disproportion between the material and the energy of culture' (Musil 1990, p. 283). That is to say, intelligent stupidity produces energy far beyond the capacity of its cultural material to direct it wisely. Such energy continues to mount until it is expended with simple but cataclysmic violence. Musil further contended that such stupidity 'is no mental illness, yet it is most lethal; a dangerous disease of *Geist* that endangers life itself' (Musil 1990, p. 284).

Before Musil, who had a doctorate in philosophy, turned to his epic pursuit of the problem of stupidity, Flaubert's posthumously published *Bouvard et Pécuchet* (1881) demonstrated that he too had been obsessed with this delicate, but inherently catastrophic problem. This unfinished novel chronicles the relentless intellectual pursuits of these two former Parisian copyists (i.e., those who, like a parrot, merely repeat, unburdened by the desire to understand what they are repeating). When Bouvard's uncle dies, he inherits a substantial sum of money and the duo soon move out to the country and devote themselves to their intellectual pursuits, which, in a series of disasters, moves through what they imagine to be agriculture, landscape gardening, food preservation, anatomy, medicine, biology, geology, archeology, architecture, history, mnemonics, literature, drama, grammar, aesthetics, politics, love and sex, gymnastic training, occultism and esoteric spirituality, theology, philosophy, religious life, education, music, and urban planning before they return, with an immense sense of relief, to the life of copyists.

Borges cites Emile Faguet's exasperated complaint in 1899 that 'Flaubert makes them read an entire library *so that they will not understand it*' (Borges 1999, p. 386). In fact, Flaubert himself had worked through 1,500 often difficult tomes to be able to dramatize Bouvard and Pécuchet's bêtise with regard to these ideas (Borges 1999, p. 387). Flaubert had to in some way understand a vast range of material in order to locate with precision his two protagonists' inability and unwillingness to master the skills requisite to write a novel about bêtise. Flaubert attempted to surgically locate stupidity's ill-will. Just as Musil's *Man without Qualities* is enormous, yet no where near finished at 1,500 pages, so obsessed was it with exploring the seemingly endless variety of forms of human stupidity, Borges notes that the late Flaubert was like Swift: 'Both hated human stupidity with minutious ferocity; both documented their hatred with trivial phrases and idiotic opinions compiled across the years' (Borges 1999, p. 388). It is not without irony that in his *Dictionnaire des idées reçues*, a collection of habitual exercises of la bêtise which Flaubert developed as a supplement to *Bouvard et Pécuchet*, we find the following definition for IMAGINATION: 'Always "lively." Be on guard against it. When lacking in oneself, attack it in others. To write a novel, all you need is imagination' (Flaubert, *Dictionary* 1954, p. 47). If all you need is imagination to write a novel, then you cannot understand what the novel, on its own terms, seeks to understand. Bouvard and Pécuchet, the personification of bêtise, cannot write a novel or even a philosophical treatise about bêtise because they cannot stand in thoughtful relation to it, despite the fact that what thinking stands for, in relationship to such encounters, threatens to stupefy thinking.

And what of Flaubert, who both, writes a novel and seeks to understand his characters as they are mired in an uncomprehending bêtise? Derrida has alerted us to Flaubert's 1875 letter to Edma Roger des Genettes where he exclaims 'Bouvard and Pécuchet fill me up to the point that I have become them! Their bêtise is mine and it's killing me!' (Derrida 2009, p. 158). If one understands either the novelistic or the philosophical account of bêtise to be wholly uncontaminated by bêtise, somehow wholly evading it, standing above it, purely its opposite as one reigns down upon it, excoriating and capturing it, then paradoxically one cannot understand bêtise. Flaubert, Derrida claims, was 'scared by the bêtise that he has made and put to work, by the bêtise he was intelligent and *bête* enough to secrete in order to see, to see it, him too, and no longer tolerate it' (Derrida 2009, p. 159). Bêtise is not the idiocy of everyone who is supposedly not as bright as myself.

Even in negotiating and delineating stupidity's seemingly infinite borders, one cannot fully extricate oneself from it. The thought of stupidity demands an impossible double gesture: *to mire oneself in it so that one can analyze it* AND *simultaneously to remain above it so that one does not merely say stupid things about stupidity*. Musil concluded that there was no clean escape from the problem: 'Occasionally we are all stupid;

occasionally we must also act blindly or half blindly, or else the world would stand still' (Musil 1990, p. 286). If we withheld judgement from all that we did not understand, we would be paralyzed, much like Ulrich, the man without qualities himself, who cannot strongly commit himself to any predicates until he understands which would best suit him. Ulrich is consequently hardly able to decide on anything. 'If he is told that something is the way that it is, he will think: Well, it could probably just as well be otherwise' (Musil 1996, p. 11). Musil warns against the futility of a clean escape from stupidity: 'because our knowl-edge and ability are incomplete, we are forced in every field to judge prematurely.' Dogmatism aggressively avoids what Musil counseled as our only 'weapon' against a force form which we cannot extricate our-selves, namely, *modesty*. It teaches us an indispensable principle of think-ing: 'Act as well as you can and as badly as you must, but in doing so remain aware of the margin of error of your actions' (Musil 1990, p. 286). Hence we come to the second variation of the double gesture that the problem of stupidity demands: If one waits for wisdom in all situa-tions to act, one will be paralyzed, condemned to having no qualities. If one acts too quickly, one knows only the violence of dogmatism, the violent immodesty that avoids stupefaction at all costs.

Let us return to Bouvard and Pécuchet as they take the new inheri-tance and move out to the country and try their hand at farming. Rather than seek the advice of the farmer already there working the land—what do these idiotic peasants knows anyway?—they decide to figure out the agricultural sciences for themselves. After many disasters, they come upon the following hypothesis: They had not sufficiently amended the soil.

Egged on by Pécuchet, he had a frenzy for manure. In the compost trench were flung together boughs, blood, entrails, feathers—everything that could be found. He employed Belgian dressing, Swiss fertilizer, lye, pickled herrings, sea-weed, rags; he sent for guano, and tried to manufacture it; then, pushing his tenets to the extreme, would not let any urine be wasted. He suppressed the privies. Dead animals were brought into the yard with which he treated the soil. Their carcasses were scattered over the country in fragments. Bouvard smiled in the midst of the stench. A pump, installed in a tumbrel, spurted liquid manure over the crops. To those who put on airs of disgust he said: 'But it's gold! It's gold!'

And he regretted not having still more dung-heaps. Happy is the country where are natural grottoes filled with bird-dropping! (Flaubert 1954, p. 50).

Needless to say, the harvest was not robust: 'the rape was meager, the oats poor, the corn sold badly because of its smell' (Flaubert 1954, p. 50).

Their 'studies' continued unabated and when, after many other intellectual debacles, they are confounded by literature, they turn to the study of aesthetics, even reading Schelling, who teaches them that beauty is the 'infinite expressing itself in the finite' (Flaubert 1954, p. 166.). The new academic enterprise goes into crisis before it can come into itself, foundering on the duo's inability to distinguish successfully the beautiful from the sublime:

A character is beautiful when it triumphs, sublime when it struggles.

'I understand,' said Bouvard, 'beauty is beauty, the sublime is great beauty. How can they be distinguished?'

'By intuition,' replied Pécuchet.

'And where does intuition come from?'

'From taste.'

'And what's taste?'

It was defined as a special perception, swift judgment, the gift of perceiving certain relationships.

'So taste is taste; and all that says nothing about how to acquire it.'

'It is necessary to observe the proper rules, but these rules vary: and however perfect a work may be, it will not be altogether free from reproach. Still, there is an indestructible beauty, whose laws we do not know, for its origin is a mystery (Flaubert 1954, p. 167).

When their gardens fail, they conclude that 'arboriculture is probably all humbug,' just 'like agriculture!' (Flaubert 1954, p. 59). And then there is their spastic political involvements, in which their commitments run the gamut from solidarity with the people of the 1848 revolution to a defense of Napoleon—'Let him gag the mob, stamp it under foot, crush it! That will never be too great a penalty for its hatred of the right; its cowardice, its ineptitude, its blindness!' (Flaubert 1954, p. 203). Exasperated by all of this floundering in the world of ideas, they no longer pursued their studies, for 'fear of disillusionment' (Flaubert 1954, p. 204); 'sometimes they opened a book, only to close it again—what was the use' (Flaubert 1954)?

Their experiments and forays into animal magnetism and other forms of occultism eventually led them to a philosophical quandary: Ecstasy depends on a material cause, but what is matter and what is spirit (Flaubert 1954, p. 240.)? This led them to the study of philosophy and what is now called the mind-body problem. Trying to understand Spinoza and concluding that the universe 'is impenetrable to our consciousness' (Flaubert 1954, p. 244), they were quickly overwhelmed. 'All this was like being in a balloon at night, in glacial coldness, carried on an endless voyage towards a bottomless abyss, and with nothing near but the unseizable, the motionless, the eternal. It was too much. They gave it up' (Flaubert 1954).

They turned to philosophy primers, but these, too, proved vexing until 'both avowed their weariness of philosophers. So many systems serve only to confuse. Metaphysics has no use. One can exist without it' (Flaubert 1954, p. 249). Still, despite pressing quotidian demands, metaphysics returned because once again 'thoughts had come bubbling up' (Flaubert 1954, p. 250). Their metaphysical endeavors, alas, were to no avail. Although 'they began reasoning on a solid basis' (Flaubert 1954), 'suddenly an idea would vanish, as a fly darts off when one tries to catch it' (Flaubert 1954, p. 251). Pécuchet turns to Hegel, but soon Bouvard is exasperated: 'One explains what one knows little about, by means of words that one doesn't understand at all' (Flaubert 1954, p. 255). This soon drives them to the depths of nihilism: 'The certainty that nothing exists (however much to be deplored) is not the less a certainty. Few people are capable of holding such a belief' (Flaubert 1954). Soon Bouvard is defending even rogues. 'When a man's born blind, or an idiot, or a murderer, that seems disorder to us, as though order were known to us, as if Nature acted with a purpose' (Flaubert 1954, p. 257). Bouvard and Pécuchet continue to routinely undermine 'all foundations' (Flaubert 1954, p. 258).

Although they are threatened with prison and slandered for being immoral, something much worse transpires. In their heroic nihilism, something strange begins to emerge, something to which Deleuze also alerts us: 'the presentiment of a hideousness proper to the human face, a rise of bêtise, an evil deformity, or a thought governed by madness. For from the point of a philosophy of nature, madness rises up at the point at which the individual contemplates himself in this free ground,—and, as a result, bêtise in bêtise, cruelty in cruelty—to the point it can no longer stand itself' (Deleuze 1994, p. 152; Deleuze 1968, p. 197). As we shall develop shortly, Deleuze admits in a footnote that this kind of articulation of the problem borrows from Schelling's *Freedom* essay[1], but at this point he also turns to *Bouvard et Pécuchet* when Flaubert famously tells us that 'then a pitiable faculty developed in their spirit, that of perceiving bêtise and no longer tolerating it' (Flaubert 1954, p. 258; Deleuze 1994, p. 152; Deleuze 1968, p. 197).

What comes of this 'pitiable faculty'? The bêtise that imagines everyone else to be idiotic, grows to spite itself and then succumbs to melancholy, the melancholy that Schelling in the Freedom essay spoke of as the attractive force of the re-emerging abyssal ground that pulls the stupidity of self-grounded ideas into its vortex: 'The human never receives the condition within their power, although they strive to do so in evil … Hence, the veil of melancholy that is spread out over all of Nature, the deep, indestructible melancholy of all life' (I/7, 399).[2] Poor Bouvard and Pécuchet sink deep into the burgeoning evil and flaring illness of their aggressive bêtise:

Insignificant things made them sad; advertisements in the newspapers, a smug profile, a foolish remark heard by chance … they felt as though the heaviness of all the earth were weighing on them. They no longer went out, or received visits … The world was diminishing in importance; they saw it as through a cloud, come down from their brains, over their eyes (Flaubert 1954, pp. 258–259).

In the *Dictionnaire* we learn under the entry TO THINK: 'painful. Things that compel us to think are generally neglected' (Flaubert, *Dictionary* 1954, p. 79). This is the evasion of thinking that hides, initially and for the most part, in the bêtise of what passes for thinking, much in the way that Franziska 'thought' that she was consoling her son by telling him that his 'books are now world shaking.' This is the kind of 'thinking' that manifests in the Dictionnaire entry for 'MISTAKE': 'It's worse than a crime, it's a mistake' (Talleyrand). 'There is not a mistake left to commit' (Thiers). These two remarks must be uttered with an air of profundity' (Flaubert, *Dictionary* 1954, p. 58). The problem with this entry is not that it is a mistake about mistakes, but rather that it protects thinking ('painful') from the 'stupidity' of its ground by making oneself the ground of thinking. This reversal or inversion—the force of illness, evil, madness, and melancholy—does not originate in myself nor is it simply dwelling in the ground that we shun in our anxiety before the possibility of being stupid.

In English, the word 'stupid' derives from the Latin *stupidus*, to be 'confounded and amazed,' itself derived form the literal meaning of stupidus as 'struck senseless,' from *stupere*, to be stunned and confounded, and hence, retaining a relationship, which was preserved in English until sometime in the 18th century, with the word 'stupor,' itself the result of being paralyzed by surprise. *Dumm*, whose origins are less clear, suggest inexperience, but seems also to be related to *stumm*, to be mute, as if the experience of stupidity swallowed up all other experience, leaving one with nothing really to say, unable really to use language. It is to be left speechless in the sudden muting of what one has imagined to be one's experience. For Deleuze, la bêtise 'is the faculty for false problems; it is evidence of an inability to constitute, comprehend or determine a problem as such' (Deleuze 1994, p. 159; Deleuze 1968, p. 207). As is the case with slaves, stupid thinkers 'do not control the problems themselves' and do not see themselves as having a right to the great problems, questions whose power outstrips the force of a dogmatic answer or the sterility of a melancholic response. Stupidity avoids the abyss through its incessant platitudes, clichés, kitsch, and takes refuge in common sense, the natural attitude, the self-evident, and other snares of 'idiocy.' The latter is not to be conflated with stupidity, for it specifically names the subjective assumptions that surreptitiously govern thinking, taking the form of 'Everybody knows [*tout la monde sait*]' (Deleuze 1994, p. 129; Deleuze 1968, p. 170). If it cannot rely on its arsenal of mechanical repetitions, it stares into the abyss, unable to creatively transform it, that is, to think philosophically.

Such unexpected muting and dumb staring cannot be wholly separated from being-unto-death, and when Bouvard and Pécuchet joylessly walk the countryside they come upon the corpse of a dog.

The four legs were dried up. The grinning jaw revealed ivory fangs beneath blue chops; instead of the belly there an earth-colored mass that seemed to quiver, so thickly did it pullulate with vermin. It stirred, beaten by the sun, under the buzzing of flies, in that intolerable stench—a fierce, and as it were, devouring odor ... Pécuchet said stoically: 'One day we shall be like that' (Flaubert 1954, p. 260.).

They were under the sway of the idea of death, and 'they tried to imagine death in the form of a very dark night, a bottomless pit, a never ending swoon—anything at all was better than this monotonous, absurd and hopeless existence' (Flaubert 1954, p. 260.). They considered what they had missed out on. Bouvard yearned for wealth, wine, and 'beautiful yielding women,' while Pécuchet dreamt of mastering philosophy so that he could solve all problems by solving a problem so vast that it contained, and thereby simultaneously resolved, all other possible problems. And then they contemplated suicide, but averted it by discovering religion. Facing the silent stupor of the noose, a song about the King of Angels made them feel as if 'a dawn were rising in their souls' (Flaubert 1954, p. 264). Religious life brings them back from the abyssal stupidity of death, and soon they are back at work 'thinking' in their serial progression of intellectual catastrophes about education, music, and urban planning.

How does bêtise so easily escape the stupefying silence of the noose and remain so 'unshakable' such that, Flaubert reflected, 'nothing can attack it without breaking against it' (Quoted in Derrida 2009, p. 160)? *La bêtise* is as relentless as death itself, much like Sancho Panza characterized it in Cervantes masterpiece: Death is 'more powerful than finicky; nothing disgusts her, she eats everything, and she does everything, and she crams her pack with all kinds and ages and ranks of people. She's not a reaper who takes naps; she reaps constantly and cuts the dry grass along with the green, and she doesn't seem to chew her food but wolfs it down and swallows everything that is put in front of her, because she's as hungry as a dog and is never satisfied' (Cervantes 2003, p. 590). As such, it drives us from its ground to the violent safety of ourselves as the unquestioned authors of fixed positions, self-assured answers, and comfortable conclusions.

Borges admires Flaubert's sense of this in the latter's appreciation of Spencer's critique of science as 'a finite sphere that grows in infinite space; each new expansion makes it include a larger zone of the unknown, but the unknown is inexhaustible.' Hence, Flaubert concluded that 'we still now know almost nothing and we would wish to divine the final word that will be never revealed to us. The frenzy for reaching a conclusion is the most sterile and disastrous of manias' (Borges 1999, p. 388). Let us be clear: the violence of la bêtise lies in a madness, but a very particular one and one that is supremely destructive, namely, the insanity of the self-grounded ego to still the ground of thinking with grand conclusions, lest it stupefy one with the abyssal force of death itself. Was this not Pécuchet's greatest desire, standing before the noose, of utterly mastering philosophy so that he could solve all problems by solving a problem so vast that it contained and thereby simultaneously resolved all other possible problems? In his critique of Auguste Comte's positivistic bêtise, Flaubert warns that 'Ineptitude consists in wanting to conclude ... It is not understanding twilight, it's wanting only noon or midnight ... Yes, *bêtise* consists in wanting to conclude' (Derrida 2009, p. 161).

We also find this paradoxical conclusion about the danger of conclusions in Schelling who considered philosophical errors not as the incapacities of intelligence, but as the moments in which thinking inhibits itself, clots, refuses to go on, stops cold. 'There are no universally valid propositions, only propositions that are valid for *the* moment of development of which they are an expression' (Schelling 1969, pp. 6–7). Ideas do not have free-floating veracity, lying about, ready to be picked up and contemplated. They must be thought genetically, in their becoming within a domain in which they can have meaning. Deleuze, in this Schellingian vein, argues that 'all determinations become bad and cruel when they are grasped only by a thought that invents and contemplates them, flayed, and separated from their living form, adrift upon this barren ground. Everything becomes violence on this passive ground.' This, for Deleuze is the site of 'the Sabbath of bêtise and malevolence [*méchanceté*]' (Deleuze 1994, p. 152; Deleuze 1968, p. 198). On the Sabbath, the genetic dynamism of the ground is given a rest in the malevolence of conclusions that allow the ground to be usurped by a thinking that cannot affirm it and, in failing to do so, takes refuge in itself as the ground, thereby inverting the original relationship.

The anxiety that the threat of bêtise evokes is the threat to a ground whose life cannot be settled in final conclusions. Hence, in the *Freedom* essay, Schelling famously argued that 'the anxiety of life itself drives the human from the center in which they were created' (I/7, 382; in English translation: Schelling 2006, p. 47).[3] It is as if, Schelling tells us, one were to stand at a great height and suddenly, as if from nowhere, one felt tempted to jump or as if one suddenly rushed to the sirens. This is the anxiety at the heart of stupidity. It is not something in itself (hence the endless variation of possible forms of stupidity and Flaubert's exhaustion and Musil's gargantuan but still unfinishable novel). It is, as Deleuze argues, following Schelling, 'neither the ground nor the individual' but rather the relation in which the relation between ground and presence is reversed and hence it is 'this relation in which individuation brings the ground [*fond, (Un)grund*] to the surface without being able [*sans pouvoir*] to give it form (this ground rises by means of the I, penetrating deeply into the possibility of thought and constituting the unrecognized in every recognition)' (Deleuze 1994, p. 152; Deleuze 1968, pp. 197–198). The I, anxious before a ground which consumes the very determinations that it births, confronts it as a dark night when all cows are black,' fleeing from it to the alleged safety of her I. This, Deleuze tells us, is what is 'the most tempting in the most stupefied moments [*les moments de stupeur*] of an obtuse will. For this ground, along with the individual, rises to the surface yet assumes neither form nor figure. It is there, staring at us, but without eyes' (Deleuze 1994, p. 152; Deleuze 1968, p. 197). The abdicated ground of thinking, inverted in thinking's flight to the self as its own ground, returns as the haunting force of stupefaction.

Michel Foucault very much admired Deleuze's courage with regard to this problem, arguing that 'within categories, one makes mistakes; outside of them, or beyond or beneath them, one is stupid. Bouvard and Pécuchet are acategoriacal beings' (Foucault 1998, p. 361). When they cannot complete a thought, they immediately dismiss it as hopeless. 'It's the same either way' stupidity says' (Foucault 1998, p. 362). It is catatonic stupefaction in which all thoughts are arbitrary. Drugs, which unless you are a fortune-teller, have nothing whatsoever to do with the problem of truth and falsity—they, too are acategorical, but unlike stupidity, they are not paralysed by the dark night when all cows are black. They 'displace the relative positions of stupidity and thought by eliminating the old necessity of a theater of immobility' (Foucault 1998, p. 363). As Deleuze, following Schelling, puts it, Flaubert's 'pitiful faculty'can become the 'royal faculty' as it renders possible a violent reconciliation between the individual, the ground, and thought' (Deleuze 1994, p. 152; Deleuze 1968, p. 198). The royal repetition, when the groundlessness of death is longer than the stupefaction of the dark of the black cows, is 'a belief in the future [*croyance en l'avenir*]' (Deleuze 1994, p. 90; Deleuze 1968, p. 122). Death becomes the productivity of thinking. 'In this manner, the ground has been superseded by a groundlessness, a universal ungrounding which turns upon itself and causes only the yet-to-come to return' (Deleuze 1994, p. 91; Deleuze 1968, p. 123).

Stupidity flees the ground as if it were the mere opacity of death, the dark night when all cows are black, but this is the violence in which the ground of life is bracketed by the dogmatic image of thought, as mere stupefaction. Hence, I agree wholeheartedly with my colleague Julián Ferreyra that, in contradistinction to the kind of Deleuzian who drunkenly rushes, intoxicated by rhizomes and promises of lines of flight, to an undifferentiated abyss as if they were glibly not as stupid as Bouvard and Pécuchet, 'becoming a philosophy of indifference is the greatest risk for the philosophy of difference' (Ferreyra 2012). How stupid to have spoken of the dark night! Bêtise is not the stupefaction of utter indeterminacy, i.e., Moosbrugger's insane experience and conviction were that nothing could be singled out by itself, because things hang together. As Deleuze argues in the conclusion to *Difference and Repetition*, defending Schelling from Hegel's charge of the night of the black cows, the illusion internal to all representation is that that 'groundlessness (*le sans fond*) should lack differences, when in fact it swarms with them' (Deleuze 1994, p. 277; Deleuze 1968, p. 355). As the I fractures, the abandoned relationship to the *Ungrund* reasserts itself and we succumb to melancholy and malevolence or, as Ferreyra notes, 'we attain the point of view of genesis' and 'ideas spring in the apparent groundlessness of *bêtise*' (Ferreyra 2012). As Deleuze had already argued in 1962, Nietzsche had made active thought a 'critique of *la bêtise* and baseness [*la bassesse*]' and in so doing, proposed a new image of thought, liberated from the malevolence and stupidity of the dogmatic image of thought. 'Thinking depends on forces which take hold of thought. Insofar as our thinking is controlled by reactive forces, we must admit that we are not yet thinking' (Deleuze 1983, p. 108; Deleuze 1962, p. 123).

This finally, was the guiding insight into Schelling's classification of our species into three fundamental types. In the third draft of *Die Weltalter* (1815), he dissects the problem of the *Verstandesmensch* (the 'intellectual') as a problem of stupidity:

One could say that there is a kind of person in which there is no madness whatsoever. These would be the uncreative people incapable of procreation, the ones that call themselves sober spirits. These are the so-called intellectuals [*Verstandesmenschen*] whose works and deeds are nothing but cold intellectual works and intellectual deeds. Some people in philosophy have misunderstood this expression in utterly strange ways. For because they heard it said of intellectuals that they are, so to speak, low and inferior, and because they themselves did not want to be like this, they good-naturedly opposed reason [*Vernunft*] to intellect instead of opposing reason to madness. But where there is no madness, there is also certainly no proper, active, living intellect (and consequently there is just the dead intellect, dead intellectuals). For in what does the intellect prove itself than in the coping with and governance and regulation of madness? Hence the utter lack of madness leads to another extreme, to imbecility (idiocy), which is an absolute lack of all madness. But there are two other kinds of persons in which there really is madness. There is one kind of person that governs madness and precisely in this overwhelming shows the highest force of the intellect. The other kind of person is governed by madness and is someone who really is mad. (Schelling 2000, pp. 103–104; I/8, 338–339)

Thinking finds itself before the crossroads of two great violences: the stupidity of dogmatism (the malevolence, incipient or manifest, of the self-assured dogmatist) and the dark night of ungoverned madness. Philosophy negotiates madness as its vocation, with all due modesty, in its attempt to keep the upper hand on stupidity and stop being the only beast that can be beastly.

By the phrase 'keep the upper hand,' I would like to evoke Heidegger's argument that one cannot overcome (*überwinden*) metaphysics, but rather that one must do one's best to 'keep the upper hand [*verwinden*]' on them. Of course, I do not disagree with the danger of metaphysics, but I hope that I have successfully suggested that the problem of metaphysics cannot be extricated from the more fundamental problem of the violence of stupidity. This requires the kind of double gesture that has been the transcendental concern of the present essay, a gesture in which *die Verwindung* negotiates the twin violences of metaphysical dogmatism and melancholic paralysis. It cannot fully evade the two, but the dignity of philosophy lies in the attempt not to be utterly consumed by them.

Finally, there are a host of issues regarding the metaphorical animality at the heart of the problem of la bêtise. *L'animal*, Deleuze tells us, is 'protected' from la bêtise 'by specific forms' (Deleuze 1994, p. 150; Deleuze 1968, p. 196) and that 'animals are in a sense forewarned against this ground, protected by their explicit forms' (Deleuze 1994, p. 152; Deleuze 1968, p. 197). The human is the only *bête* with a faculty (in the Kantian sense) of la bêtise, the only bête that can be bête, the only beast capable of being beastly. This is perhaps also a reference to Schelling's claim in the Freedom essay, following Franz von Baader, that the human can 'only stand above or below animals' (I/7, 373; Schelling 2006, p. 40). Perhaps the language of above and below does not take us far enough away from the history of the human subjugation of animals, even though both Schelling and von Baader here link such a history with the human being finding itself beneath animals, that is, having a beastly relationship to beasts. Only human beings can be evil and only human beings can be stupid. That being said, the claim is not that animals are lost in some kind of permanent stupor, lost in the non-philosophical default mode of species specific natural stupidity. The burden is rather on our species to stop having such a *stupid—and I daresay evil—*relationship to our non-human animal sisters and brothers.

As Whitehead lamented in *Science and the Modern World*, the stupidity of our age is characterized not by thoughtlessness, but by the 'restraint of serious thought within a groove. The remainder of life is treated superficially, with the imperfect categories of thought derived

from one profession' (Whitehead 2011, p. 245). As a result we are direc-
tionless, imbalanced, with the whole 'lost in one of its aspects'
(Whitehead 2011, 246), and as the violence that Musil's endless committee meetings could not foresee, let alone forestall, teaches us, unless
we claim our right to the problems of thinking, this explosive force continues to acquire catastrophic energy. Religion cannot intervene, if it
too, is claimed by the stupidity that Rick Santorum demonstrated to the
world in his beastly 2011–12 run for the presidency of the United
States, a run that reminds us that religion's capacity for emancipatory
awakening must not fail to struggle to keep its upper hand on its pro-
clivity (in the Schellingian and Kantian sense of radical evil: Wirth
2003) for devastating—and devastatingly dogmatic—violence.

Notes

1. 'Schelling wrote some splendid pages on evil (stupidity and malevolence), its source which is like the Ground becomes autonomous (essentially
related to individuation), and on the entire history which follows from this ...'
(Deleuze 1994, pp. 321–322; Deleuze 1968, p. 198).

2. Schelling citations follow the standard pagination, which follows the
original edition established after Schelling's death by his son, Karl. It lists the
division, followed by the volume, followed by the page number. Hence, (I/1, 1)
would read, division one, volume one, and page one. It is preserved in Manfred
Schröter's critical reorganization of this material. The Schelling translations are
my own responsibility, although I also provide the citations for the English
translations, in this case (Schelling 2006, p. 63). The German original for the
passage at hand reads: 'Der Mensch bekommt die Bedingung nie in seine
Gewalt, ob er gleich im Bösen danach strebt ... Daher der Schleier der
Schwermut, der über die ganze Natur ausgebreitet ist, die tiefe unzerstörliche
Melancholie alles Lebens.'

3. In the third draft of *The Ages of the World*, we find the following description: 'Hence, since the first potency unites within it conflicting forces, of which
one always craves the outside and of which the other is always inwardly
restrained, its life is a life of loathing [*Widerwärtigkeit*] and anxiety since it does
not know whether to turn inward or outward and in this fashion falls prey to an
arbitrary, revolving motion' (Schelling 2000, p. 246).

References

Borges, Jorge Luis, 'A Defense of *Bouvard et Pécuchet*' (1954), *Selected Non-
  Fictions*, ed. Eliot Weinberger (New York: Viking, 1999).
Cervantes Saavedra, Miguel de, *Don Quixote* (1605–1615), tr. Edith Grossman
  (New York: Ecco, 2003).

Deleuze, Gilles, *Difference and Repetition*, tr. Paul Patton (New York: Columbia University Press, 1994).

——, *Différence et répétition* (Paris: Presses universitaires de France, 1968).

——, *Nietzsche and Philosophy*, tr. Hugh Tomlinson (New York: Columbia University Press, 1983).

——, *Nietzsche et la philosophie* (Paris: Presses universitaires de France, 1962).

Derrida, Jacques, *The Beast & the Sovereign*, volume 1, tr. Geoffrey Bennington (Chicago and London: University of Chicago Press, 2009).

Ferreyra, Julián, 'Flaubert's *Bêtise* as a Way into Deleuzian Ideas,' unpublished manuscript presented at Harvard University, February 16, 2012.

Flaubert, Gustave, *Bouvard and Pécuchet*, tr. T. W. Earp and G. W. Sonier (New York: New Directions, 1954).

——, *The Dictionary of Accepted Ideas*, tr. and ed. Jacques Barzun, included as a supplement to *Bouvard and Pécuchet*.

Foucault, Michel, 'Theatrum Philosophicum,' tr. Donald F. Bouchard and Sherry Simon, *Aesthetics, Method, and Epistemology: Essential Works of Foucault*, volume 2, ed. James D. Faubion (New York: The New Press, 1998).

Gilman, Sander L. ed. *Conversations with Nietzsche: A Life in the Words of His Contemporaries*, tr. David J. Parent (New York and Oxford: Oxford University Press, 1987).

Musil, Robert, *The Man Without Qualities*, volume 1, tr. Sophie Wilkins (New York: Vintage, 1996).

——, 'On Stupidity' (1937), *Precision and Soul*, tr. Burton Pike and David S. Luft (Chicago and London: University of Chicago Press, 1990).

Nietzsche, Friedrich, *Kritische Studienausgabe*, volume 3, ed. Giorgio Colli and Mazzino Montinari (Munich and Berlin: Deutscher Taschenbuch Verlag and Walter de Gruyter, 1988).

Ronell, Avital, *Stupidity* (Urbana and Chicago: University of Illinois Press, 2002)

Schelling, F. W. J., *The Ages of the World*, tr. Jason M. Wirth (Albany: SUNY Press, 2000).

——, *Initia Philosophiæ Universæ* (1820–21), ed. Horst Fuhrmans (Bonn: H. Bouvier, 1969).

——, *Philosophical Investigations Into the Essence of Human Freedom* (1809), tr. Jeff Love and Johannes Schmidt (Albany: SUNY Press, 2006).

——, *Schellings Werke: Nach der Originalausgabe in neuer Anordnung*, ed. Manfred Schröter (Munich: C. H. Beck, 1927).

Singh, Rustam, *'Weeping' and Other Essays on Being and Writing* (Jaipur, India: Pratilipi Books, 2011).

Whitehead, Alfred North, *Science and the Modern World* (1926), (Cambridge: Cambridge University Press, 2011).

Wirth, Jason M. *The Conspiracy of Life: Meditations on Schelling and His Time* (Albany: SUNY Press, 2003).

4 'No Eye Has Seen It'
*The Renewal of the Human Condition in Marx and Lévinas**

Aïcha Liviana Messina

In a recently published book, *Le Consentement Meurtrier* (*Murderous Consent*), Marc Crépon faces one of those problems that must be addressed, that in some way defines the challenge of responsibility, and yet lacks a solution: the fact that the practice of violence is not always voluntary but, more often, even constantly, takes place despite ourselves. This fact, in the very impossibility to respond to it, structures not only society but also humanity in the 'murderous consent.' Thus Crépon writes:

> We are caught between two forms of 'murderous consent'. On the one hand, we are exposed to the paradox of revolt, which states that the introduction of unity in the world (such as a dream of justice that needs to become reality) shall change the protest against death (which had inspired it) into murderous consent. On the other hand, denial of the necessity of such a unity is also an acceptance of the death of others. (Crépon 2012, p. 50)

On the one hand, injustice (which is a form of violence) that structures, haunts, and perhaps constitutes our societies requires revolt, revolution—that is, the radical (and not only partial) change not only of society but of humanity itself. But the revolt itself entails violence, so we end up doing what is to be denied. On the other hand, adhering to the

* Acknowledgement: This article was written under the auspices of the FONDECYT research program 11,090,366 (Conicyt, the government of Chile) and of the SEMILLA research program (Universidad Diego Portales, Chile).

belief that nothing can be done is still an acceptance of violence and injustice, and therefore its practice.

This problem is at the heart of Emmanuel Lévinas' thought. For Lévinas, in fact, I am responsible not only for my own faults but also for those of all humanity, so that the violence perpetrated in spite of myself every day is also one to which I must respond every day, at every moment. But for Lévinas, we cannot respond to this violence by committing violence in turn. One cannot fight evil via evil means. The struggle that justifies evil in the name of Good cannot hope to end the evil. Thus, Lévinas draws a new figure of the revolutionary: 'The Revolutionary action,' Lévinas writes, 'is primarily that of an isolated man who prepares the revolution in danger, but also in the tearing of consciousness—in the catacombs and consciousness's double clandestinity' (Lévinas1977, p. 38). In other words, for Lévinas, the revolutionary man is not justified by the Good he projects and by which he would redeem mankind. If he remains separated and concealed in 'consciousness' clandestinity,' this means he is not at peace with himself. He does not conform to his conscience animated by the idea or hope of a future good, but neither is he even at peace with regard to the dead men around him, with the violence he is doing in the name of Good. But then, how can this man act? While describing the revolutionary man in the 'tearing of consciousness,' Lévinas himself is aware of the threat of inaction: 'the tearing of the conscience' 'may make revolution impossible, because what is at stake is not only to seize the criminal, but to prevent making the innocent suffer' (Lévinas1977, pp. 38–9). Should we conclude that Lévinas calls us to remain paralyzed in a state of bad conscience? But is a torn conscience reducible to a bad conscience? While it is difficult to imagine a humanity freed from violence, is there still a form of revolutionary action, which is an action that aims at not only partial but total transformation of society, which can be done on behalf of the Good without violence? And how is that Good designed without relying on axiomatic values, that is, an ideology that ultimately, whatever it pretends to be, will always be maintained by violence?

Surprisingly, it is especially in his Talmudic commentaries and readings that Lévinas explicitly raises this question. In 'Judaism and Revolution' for example, Lévinas writes: 'I do not think… we must define revolution in a purely formal manner, by violence or by the reversal of a given order…. We must define revolution by the content, by the values: revolution is where there is freed man, that is, where man is pulled up from economic determinism' (Lévinas1977, p. 24). And in 'State of Caesar, State of David,' Lévinas stops for a moment to consider the biblical problem of the 'future world' by saying that if one can assign a purely religious meaning to issues of redemption, one can also interpret them from a social perspective. Thus, about the future world, of which interpreters of the Talmud say 'No eye has seen besides You, O Thee Lord, who rescues the one who waits for You,' Lévinas adds in a note this surprising comment: ' "no eye has seen," recalls singularly the strange passages where Marx expected the socialist society of changes in the human condition, evading any predictions because of their revolutionary essence itself.' (Lévinas1982, p. 217). That is, for Lévinas, the strictly religious problem of redemption, of individual salvation expected at the end of time once the Messianic era is completed, is inseparable from a social problem, from the problem of the human condition in its entirety. The expectation of a 'future world' makes sense only if it announces 'a new way of life, new relationships with others' (Lévinas1982, p. 217). But how is it possible to relate the problem of the 'future world' to each other, that would be the 'real term of eschatology' (Lévinas1982, p. 217), with changes of the human condition that could induce the Marxian socialism? If the 'future world' cannot even be prophesied, if 'no eye has seen it besides You, O Thee Lord' doesn't this awaiting of divine action entail the curbing of any possible revolution? Doesn't it thereby implicate consent to all injustices, and, in the acceptance of powerlessness, consent to murder?

Back to the question of good and evil which I mentioned earlier. In 'Judaism and Revolution,' Lévinas is clear about the dialectic of good and evil: 'The dialectic where evil serves the good, where evil can objectively be a force of good, is confusion and night' (Lévinas1977, p. 33). In other words, the historical pattern that suggests that the Good comes from evil, that evil is a necessary step in human progress, ends up confusing good and evil, and can only lead to be held in the meshes of the latter. This is thus contrary to Marx, who in 1843 wrote to Ruge: 'You will not say that I overstate the present world, however, if I do not despair of it, that is precisely because its desperate situation fills me with hope' (Marx and Engels 1971, p. 29). Still Hegelian, Marx trusts the idea that evil can promise a good to come, the first being necessary to the second. However, for Lévinas, good and evil are not opposed dialectically. If

Good is a renewal of the human condition and not just a final destination that can logically be deduced or induced from a historical process, and must be thought of like the action of newness in history as what cannot be deducted from any logic. In this sense, 'the dialectic where evil serves good' does not bode anything radically new. We cannot expect a renewal of humanity from a science of history—that is, either the achievement of Reason or, in contrast, of historical materialism. The freedom of humanity simply cannot come from what alienates it. Good cannot be spoken in the language of evil, otherwise humanity is not renewed, and revolution remains partial—that is, not realized. Separating good from evil, so as not to understand these two terms dialectically, is the condition for a real revolutionary action, that is, for a revolution that commits humanity to a destiny of total renewal. Thus, it is to adhere to the revolutionary ideal without diminishing its scope and effectiveness that Lévinas extricates revolution from its formal, dialectical sense, where evil is a force of good.

Before asking what is this good that could act to forge the renewal of humanity, let us examine the problem of evil. Like Marx, Lévinas could associate evil with alienation. As we have already said, in 'Judaism and Revolution,' Lévinas explicitly talks about the revolution as the need to free human beings from economic determinism, which is, for Marx as for Lévinas, to release mankind, to restore its humanity. Indeed, for Marx, injustice encompasses more than the terms of economic inequality. It's not just that some are bourgeois-owners, and that the proletarian is deprived of the object of his work. Of course, for Marx, alienation is a form of dispossession, but is so in ways that exceed a purely economic condition. Previously, for the young Marx, alienation is what strips human beings of their humanity. Reduced to a mere 'workforce,' the proletariat is not only reduced to economic misery, it is deprived of a genuinely human world. What in fact is such a humanity to Marx? It is inseparable from the possibility of expressing oneself through the object of work and thereby through the mediation of the object, of creating a common world, of being 'oneself' while being 'for others' (Marx 1996, p. 145). Through work, human beings become human by becoming social beings, by sharing a common world. The common world that results from the means of work is that by which humanity self-produces itself. Socialization is therefore inherent to humanity. In this sense, alienation does not only mean that human beings are dispossessed of the objects of their labour but of their very humanity itself. Separated from the objects of its work, the proletariat is mostly bereft of what Marx calls the 'generic life,' that is, the life that comes from the ability to self-produce oneself, which is constitutive of its humanity:

Thus, while the alienated work takes out from the man his production, it snatches his generic-life, his true generic objectivity, and transforms his superiority over the animal into inferiority, since his non-organic body, the nature, has been stolen. (Marx 1996, p. 116)

Hence, we see that the violence and injustice denounced by Marx is not inequality of thought only in economic terms. Human beings do not recover their humanity through distributive justice. If economic determinism deprives humans of their humanity, we must transform the means of production as well as distribute the goods in a more equitable fashion. Thus, the socialist project aims to restore humanity by abolishing private property. The revolution does not aim thereby to recover an innate essence, a 'human nature' that a human being should possess in an unhistorical way. Humanity is not an essence but a self-produced nature: 'But for the socialist man, the so-called universal history is nothing other than the production of man by human labour, rather than the fate of nature for man' (Marx 1996, p. 156).

We can now understand how socialism, as projected by Marx, based on its scientific basis, can change the human condition. Socialism is not only social justice thought in economic terms but the modification of the human condition through the transformation of what relates one human being to another. It is in a human world that a human being can relate humanly to another. Therefore, as Marx wrote, communism is the way to transform this world, but it is not its end. The aim of the revolution is not merely the overturn of the system, the abolition of private property, but the transformation of the human condition:

Communism is the necessary form and the dynamic principle of the immediate future, but communism as such is neither the goal of human development and nor the way of human society. (Marx 1996, p. 157)

If Lévinas indirectly shares the values of the socialist project, that is, its humanist content—, that is, a materialistic humanism[1]—however, as we have seen, he parts ways with the form which such values and content would take. In fact, for Marx, alienation is the way by which the human being can historically understand and thereby regain his humanity, a humanity that by itself is a historical product[2]. But for Lévinas, Marx's analysis of the problem of alienation remains a prisoner of what is detected as evil. In fact, even though Lévinas doesn't offer such an explicit formulation, we could say that for Lévinas the problem of alienation isn't focussed solely on the means of production but is already inherent to what Marx describes as a generic life. In Lévinas' view, such a 'generic' understanding of humanity reduces the singularity of each being to a generality or a type–even if this type is not presupposed and abstract, but self-produced and strictly conditioned by the means of production (by a material context). Now, it is precisely this conception of mankind as subordinated to a context or as encompassed in a generality that Lévinas could define as an alienated condition.[3] In fact, understood through their 'generic life,' human beings are dependent on the context in which they become meaningful. The meaning itself is no longer human but rather contextual or structural. In such a context, humans are parts of a whole, they are never themselves; they disappear behind 'coherent discourses to which the speaker lends his tongue and lips' (Lévinas 1963, p. 290). In other words, for Lévinas, Marx's conception of humanity remains inhuman in that it makes humanity dependent on general structures which end up *silencing* each human being. As Lévinas writes, criticizing not only structuralism, but more generally all western philosophy, where humans can be determined only as a generality (as man*kind*), 'no *one* can talk,' 'words-have become—the silent signs of anonymous infrastructure, such as utensils of dead civilizations or as missed acts of our daily lives' (Lévinas 1963, p. 290). Conceived as a generic essence, humanity would remain silent. Thus, in 'Freedom of Speech,' Lévinas puts on the same plain Marxism, sociology, and psychoanalysis (that is, structuralism), as symptoms resulting from this 'civilization of aphasia.' Explaining man by conceptions such as the means of production, social structures, or unconsciousness entails dissolving human beings in a structure, so at every turn one understands man as being what alienates him. Here we find ourselves in a perfect circle where alienation is described by the very means by which humanity is alienated.

In this sense, Lévinas' conclusion can only be pessimistic: 'no word has more authority to tell the world the end of his own downfall' (Lévinas 1963, p. 290). In other words, if we are always immanent to what we criticize, we do not see how, as Marx addresses Ruge, a 'desperate situation' may 'fill with hope.'

This displacement in the analysis of the problem of alienation leads to the disablement of the very processes that would lead, according to Marx, to the liberation of humanity, and the transformation of its condition. In fact, while for Marx humanity requires the object that it shapes in order to express itself, Lévinas will see in this objectification the very dissolution and therefore alienation of humanity. Therefore, while Lévinas coincides with Marx in understanding alienation as a dispossession, he does not believe that the end of alienation coincides with the reappropriation of power of human beings. On the contrary, he defines alienation as being inherent in the power of human beings and their ability to produce themselves (i.e., their humanity) through their objects. This point can be exemplified by a passage of *Totality and Infinity*, where Lévinas explains that when I produce, my work is no longer mine because the sense of what I do exposes me to the vagaries of otherness, to alien forces, to the unknown. Through work, I am certainly shaping a human world, a world where I can feel 'at home,' but as long as that world goes through the mediation of the object, it is also anonymous. We cannot be in that way fully contemporary with our essence, fully immanent to our activity. Even in a world free of capital, alien forces will take hold of us. Thus, Lévinas writes: 'the part of eternal truth that materialism consists of in the fact that the human will can be taken hold of by its works' (Lévinas 1961, p. 253). If Man can, by his activity, express himself through his work, he cannot, however, control the destiny of this work. The meaning that it will take will necessarily escape him. Therefore, if the work can take 'the anonymity of merchandise, an anonymity where, as an employee, the worker may himself disappear' (Lévinas 1961, p. 250), then this is not due only to economic determinism as embedded in the means of production; as well as how other people will take hold of my work: it is inherent to the duplication produced by the action, namely, to the fact that the object of the action is immersed into the anonymity of things—things that certainly, as Lévinas says, have 'meanings' but remain 'silent' (Lévinas 1961, p. 250). As Lévinas writes:

It is important to note that the destination of the work devoted to a story that I cannot predict—because I can't see it—is part of the essence of my power and doesn't result from the contingent presence of other people at my side. (1961, p. 251)

We can observe here how Lévinas' critique of the understanding of humanity as self-produced, as well as his conception of alienation as inherent to Man's power (and in this way, to his essence), entail the denial of any possible hope in a freeing History. More precisely, if Lévinas pointed out the insufficiency of an understanding of alienation as historical and as dependent on the means of production, he is now pointing out that History, by its very objective structure, is doomed to fail in freeing humanity because it cannot be understood otherwise than as an objective form which ends up silencing humans. Rather than freeing humanity, History would therefore be the very manifestation of its alienation. In fact, Lévinas notes that the historic character of Man does not make him the holder of his destiny. Human action that passes through the object, once expressed, turns against the one who would, by it, become a subject of his history. In this sense, heroism necessarily fails; the freedom of the hero who wants to take control of destiny is always coupled with a shadow, which, ultimately, will turn against him: 'The hero finds himself playing a role in a drama that is overflowing his heroic intentions, which by their very opposition to this tragedy, hasten the accomplishment of designs foreign to these intentions' (Lévinas 1961). If the human being's history requires work, and if work is that by which humanity produces its 'generic-life,' its historical essence, and thus its future release, that one thing that could make possible a solution to the alienation of human beings turns against itself, against the one who seeks, through history, to be free: 'the absurdity of fate,' writes Lévinas, 'thwarts the sovereign will' (Lévinas 1961). So, if Lévinas challenges the dialectic of good and evil, he does so not only on the behalf of a revolutionary ideal, but because the dialectic of history is not able to release humanity, because in the ultimate instance, human beings find themselves speechless in front of events, in front of the objective forms taken by their actions.

At this stage, it should be observed that this new understanding of alienation does not lead to the denial of any possibility of finding an issue of alienation. But if the understanding of alienation is different, the outcome will be different. It is therefore worth deepening such an understanding in order to think of the possible solutions that Lévinas brings to the problem of alienation. In fact, as we have yet only suggested, alienation is made manifest as a silenced humanity, as a humanity that has lost its speech (*qui a perdu la parole*). If, as Lévinas states, alienation is 'part of the essence of my power' (Lévinas 1961), it is in that the power to create objects—humanity's self production—destines humanity to the anonymity of these objects, to the anonymity of their objectivity, to their merely formal determination, to what Lévinas calls the 'plastic forms of epics' (Lévinas 1961, p. 9). Indeed, to its silence. Therefore, in order to break the circle of alienation, we have to think of what allows humanity to recover speech, of what allows a human being to speak in the first person. This is why, within the problem of revolution and of what might allow for a transformation of the human condition, there lies the question of language and the idea that only through speech can human beings—alienated beings, as Marx would write recover their humanity, and find a way out of alienating structures.

And indeed, coming back to Lévinas' writings, which are directly connected to the problems of revolution and of good and evil, we see that Lévinas describes evil as an impossibility of communication. In 'Judaism and Revolution,' for example, Lévinas writes: 'Evil—or bestiality—is non-communication, being absolutely locked inside oneself, to the point of not appearing to oneself' (Lévinas 1977, p. 36). Although Lévinas does not say so, one might hear in 'absolutely locked inside oneself' a form of alienation, or rather, the very mechanism of alienation. Indeed, in its clinical sense, alienation has two meanings correlative to one another: being alienated means that an Other speaks within oneself (in this sense, the alienated being is a possessed being), but being alienated also means that one is locked up inside oneself. In the clinical sense, the alienated person is the one who moves in a system which is absolutely its own. But if the alienated being is possessed, this is precisely because this being is locked into a system, a system of unique significance. That system, the system of significance in which this being is enclosed, fully determines it and possesses it. Therefore, by linking evil to bestiality, Lévinas intends to say not that evil is the animal, the non-reasonable being, the being of passion, but that evil is a system of significance that prohibits the emergence of the human in Man, because this system is perfectly closed, self-sufficient. Bestiality in that sense is not a lack of reason; in a certain sense, we could say that it is full of reason, or that it is the fullness of reason: it is the perfect immanence to one's sense or world of meaning—immanence that leads to it being impossible to break out of one's own world, to meet another and to be opened to its otherness.

This conception of evil as 'non-communication' makes it even more necessary to understand that Good, or what Lévinas calls the content of revolution (which might simply be what Good is the name of), happens as a birth of language, as a humanity newly born to language. If we consider together texts such as 'Judaism and Revolution,' where Lévinas draws a new figure of the revolutionary, and 'State of Caesar, State of David,' where Lévinas associates the problem of the redemption of humanity, with the question of the transformation of the human condition, such as hoped for and even expected by Marx, and finally the numerous passages of *Totality and Infinity* where Lévinas denounces the formalism that is still inherent to the historical materialism, we can make the hypothesis that Lévinas indeed seeks to rethink both the idea of revolution—or more precisely its content—as well as the renewal of the human condition through the problem of language: through the need to break the silence in which humanity is locked in. The preface to *Totality and Infinity* suggests, for example, that violence, and therefore the dialectic of good and evil—its justification—can be interrupted only through the one who has recovered the 'capacity to speak' (Lévinas 1961, p. 11). More precisely, this preface indicates that evil's forms or evil's formalism, namely evil's silence or evil as a silenced humanity, can be interrupted through another way of practicing language, a practice that could be associated with what we could call 'eschatological prophecy.' In fact, in the preface to *Totality and Infinity*, Lévinas opposes eschatology to teleology, suggesting that eschatology coincides with a humanity newly born to language. But what is interesting is the fact that language becomes human, in that it inaugurates a new relation to time. The mention of eschatology in *Totality and Infinity* allows, in fact, for the description of another way of relating to time and language. Whereas in a teleological conception of history, both the individual and the singular instants of time are subordinated to the future meaning that history will reveal and achieve, eschatology is for Lévinas not so much a prophecy that concerns the end of time but a way of relating to each instant as if it were an end in itself. In this sense, 'eschatology' wouldn't refer to an 'end of times,' but would rather mean that the end happens at each instant. Following this way of understanding messianism, 'eschatological prophecy' gives a voice to individuals while interrupting the continuity of time where evil is a force of good. Freeing the instant from the objective (and anonymous) forms of History, prophets are unsubordinated to what Hegel would call the 'Spirit of the Age', in which individuals dissolve, or to the hyperstructures that individuals produce but beneath which they remain silent. In this sense, human beings can recover a singular voice only if they relate newly to the instant. If we follow this understanding of eschatological prophecy, the figure of the revolutionary that Lévinas seeks to draw in 'Judaism and Revolution' is in fact a prophet—and conversely, the prophet's speech is the truth-content of revolution. But how can a form of speech overcome the formalism of language? And how can eschatological prophecy assume revolutionary goals?

Back to the question of Good and to the figure of the prophet that allowed us to evoke a humanity newly born to language. It's the way humanity recovers speech that makes possible the understanding of what Good is for Lévinas and what is at stake—, that is, what is the content—in a revolution that does not negotiate with evil's forces. In fact, while Lévinas defined 'evil' as the absence of communication, as a way of 'not appearing to oneself' and in that sense as an absolute imprisonment (within oneself), Good is exactly what breaks any kind of imprisonment, any form of belonging in which humanity would be subsumed to an essence, a type, a form. Yet, if Lévinas puts on the same plane not only Marxism, sociology, and psychoanalysis (namely, structuralism), but also ontology and more generally all Western philosophy, this is because these forms of knowledge reproduce each time the same structure of subordination. Each time, the understanding of humanity depends on a structure (the structure of Reason, of the ontological difference, of society, of the psyche, etc.). Therefore, each time, the human in Man is silenced (or subordinated) by the structure that makes possible its understanding, by the structure to which he ultimately belongs and that possesses him. Conversely, while coinciding with the rupture of this alienating circle, Good happens as a particular way of assuming speech. In that sense, for Lévinas Good is not a system of value to which reality should be ordered or newly subordinated; it is, on the contrary, *the rupture of any system*. To put it another way, there can be Good only because there is insubordination, only because reality is not fully reducible to the structures that make it meaningful.

We should recall at this stage that it is this situation of insubordination that allows Lévinas' descriptions of speech to be associated with the figure of the prophet. In *Totality and Infinity*, Lévinas describes, in fact, the birth of language through the way the Other (*Autrui*: the Other man) appears to the subject and resists its power, its system of recognition, and understanding. Calling the self out of the system to which it belongs, the Other breaks the system of belonging that makes a subject identical to itself. Therefore, the subject of speech is bound to speak out of any relation of cognition, out of any system to which his language would be subordinated: he is bound to speak *in the first person*. And indeed, if there is any reason to speak, isn't this because meaning is not already constituted? Indeed, by speaking, we are *relating* to the unknown. Now, it is such a relation to the unknown that makes it possible to explain eschatological prophecy. If the prophet speaks on behalf of the time to come, it is because the Other which is not subordinated to any system of pre-comprehension breaks the continuity of time. The Other, in fact, calls for a renewal of time. The language to which the Other gives birth summons a response to the time to come in the very instant when the continuity of time is interrupted—an instant which is not subordinated to an external end. If evil is 'non-communication,' the closure within oneself, then Good, as we can see, requires a relation of non-subordination that breaks any system of belonging—rupture that calls for an 'I' who speaks in the first person precisely and in that his speech will effect a new beginning.[4]

We can now try to come back to the main topic of our reflection. As we have seen, Lévinas tries to renew the problem that besets Marx's revolutionary thought and project concerning the renewal of the human condition. Lévinas rejects Marx's hopes and expectations (their form, not their content) not only because they would not be revolutionary enough, but, more deeply, because the dialectical pattern they follow is not able to release humanity from alienation. On the contrary, such a pattern is essentially alienating. For Lévinas, alienation is what roots humanity in a system of belonging and deprives it of a singular voice. Now, while Lévinas opposes this dissolved humanity to eschatological prophecy, how can the prophetic word change the world? Is it enough to move from historical materialism to eschatological prophecy in order to change both the human condition and the world it shares?

Lévinas certainly lacked the pretentions to describe what could allow the move from a description of the world to its transformation. Yet, the fact that for Lévinas, beings become human only through language doesn't preserve humanity in any kind of abstraction or ideality that would have no incidence in the world. On the contrary, if Lévinas suggests that a human being is humanized through speech, it is in that speaking—namely: relating to the unknown[5]—human beings break the system that preserve them in their *own* world; they are made to question the *right* they have on their world (their natural right to be owners and to dominate the world). Precisely because speech is not based on a previous system of meaning but is summoned by another who breaks this system, language takes place as what I *own* to the Other that is not part of *my* world (for it appears as *unsubordinated*), but with whom a world is to be constituted. As Lévinas writes: 'Language is spoken where the community between the terms in relation is lacking—where a common plan lacks, where it should only be constituted' (1961 p. 71). Therefore, if prophetical eschatology doesn't give itself the means to transform the world, we can say that it transforms our relation to the world. In fact, speech—that speech that relates to the unknown— deposes humanity of its natural quality of ownership; it moves humanity from the solidity of a homeland (of systems of meaning where humanity is both protected and possessed); it discovers that the world doesn't become human once it's meaningful or useful, but only once the right to possess it is put into question, therefore, only because it can be offered and shared.[6] In that sense, Lévinas might agree with the potential promise of communism regarding the human condition: a human world is a shared world. The human condition can be transformed only if it relates otherwise to the world. Yet, for Lévinas, a world can be shared, a common plan can be constituted, solely because I previously own it to another. Language or speech (*Dis-cours*), is what discovers and makes concrete this situation of owner or of host (or what Lévinas calls the 'superiority of my duties over my rights') that constitutes subjectivity and that disturbs the security that confers a homeland (a world of meaning). By relating to the unknown, language makes concrete the *displacement* of a humanity, which, instead of reappropriating its essence, its power (and therefore of being appropriated, alienated by an essence), relates to an infinite exigency in which I own more than I can ask for myself. In that sense, humanity is *u-topic*: it is literally out of place: displaced by the Other who breaks the security of a homeland, of a world of meaning). But the 'utopia of the human' is not, like in Marx in a hypothetical future, it is here and now: it is what questions human nature in the moment in which the human relates to what exceeds its own power, its own limits. There is humanity only when the human system or sphere is broken and when human beings are called to do more than simply stick to their essence, when they are called beyond their limits.

We can now come back to the figure of the revolutionary as Lévinas redefines it in 'Judaism and Revolution'; and to the question of what exactly the 'content' of revolution might be, a content that would be inadequate to its form. With Marx (at least the young Marx), we could say that this content is nothing else than humanity itself—nothing less than the transformation of its condition! But for Lévinas, what is at stake is not the transformation of humanity *as a whole*, but the humanization of each instant in which each human being is called to respond to what exceeds its self-centered definition, to what breaks the autonomy of its worlds of meaning. While the Marx revolution transforms the human condition because it transforms the world (the means of production), for Levinas, each 'creature' is made responsible for the whole creation. The newness of the world and of humanity is at stake in each instant precisely because language is a relation to the unknown, a relation in which one is made responsible for the unknown, for the 'to come': for the renewal of the world and of humanity. If the content of revolution is not identical to its form, it is precisely because the human being's humanity exceeds its nature, its essence, and its form. In fact, any adequacy of a form, an essence, ends up legitimizing violence. Conversely, while Good in Lévinas does not correspond to a new order (a new system of valuation), but to the relation to what exceeds and breaks such an order or system of belonging, it calls for an action that exceeds what is properly legitimatized. In that sense, if the revolutionary, as Lévinas conceives such a figure, rejects violence, this denial of violence is not a passive acceptance of violence. What tears his conscience takes on the *urgency* of an action. If he is acting in hiding and in isolation, he does so also because no previous meaning (no objective meaning) informs his decision. Therefore, the fact that he has a torn conscience does not mean that he is immobilized in a bad conscience. Conscience is bad only if the adequacy of a system can define it as good. But the good conscience is not in itself fair. The prophet—and such is, for Lévinas, the revolutionary who acts in isolation—is the one who is called to a justice that goes beyond law (1961, p. 274), beyond what time can define as good or bad, beyond the cultural forms of legality, which, as we know, are never far from indulging in evil. Therefore, the human condition can never be guaranteed to stick to Good. What makes humanity possible is instead what prevents consciousness to be finally at peace with itself. Humanity, indeed, is at stake at every instant and not as a hope that concerns future time. If, as Marx wrote to Ruge, a 'desperate situation' may 'fill with hope,', hope is, as Lévinas reflects, a hope for the present, for the infinity that crosses each instant of time.

But this also means that what 'no eye has seen,' the transformation of the human condition, is what summons us daily, not in order to *correspond* to an idea of Good or of humanity, but in order to *do more* than expected: we are to respond to it and it bounds us *infinitely* to language. The transformation of the human condition is at stake at every instant because through language the world can be questioned, opened, and offered; through language, humanity is more than 'itself,' more than its sphere of belonging. However, there is no doubt that this speech to which we are called and that obliges us to Good cannot unequivocally erase the eventuality of a return of Evil (Lévinas 1961, p. 318). Yet, Evil is not merely the destruction of the world. Evil, what is inherently radical in it, is, to quote Lévinas once again, 'the non-comunication, being absolutely locked within oneself, to the point of not appearing to oneself.' Radical evil is our lack of awareness that we are committing such evil, as when we are absolutely locked and legitimized in our own silence, or when outside forces and systems of understanding, predominate (evil in this sense is the world as a totality: its adequacy to the systems that predominate). The language which summons the Other certainly doesn't have the power to transform 'the world,' to definitively redeem mankind and fulfill 'the utopia of the human.' The world is never safe from evil, from what 'locks inside oneself to the point of not appearing to oneself.' But the fact that the 'utopia of the human' requires language, requires a communication which relates to the unknown, which moves human beings out of the security of their homelands and system of meanings, means that the humanity in each human being can only be out of place (in what displaces, dis-arranges human—inhuman—orders or systems), that it consists solely in a non-place ('non lieu') and is therefore the 'utopia' to which we deal with, at each instant, anew. Humanity is the very fragility that must make fragile all that has given itself the appearance of solidity, of having strong and secure essences. That also means that the human being's world is always close to being an inhuman world. The human inside Man is what is more fragile, less proven, and that, for this precise reason, bears the obligation of an infinite task. Now, even though Lévinas seems to oppose eschatological prophecy to historical materialism, it is indeed important to remark that this task does not require divine intervention. Yet, if it were not infinite, it would be accomplished so quickly that Man would lock himself up again in the sphere of his inhumanity. To summon the human being to speak in the first person surely does not convey to divinity any role in History, but neither does it entail making divine the human. On the contrary, it recalls the fragility of humanity and it also means that the worst violence, with the greatest brutality, happens when nothing calls humans to speak in the first person, out of the system that legitimize one's actions—it happens when humanity is in peace with itself, with its own silence, with its definition, namely, with the limits that defines it and secures its essence. Indeed, when nothing makes fragile our system of meaning, our world, when, in this sense, human condition is adequate to its essence, when humans only speak their own language and not the one summoned by another (the one that relates to the unknown), humanity feels legitimized in bestiality because it doesn't know about it; all it knows about is itself. The only world it recognizes is the one that secures its essence and legitimizes its violence. As Crépon remarks in *Le consentement meurtrier*, 'butchers never speak of their victim's world. On the contrary, what they signify to their victims is always the same: "you don't exist!", "there is no world within you!–Nor for you!"' (Crépon 2012, p. 153).

Notes

1. One might think, because of the passage of the Talmud he cites and comments on, that Lévinas feels close to a certain type of Marxism, that which he himself calls 'humanistic Marxism,' 'the one,' he writes, 'that keeps on saying

that "man is the highest good for man" and that in order for "man to be the supreme good for man," must be truly human' (Lévinas 1982, p. 17). We will see that this version of Marxism is not based on the abstract ideal of Humanism, namely on a humanism that comes from an Enlightenment ideal. Moreover, Lévinas specifies in this same article that he is claiming a 'materialist humanism': 'No humanistic rhetoric comes to damage this text that actually defends Man. Authentic humanism, materialist humanism' (Lévinas 1982, p. 6).

2. On the question of the historical dimension of sensibility and more precisely of what Marx calls the 'humanity of the senses,' see Marx and Messina (2011).

3. Lévinas does not use the term *alienation*. In 'Judaism and Revolution,' he reflects rather on the problem of good and evil. This could make us think, at first glance, that Lévinas' problem is above all theological. Yet, as we will show, Lévinas' analysis of Evil is not theological but ontological and allows for another understanding of the problem of alienation.

4. In this sense, Lévinas writes in *Totality and Infinity*, discourse is 'rupture and beginning' (1969, p. 221). If speech is a relation to the unknown, it breaks with the already known, and therefore, with the past.

5. Relation which Lévinas calls religion but that results from a phenomenological understanding, and not from faith.

6. This point suggests that if Lévinas seems to prefer eschatological prophecy to historical materialism, yet the prophetic language (the language that relates to the unknown) has a material dimension: it is the words of things and of things as belonging to one's own world that a language summoned by the Other puts into question.

References

Crépon, Marc, *Le Consentement Meurtrier* (Paris: Cerf, 2012).

Lévinas, Emmanuel, *Totalité et Infini* (Livre de Poche, SD; première édition 1961). *Totality and Infinity: An Essay on Exteriority*, trans. Alphonso Lingis (Pittsburgh: Duquesne University Press, 1969).

————, *Difficile Liberté* (Livre de Poche, SD; première édition 1963); *Difficult Freedom: Essays on Judaism*, trans. Sean Hand (Baltimore: The John Hopkins University Press, 1997).

————, *Autrement Qu'être ou Au-Delà de L'essence* (Livre de Poche, SD; première édition 1978); *Otherwise than Being: Or, Beyond Essence*, trans. Alphonso Lingis (Pittsburgh: Duquesne University Press, 1998).

————, *L'au-Delà du Verset. Lectures et Discours Talmudiques* (Paris: Les Editions de Minuit, 1982).

————, *Du Sacré au Saint* (Paris: Les Editions de Minuit, 1988).

Marx, Karl and Engels, F., *Correspondance t.I* (Paris: Editions sociales, 1971).

Marx, Karl, *Manuscrits de 1844* (Paris: Flammarion, 1996, trad.-P Gougeon); *Economic and Philosophic Manuscript of 1844,* trans. Martin Milligan (NY: Dover Books, 2007).

Marx, Karl and Messina, A, *Argent/Amour. Le Livre Blanc des Manuscrits de 1844* (Paris: Phocide, 2011).

5 The Necessity for Clean Air and Space is Stronger than Any Kind of Hatred
An Essay on the Concept of Violence and Religion in Walter Benjamin

Maria João Cantinho

To my beloved friend and teacher Gérard Bensussan

The destructive character knows only one motto: creating space; it knows only one activity: opening a path. Its necessity for clean air and space is stronger than any kind of hatred.

—Walter Benjamin, *Der Destruktive Charakter* (*G.S.*, IV, 396).

Normally we connect violence with a destructive and useless sentiment, which, in light of the political actuality and the concept of democracy, presents itself, either in a gratuitous character, or a brutal and tyrannical one, but rarely in a positive way and as a bringer of a new, just, social, and political order. The text *The Destructive Character* by Walter Benjamin can be one of the keys to a better comprehension of the violent gesture, one that is simultaneously capable of destruction and openness. As he says, its objective is 'creating space' (*Platz schafen*, see Benjamin *G.S.*, IV, 1,)[1] and opening new roads. The characteristics of the 'destructive character' are regeneration and renovation and the one who defends the 'destructive character' 'sees ways everywhere'. To put it in another way, the destructive character's goal is destruction, not as an end in itself, but as a means to an end (in the case that I am speaking of justice as the end). This is what constitutes violence as a revolutionary gesture, in the light of Benjaminian thinking and it is also what I am proposing in this text. On the other hand, I intend equally to show

how this destructive gesture configures the 'instance of religious founda-tion' and how one cannot open this 'religious'[2] instance without its pre-vious destruction (or 'deconstruction', to justly use Derrida's term). This is what we will see.

History shows us that since the beginning of times violence is a dynamic immanent to its metamorphosis, from its big turning points to its interruptive moments; it is almost always by violence that the revolu-tionary gesture throws its seeds, originating a new order. The question is what distinguishes the violent and the revolutionary gesture, founder of a new order, from justice, violence, and barbarism, which we have so many times witnessed in the recent past.

There is another question that imposes itself above all others. Lately we have seen violence associated with religion, which vulgarly polarizes itself in Christian against Islamic conflicts. Is it still legitimate to associ-ate divine violence, which Benjamin speaks of, to the idea of justice? These questions intersect each other and relate, in my point of view, with Walter Benjamin's text analysis, justly proposing as the object of analysis the paradigmatic text *Critique of Violence* (*G.S.*, II, 1, pp. 75–87).

Schopenhauer, as Nietzsche, was fundamental in the comprehen-sion of the way in which man's evolution and history rule themselves by a longing of power, which gives way to an overwhelming and irrational violence. And it is from Nietzsche[3] that the young Walter Benjamin draws the strength of the concept of violence and of the 'longing of power' early on. On the other hand, the presence of the messianic think-ing—considered from the point of view of its many capabilities: politi-cal, ethical, religious, and historic—contains that violent and apocalyptical dimension, which consubstantiates in various moments and fundamental texts such as *Critique of Violence* (*G.S.*, II, 1, pp. 179–203), *Theological-Political Fragment* (*G.S.*, II, 1, pp. 203–04), *The Destructive Character* (*G.S.*, IV, 1, pp. 396–98) and many other later texts which approach this articulation between violence and religion.

Since the beginning of his work Walter Benjamin defends the importance of religiosity, in a world increasingly devoid of holiness and undermined by individuality. Coming from an uncultured background, where the Jewish religion was becoming increasingly distant to a wealthy central European youth (it is worth mentioning the famous *Letter to His Father* by Franz Kafka (1966), in which a son berates his father for their separation from Judaism, just like the controversy that opposed Gershom

Scholem to his father, from an early age). Such an uncultured perspective created a spiritual emptiness in these young men, sharpened by their obsession with rationalization and specialization, as well as the fundaments of the traditional pedagogy. It is the youth's reaction, closing in on Martin Buber and other thinkers of its time who were connected to the reappearance of Jewish tradition, was swift. And if Walter Benjamin, who never revealed himself as a practicing Jew, was no stranger to the question, it was because he understood how the Jewish tradition could serve as a counterpoint and as a critique to the notion of history as progress, based on the idea of time as something continuous, quantitative, and homogenous, something that is, by himself, since a very young age, strongly refused. The Jewish religion and tradition appear to Walter Benjamin as a possibility to understand history in the light of a new perspective, the messianic one, in which time appears to us in a completely different form, which is, heterogeneous, qualitative, and synchronic.

Therefore, since Walter Benjamin's earlier texts, this search for 'religiosity'[4] is always present and appears most of all, in the search for an ideal community which defended a new pedagogic vision. This free and spiritual community is based on the idea of rupture with the bourgeois ideal of education and in the return to a more humanistic conception of education, in which its essential leitmotif is the idea of messianicity/messianic kingdom, as a real and effective presence immanent on the stage of history (but not overall, just in this specific case, in which Walter Benjamin distances himself from his mentor Gustav Wynecken).

For that community (*Gemeinschaft*) to be founded, it is necessary to break away from its former pedagogy. This community's ideal is found all throughout Walter Benjamin's earlier texts. It appears in *Dialogue on Religiosity* (*G.S.*, II, 1, pp. 17–35), from 1912, where Benjamin defends the existential concept of community, and in its correspondence, mainly with Carla Seligson (Benjamin 1966, p. 1), from 1913 to 1914, as well as in its corresponding texts in this time period, respectively, in *Der Moralunterricht* (*G.S.*, II, 1, pp. 48–54) and *Die Religiöse Stellung der neuen Jugend* (*G.S.*, II, 1, pp. 72–74). In the texts written in his youth, Benjamin insists in the articulation between youth, religion, and community, as an attempt to overcome the individualistic mysticism (G.S. II, 1, pp. 72–74). One of the main keys to the understanding of the articulation between the concept of violence and religion seems to be found in the enigmatic text *The Life of Students* (G.S., II, 1, pp. 75–87) of 1914, where Benjamin clearly talks about a 'messianic kingdom' which presents and codifies itself historically. But for this to happen, the new historical order demands the suppression of the profane order of history, an idea that is repeated in 'Theological-Political Fragment'. When Benjamin declares, in the beginning of 'The Life of Students', that 'the historical task is to disclose this immanent state of perfection and make it absolute, to make it visible and dominant in the present(G.S., II, 1, p. 75), that seems to be the meaning of 'showing the true shape of religion', which is, showing it in the field of history, in its state of perfection, namely, in the shape of messianic and metaphysical historical perspective, made immanent to history. In that sense, messianic history matches the emergence of a metaphysical state that presents and configures itself in this way, in an immanent way, in 'the stage of history'. And here we also find the articulation between violence and religion, because to give way to this state of perfection in history, it is necessary to break away from history itself, seen as continuity, so that the 'messianic kingdom'—the state of perfection—reveals itself. This revelation can only emerge from the rupture and destruction of homogeneity of historical time as a continuity, as Benjamin will later explain, as in the later texts of *Arcades Project* (G.S., V, I and II) as 'a flash', at a time, causing blindness and illuminating the dialectical instant, relentlessly violent and apocalyptic. In this way, these dialectical and messianic instants are the true 'revolutionary moments in the course of the history' (G.S., V, 1, *Das Passagen-Werk*, [N 9 a, 5], p. 592).

Violence always appears, in Benjamin, in a positive sense of breaking away from what appears as apparently continuous, that is, falsely continuous, because in reality all of humanity's development, on a historical and knowledge level, steers away from this postulated continuity, showing, therefore, its internal fissures and its own defects. Contrary to the systems, which asphyxiate thinking and would not let it breathe, Benjamin defends this discontinuity, declaring that, for the philosopher, thinking is an irregular activity and that the philosopher should 'renounce the continuous course of intention', continuously coming back to the beginning, like an 'indefatigable breathing motion' (G.S., V, 1, *Das Passagen-Werk*, [N 9 a, 5], p. 208), paused by the irregularity/discontinuity of its own vital flow. Therefore, life of every thought is marked by interruption, and violence is not an external movement, it is instead embedded in life, either in living and thinking, or in history herself.

The conception of violence, as is presented to us in the work *The Origin of German Tragic Drama* (*G.S.*, 1.1) is violence in an allegoric connotation—another great Benjaminian theme—in the sense of saving the *physis* from its unstoppable catastrophe and saving it (in an apocalyptic and redeeming movement) by annihilation, as a way to integrate to a new order: the durable order of the messianic kingdom. This notion that runs through Benjamin's thought brings him closer to Nietzsche's critical tone and demolishing violence. Destructive violence should be understood as the moment prior to the creation of something new, of the new order of values[5]. In this way, violence as such is, not only a destructive gesture (and gratuitous) but also profoundly revolutionary[6], in the complete sense of the term.

Likewise, in the first texts one can already see the presentation of a political and revolutionary project, of messianic character (*G.S.*, 1.1, p. 75)[7]. By cross reading the texts of 'Critique of Violence' (1921) and 'Theological-Political Fragment' (1920), we clearly understand how that destructive violence, as a *modus operandi*, makes the possibility of a new political order emerge, in which justice, that in this context means messianic justice, is the new catchword. It is not in Theological-Political Fragment that justice is asserted as the fundamental of a new messianic order, but mostly in his text 'The Critique of Violence' (Zur Kritik der Gewalt). However, this demand of legitimacy of justice goes precisely through the gesture of divine violence, fundamentally and absolutely revolutionary, in the sense that it is introduced by it. We shall treat this text next, and as we will see, violence is the gesture that legitimates violence, far from the mere force and authority that only enforces the law.

First published in the magazine *Archiv für Sozialwissenchaft und Sozialpolitik*, 'The Critique of Violence' dates from 1921. The Benjaminian analysis reflects here the crisis of the European bourgeois democracy model, liberal and parliamentary, and the concept of right that is inherent to it. Ahead of the major changes that occurred during the war, political, social, etc., the big questions of the death sentence and the right of punishment have an immense actuality and pertinence. Sorel[8] wrote, in 1908, *Réfléxions sur la violence*, a very well-known work attentively read by Benjamin's generation. In a way, Benjamin's text can be understood as a response to Sorel and his work, but it is also a reaction to the theories of the German jurist Carl Schmitt[9].

The demonstration that Benjamin tries to carry through these texts is, above all, the question of right *(Recht)*. It aims to inaugurate a 'philosophy of right' from a matrix of distinction (*G.S.*, II, 1, p. 199) between the two violence of right: the positing violence, one that institutes and posits right (*die rechtsetzende* Gewalt) and the conservative violence, the one that strives to maintain and ensures the permanence and applicability of right *(die rechtserhaltende Gewalt)*. According to the author, this distinction is essential to understand the function of violence (Gewalt)[10] in its most positive meaning (and not only as an exercise of authority). As Benjamin asserts, the critical task of violence is to end the vicious and pernicious violence:

Far from inaugurating a purer sphere, the mythic manifestation of immediate violence shows itself fundamentally identical with all legal violence, and turns suspicion concerning the latter into certainty of the perniciousness of its historical function, the destruction of which thus becomes obligatory. This very task of destruction poses again, ultimately, the question of a pure immediate violence that might be able to call a halt to mythic violence (*G.S.*, II, 1, p. 199).

To Benjamin, this mythic violence concerns juridical violence *(Rechtsgewalt)*, the one that guarantees right, which conserves itself under the effect of repressive violence. It is this illegitimate and blind violence that has nothing to do with justice that should be fought, constituting the essence of the task of the critique of violence. What is violence on which justice is founded and that serves as a base for that essential difference?

The theme of violence/power (Gewalt), to Benjamin, does not imply, as such, a negative connotation, but concerns the driving force intrinsic to the Benjaminian project[11], in the sense that divine and messianic violence can found a new political order based in justice, likewise, the term *critique*, in this context, does not concern a purely negative evolution, but of evaluation of legitimacy, of examination of violence and its limits. This evaluation of the concept of violence, as we will see in Benjamin's text, cannot occur outside the field of right and justice[12] *(Recht, Gerechtigkeit)*, of law or, in the field of relations with morality and ethics. There is no natural or physical violence (as in Gewalt), in the sense that this violence, taken in a particular sense, as 'force of law', demands judgment, in the justice system. It belongs to the sphere of morality, as Benjamin says, in the beginning of the text, 'In effect, in any way that a cause acts, it does not become violent in the pregnant sense of the word, except from the moment that concerns moral relations' (*G.S.*, II, 1, p. 199).

One can speak, as such, of violence in the sense of a natural force, or even, as a physical pain, but that force is not violence (Gewalt), in the sense that it can originate a judgment. In this way, this concept of violence always belongs to the symbolic order of right, of politics, and moral, that is, all forms of authority. And it is only in this way that it can generate the possibility of a critique. Only this type of violence is worth considering as a fundamental object of the task of the critique of violence. Thus, according to Benjamin, 'that violence can first be sought only in the realm of means, not in the realm of ends', as such, 'violence is a mean to just or unjust ends' (*G.S.*, II, 1, p. 199).

Invoking the legend of Niobe, Benjamin opposes the violence of devastating divine punishment against Korah and the Levites (*G.S.*, II, 1, p. 199)[13], the privileged, in their revolt against Moses; Benjamin characterizes divine violence comparing it with *mythos* violence. While this one is bloody (*G.S.*, II, 1, p. 199)[14], imposing fault and atonement, divine violence does not threaten, nor is it bloody; it does not hesitate to annihilate, she kills them without warning, without any threat (p. 199). The nature of divine violence[15], overwhelming and unpredictable, has nothing to do with the mythic violence on which right is founded; it's of a different order. If mythic violence is gory it is because it is exerted against pure and simple life, but 'divine violence is pure power, over all life for the sake of the living' (*G.S.*, II, p. 200). This distinction between the gory and non-gory nature of violence is crucial to distinguish the various types of violence. Blood is the symbol of life, of pure and simple life, of life as it is. Now, making blood run, the mythological violence of right exerts itself in favour of the living against pure and simple life *(das blossen Lebens)*.

Instead, purely divine violence exerts itself on all life, but in favour, or for the benefit, of the living. What I mean is, as the mythic violence of right satisfies itself by sacrificing the living, then divine violence sacrifices life 'to save the living', in favour of it. Although in both cases there is sacrifice, in the case where blood is required, the living is not respected. If the living is always privileged, in the plane of divine violence, then the commandment 'Thou shalt not kill' remains an absolute imperative (Derrida 2005, p. 125), from the moment where the most destructive divine violence guides itself with its respect for the living, beyond right and judgement. This imperative is not followed by any judgement, and does not provide any criteria for it. The 'responsibility' of the decision in exceptional situations is trusted unto the individuals and the community—as is the case of Korah and the Levites, when they rose against the authority of Moses.

However, it is in this annihilation that she fulfils her purpose, because it '*washes away* the fault', the guilt, but, at the same time she positions herself outside the field of expiation, she belongs to another order, one that transcends fault and expiation, because they belong to the sphere of mythic violence. Divine violence is destructive, and it is, in effect, by brutal and unpredictable annihilation that she *washes away fault*, 'it releases the guilty, not only of fault but also of right' (*G.S.*, II, 1, p. 199). Instead of laying down the limits and boundaries of right, she annihilates them. In place of inducing, at the same time, fault and expiation, she ends them. The radical nature of this violence presupposes the suppression of right itself, in the moment it 'befalls on the guilty'. This takes us to a key point of the question: the order of right, of mythic violence, is eradicated and suppressed, by the destruction of divine violence, giving way to a new sacred order: the one of divine and messianic justice[16].

In this sense, divine violence is not only pure[17], as it also is revolutionary, originating a new order, one where justice is the catchword. According to Benjamin, this divine justice is what gives birth to the messianic order, as new and revolutionary, breaking away from order and mythic violence. But we'll go further: divine violence suppresses mythic violence, founding justice. We recognize here the same political tone of Theological-Political Fragment, integrated in the same aspiration to the messianic order, through the same gesture: the annihilation and destruction of the older profane order, which guarantees the possibility of carrying out a messianic task, breaking away from the order of violence of law.

If the critique of violence accepts and carries out the 'destructive gesture'[18], she does it, not on behalf of a gratuitous and illegitimate violence, but for a true justice that tries to reestablish itself in the profane world. The critique of violence establishes a new order, to carry out a restoration of justice and to guarantee a new political-messianic project. Because, as the author declares, 'this divine violence does not prove itself only in religious tradition, it is also found in present life, at least in a sacred manifestation.' (*G.S.*, II, 1, p. 199).

At the same time it is a moment of suspension, of *epokhé*, this founding or revolutionary instant in right, occurring as an instant of non-right. As Derrida makes clear: 'This moment always has and never has a place in a presence' (Derrida 2005, p. 89). This means that the founding moment of right, to Derrida, 'remains suspended in the void or above an abyss', because the order of right is shattered in that same messianic instant. Derrida evokes the Kafkian man as the being 'in the face of law', the one that finds himself in a terrible situation, where one never sees, or touches the law: 'because she is transcendent in the same way that he (the man) is the one who shall establish it, as forthcoming, through violence.' The paradox is evident; if, on the one hand, it is in the horizon of an inaccessible transcendence that one posits law, on the other, it is theological in the way that it depends only on the one that stands before it and that in this way produces it, founding and authorizing it' (Derrida 2005, p. 90). Transcendent and theological, law is something that always occurs, and that is always promised, precisely because of the fact that it is immanent, finite, and passing.

It is mainly in the last paragraphs of the text 'Critique of Violence' that Benjamin's position on violence is clearly defined. History and the critique of violence intertwine: 'The critique of violence is the philosophy of its history—the 'philosophy' of this history because only the idea of its development makes possible a critical, discriminating, and decisive approach to its temporal date' (*G.S.*, II, 1, p. 202). Benjamin tried, in effect, to understand violence as a driving (and founding) force of its political thought, using his personal history to diagnose its illegal forms (as well as the legitimate ones). Looming on the horizon, beyond the 'mythical forms of right' *(mythishen Rechtsformen)*, is a 'new historical era', which results, precisely, from breaking away from those mythical forces, from their annihilation, which only reveals itself under the blow of 'pure and immediate' violence, it means 'revolutionary violence' which is the 'highest manifestation between men', in the sense that she symbolizes the establishment of justice and the emergence of a new order. But this one, in contrast with mythic violence, is not known 'unless it be in incomparable effects, because the expiatory power of violence, is invisible to men' (*G.S.*, II, 1, p. 202, p. 203). Even if it's not visible to the human eye, it is her that concentrates the focus of the critique of violence, because only divine violence can found justice and create a new political order. And Benjamin ends his text by saying:

Divine violence may manifest itself in a true war exactly as it does in the crowd's divine judgment on criminal. But all mythic, lawmaking violence, which we may call 'executive', is pernicious. Pernicious, too, is the law-preserving, 'administrative' violence that serves it. Divine violence, which is the sign and seal but never the means of sacred dispatch, may be called 'sovereign' violence (*G.S.*, II, 1, pp. 202–203).

In this way, one can say that divine violence is revolutionary or makes up a revolutionary gesture[19], in the sense that, breaking away from mythic violence of right, it introduces justice, in a new messianic order. It is not hard to see the consequences of Benjaminian positions, which is bequeathed to his thought. History 'is on the side of this divine violence'; she is an opposition to myth. It is divine violence that founds a 'new historic era' (*G.S.*, II, 1, p. 202) which succeeds the end of the mythical reign, in the decisive interruption of the circle of mythical forms of right, the abolishment of the state of authority and of the state violence (*Staatsgewalt*). This 'new era' would be, according to Benjamin, a new political era, that would allow the advent of justice as a fundamental condition and responsibility of the community. In this way, by legitimizing divine violence as revolutionary violence, Benjamin ensures a legitimate statute to revolutionary violence, as pure and immediate. But is it within the grasp of men? Benjamin is clear in that aspect. The decision of the revolutionary gesture, the one that is determinant and that allows knowing or recognizing such violence as pure and revolutionary, is *a decision inaccessible to men:* 'Less possible and also less urgent for humankind, however, is to decide when unalloyed violence has been realized in particular cases' (*G.S.*, II, 1, pp. 202–203). This means that divine justice, which is, messianic, is the fairest, the most effective, the most historical, the most revolutionary, and the one that knows the greatest power of decision. However, as such, she does not lend herself to any human determination, to any knowledge or 'certainty' that may be decided upon by us, because, as he declares, violence is not known in itself, as such, but always in its 'incomparable effects', because 'the expiatory power of violence is invisible to men' (*G.S.*, II, 1, p. 203). It is not possible to reduce it to any general conceptual order or to a determining judgement. Thereby, there is no 'certainty' *(Gewissheit)* or possible determination that is not constituted only in the space of mythic

violence, of right. That is, 'only mythic violence and not divine violence', says Benjamin, let itself be known with such certainty.

In the last lines of his text, Benjamin refers to the mythical forms of
right as a 'bastardization' of the true forces. The mythical right, as we
can assert according to the author, is a violence that would have bastardized *(bastardierte)* the 'eternal forms are open to pure divine violence'
(*G.S.*, II, 1, p. 202, 203), it means myth bastardized, with right (*mit
dem Recht*), the divine violence, leaving us at the hands of injustice,
bastardizing as well the forms that guarantee justice in the world of men.
And that is exactly why it is necessary to reject all mythic violence, the
violence that founded right, because it is 'pernicious'. And 'pernicious' is
also 'the law-preserving, 'administrative' violence that serves it' (*G.S.*, II,
1, pp. 202–203). It means to refuse it in the name of divine violence,
bearer of the possibility of legitimization of the order of justice. This
one, as Benjamin declares, precisely in the last phrase, is the one that can
be described as sovereign (*die waltende heissen*).

The sovereign is in secret, without being visible to men, except in
its effects. It can be named, but never seen, never being subjected to any
conceptualization. So, the divine, the 'sovereign' violence is the potential
and founding violence. It says nothing, but names itself; it is beyond
conceptualization, but is, at the same time, a condition of all nomina-
tion. That is the sacred condition of justice, founded in the infinite
power of God, in the moment where his violence signs the revolutionary
gesture, as secret. It is up to us—by the messianic portion attributed to
us—to preserve justice, by watching over that revolutionary power of
divine violence, as an untouched flame. That is also the task of history.

The rigid nature of the divine and revolutionary gesture, which
founds justice and a 'new era' is comparable to 'the spiritual movement
of the *restitutio in integrum* which leads to immortality', through the
annihilation of the profane order and of the order of all theocracies, like
he defends in the Theological-Political Fragment. The destructive gesture makes up the desire to start a 'new historical era', the messianic one,
replacing history's dynamic with the 'rhythm' of the messianic nature
(*G.S.*, II, 1, p. 204). For this to happen it is necessary for the profane
order to fade away, to be annihilated violently, so that the new messianic
order can emerge (*G.S.*, II, 1, p. 204). The gesture of divine violence
that the author speaks of in Critique of Violence corresponds, in effect,
to that gesture of annihilation of life, to allow the start of a new and
transcendent messianic order. It means the order of founding justice.

In this way, many conclusions can be drawn. If there is a gesture that can 'save' history, interrupting it in its profane continuity, that gesture is revolutionary violence, or rather, according to Walter Benjamin, the gesture of divine violence, breaking away from the 'mythic violence' of right. Which violence is connoted with barbarism or how does one distinguish both? It is exactly the 'mythic violence' of right that upholds barbarism, expressing the divorce between right and justice. The revolutionary violence or the 'divine violence' is the one that introduces justice and a new political and historic order on which the concept of divine justice rests.

The messianic figure, in Benjamin's conception, is the foreshadowing of rupture and the unexpected, of the radically new, interrupting history, and times of continuity. Incidentally, that question was very well understood by Jacques Derrida. In Benjamin the term 'messianism', or rather, the term messianic, which is always related with temporal dimension, is a 'messianic without messianism', 'a weak messianic force'[20]. Derrida explicitly refers, here, Thesis II from Benjamin's text, *On the Concept of History*. But it is precisely in this text that we better understand the meaning of '*messianism*' in the author, as a 'weak' force trusted upon us by the previous generations.

Even if this pretention (*Anspruch*) cannot be overlooked by the materialistic historian, as Benjamin declares at the end of Thesis II, it is not formed in the way of a promise, in definite, with a figure that will come, but in the way of an expectation that is created from a 'secret agreement' (*G.S.*, I, p. 694); it means an expectation that is oriented towards redemption, without it being promised. This opening to (or its urgent demand) a horizon of occasion 'as' justice, is neither a guarantee nor a password to the divine or to transcendence; it is rather, a very human demand, that one would want in the realm of ethic and politics, as an immanent and practical reality. For that reason, the messianic, either being religious or not in its structure, has an utterly violent and revolutionary character, because otherwise, the opening wouldn't happen. And I believe that in this resides the great originality of Benjamin, when compared to the messianic thinkers and to the Jewish theological tradition. If in some instances of his youth Benjamin has seemingly welcomed a religious point of view (and our idea was precisely to analyze the linkage between violence and religion), in the traditional sense, at any time in his texts, the presence of divinity and of divine transcendence, which is the basis of all religion, are we faced with certainty, but always with the undecidability of those concepts. And the climax of that relation—absolutely secularized—appears precisely in Thesis I of the text On the Concept of History (*G.S.*, I, p. 693), which raised, and still raises, bigger perplexities, meeting Derrida's reflections which were previously discussed. In that thesis, Benjamin utilizes a powerful metaphor to talk about the relation between historic materialism—the one that violently and abruptly breaks away from the historic vision of progress—and theology, which he presents as 'an ugly, little old woman', 'dry' and that just as it appears (emptied of its power), 'has to keep out of sight.' Victory, Benjamin declares, 'The puppet, called 'historical materialism', is to win all the time'.

I believe we understand here the question of the secularization of theology, in all its clarity. Operating violence, 'opening new paths', destroying, yes, breaking the thread of historical continuity, but not without introducing the theological categories of tradition. And if this thesis clarifies Benjamin's wrongful position, it shows, however, in a final act, all the ambiguity and controversy of his positions, regarding religion and theology. Without it, we are not allowed to operate in the bosom of history, deconstructing historicism and the vision of progress, after all Benjamin's straightforward objective. To fight the winner's history and to rehabilitate the loser's history, restituting justice. But is this divine justice? No, it's up to the historic materialist the violent, the last revolutionary gesture: saving the losers from oblivion, remembering them, exactly as Jewish tradition says, fighting oblivion. This is the dialectical historian's utmost mission that recognizes himself as the 'Angel of History' (*G.S.*, I, pp. 697–98) from thesis IX, that allegoric and bug eyed figure, than the winning Messiah. It is in this prodigious tension that the historian lives and acts: in justice and expecting redemption.

Notes

1. Walter Benjamin's *Gesammelte Schriften*, has been used here as *G.S.*, IV, 1, p. 396.

2. This 'religious' in Benjamin has a very paradoxical and peculiar character, which we'll see along this text.

3. The influence of Nietzsche's works is present in Walter Benjamin's texts, in 1914, as 'III. *Die Jugend und die Geschichte*' '*Metaphysik der Jugend*', that can be found collected in *Gesammelte Schriften, II, 1*. Walter Benjamin attentively read the text 'Untimely Meditations', from which he developed his own critic to the notion of as construct of progress.

4. In the sense of working on the theological categories of the Jewish tradition.

5. Let me remind you Benjamin's text where this point is clearly expressed, in *The Destructive Character* of 1931, I will also like to refer the reader to the texts where Benjamin interprets the *Untimely Meditations* (1873–1876) by Nietzsche, reviving the debate against the vision of history as progress. I refer to the texts that were previously mentioned such as *Romantik, Metaphysik der Jugend*, collected in *G.S.*, II, 1.

6. Derrida explains in a sufficiently clear way the profoundly revolutionary character of the messianic, by the eruption of the wholly new and the non-anticipated, by the absolute and urgent demand of a radically different experience structure in the order of justice and ethics. And, in this measure, an irreducible paradox is established, an 'expectation without a horizon of expectation' (Derrida 1993, p. 267).

7. I would like to remind you of the excerpt in which he asserts: 'the historical task is to disclose this immanent state of perfection and make it absolute, to make it visible and dominant in the present. (...) This condition cannot be captured except in her metaphysical structure, as the messianic kingdom.'

8. Georges Eugène Sorel (1847/1922) had a very peculiar political trajectory, considering violence as an important driving force in politics as well as a weapon to be used in his political project. Nevertheless, Sorel clearly distinguished the brute force of violence which is in consideration here, disregarding the oppressive forms of government. A controversial author, Sorel was almost always aligned with the revolutionary socialist left, but equally admired some anarchic extreme right authors. And his ideas where accepted and highly discussed, both by the revolutionary extreme right, by the anarcho-syndicalists and some right intellectual currents.

9. Although he is considered as an 'accursed jurist' because of his close link with Nazism and the fact that his theories legitimized it, he was nevertheless, a very important jurist for the discussion and establishment of political laws and considered as one of the greatest theorists and references of political philosophy of the time. Benjamin was very influenced, mainly, by the question of the 'state of exception', which he clearly treats in the text *The Origin of German Tragic Drama*. Benjamin highly respected Schmitt and, by the time he published 'The Critique of Violence', Schmitt wrote him an enthusiastic congratulation letter.

10. The translation of *Gewalt* by violence, an option we made in this text, raises a few doubts and is wrong. If, on one hand, the term *Gewalt* refers to violence; on the other hand, it can also mean the dominance or sovereignty of legal power, the self-legitimizing authority: the power of law.

11. Like it was in Georges Sorel.

12. 'The question that would always remain open is of knowing if violence in general is moral, whether as principle, or as a mean to just ends' (*G.S.*, II, 1, p. 179).

13. 'To the legend of Niobe one can pose as an example of this violence the judgment of God against Koré's group'. Cf. In this regard see (Bojanic 2008, pp. 108–125)

14. 'Because blood is the symbol of simple life.' This allusion to blood is, to Benjamin, discriminatory. Only she seems to allow, to her eyes, the identification of the mythic and violent foundation of right in the Greek world, of the divine violence in Judaism.

15. I want to point out the reading of Andrew Benjamin's new text, *Life beyond Violence: Notes on Walter Benjamin's Zur Kritik die Gewalt.*

16. As Derrida acknowledges 'what makes the price of men, of his Dasein and of his life, is of containing capability, the capability of justice, the coming of justice, the coming of his righteous being, of his having to be just. What is sacred in his life is not life itself, but the justice of his life' (2005, p. 126).

17. In the same way that the gesture that annihilated the profane order of history was pure, to give way to another plane of messianic history, in the last paragraphs of *Theological-Political Fragment*, which were previously analyzed.

18. To this extent it is justifiable to call this violence, too, annihilating; but it is so only relatively, with regard to goods, right, life, and suchlike (*G.S.*, II, 1, p. 200).

19. On must approach the term 'revolutionary' with caution, when it is applied to violence. If divine violence is, here, revolutionary, it is so in a messianic and repairing way, because it establishes authentic justice and freeing in the way that it is repairing. However, the term 'revolutionary' will appear afterwards as an unusual force in the text *On the Concept of History*. Only here does Benjamin fully develop the notion of revolutionary, always in a direct relation with the establishment of justice and the repairing of the loser's history.

20. In that passage, in an extensive footnote, Derrida refers to a 'spectral logic of inheritance and generations, an oriented logic, in a heterogeneous and disjointed time, to the past and future alike' (Derrida 1993, p. 96).

References

Benjamin, Andrew, *Life beyond Violence - Notes on Walter Benjamin's 'Zur Kritik die Gewalt'*, http://www.cecl.com.pt/workingpapers/content/view/32/1/

Benjamin, Walter, *Briefe I,* herausgegeben und mit Anmerkungen versehen von Gershom Scholem und Theodor Adorno (Frankfurt: Suhrkamp Verlag, 1966).

———, *Gesammelte schriften,* I, 1, 'Ursprung des deutschen Trauerspiels', hrsg. von Rolf Tiedemann und Hermann Schweppenhaüser (Frankfurt: Suhrkamp Verlag, 1977); *The Origin of the German Tragic Drama*, trans. John Osborne (London, New York: Verso, 2009)

———, *Gesammelte schriften,* I, 2, 'Über den Begriff der Geschichte', hrsg. von Rolf Tiedemann und Hermann Schweppenhaüser (Frankfurt: Suhrkamp

Verlag, 1977); 'On the Theses of the Philosophy of History' in *Illuminations*, Trans. Harry Zohn (New York: Schocken Books, 1969), pp. 253–264.

Benjamin, Walter, *Gesammelte schriften*, II, 1, Zur Kritik der Gewalt, 'Theologisch-Politisches-Fragment', hrsg. von Rolf Tiedemann und Hermann Schweppenhaüser (Frankfurt: Suhrkamp Verlag, 1977).

————, 'Critique of Violence', in *Reflections*, trans. Peter Demetz (New York: Schocken Books, 1986), pp. 277–300.

————, *Gesammelte schriften*, I, 1, 'Ursprung des deutschen Trauerspiels', hrsg. von Rolf Tiedemann und Hermann Schweppenhaüser (Frankfurt: Suhrkamp Verlag, 1977).

Gesammelte schriften, IV, 1, 'Der Destruktive Charakter,' hrsg. von Rolf Tiedemann und Hermann Schweppenhaüser (Frankfurt: Suhrkamp Verlag, 1977); 'The Destructive Character' in *Reflections*, trans. Peter Demetz (New York: Schocken Books, 1986), pp. 301–303.

————, *Gesammelte schriften*, V, 1(Das Passagen Werk), hrsg. von Rolf Tiedemann und Hermann Schweppenhaüser (Frankfurt: Suhrkamp Verlag, 1977); *The Arcades Project*, trans. Howard Eiland and Kevin McLaughlin (Belknap Press, 2002).

Bojanic, Petar, La Violence divine de Benjamin et le cas de Coré (Korah). La rébellion contre Moïse comme première scène du messianisme) (Paris, Revue *Lignes,* n° 27, 2008), pp. 108–125.

Derrida, Jacques, *Spectres de Marx* (Paris, Ed. Galilée, 1993); *The Spectres of Marx: The State of the Debt, The Work of Mourning and the New International*, trans. Peggy Kamuf (New York: Routledge, 2006).

————, *Force de Loi* (Paris, Ed. Galilée, 2005); *The Force of Law: The Mystical Foundation of Authority in Acts of Religion*, trans. Gil Anidjar (New York: Routledge, 2002), pp. 228–298.

Sorel, Georges, *Reflections on Violence*, ed. Jeremy Jennings (Cambridge: Cambridge University Press, 1911).

6 Tears Are Not Yet Wiped Away on All Faces

Saitya Brata Das

For Gérard Bensussan

THE EVENT OF LANGUAGE

That certain dominant philosophy, 'the whole brotherhood from Ionia to Jena' (Rosenzweig 2005, p. 18) summons the world to its thinkability, is an originary, 'metaphysical' violence, for it must cast aside or exclude the claims of the singulars and the multiple who are bitten by the 'poisonous sting' (Rosenzweig 2005, p. 9) of death. There is something of death that is unthinkable and unknowable in all its singularity and multiplicity; or, should we say more emphatically that death is unthinkable precisely because it erupts each time as singular, irreducible to the one universal concept of death. Before we seize death by virtue of the power of our concept given in language that bears in itself the potentiality of converting the nothingness into being such is the *energia* of language death *always already* seizes us with 'fear and trembling'. This death that is singular and multiple, recalcitrant to totalization, for being too much and too little of possessing being, too much of an excess and too impoverished and fragile at the same, is that which resists the power of history on each one of us, and puts a limit to the violence waged in the name of a judgement of universal history. But is that enough to put radically into question the violence whose energia or *dunamis* is given in that, paradoxically speaking, which does not have enough of being, and precisely therefore, for the first time, *posits* itself as 'being'? Is the singular merely that being, whose singularity is its singular being-towards-its-singular-death, or there is still more of a surplus in singularity, a remnant or a remainder that is not just this 'being-towards-death, a capacity or capability to die, but an (im) mortal desire just to remain, to abide by and only then can s/he indeed be bitten by 'the poisonous sting' of death? Wherein that remainder or remnant in the singular that is, tied to the wound of death, and that resists radically the claims of a universality of the world-historical politics in its warlike march, and which is violent in its essential, metaphysical foundation? A radical critique of violence, if it must aspire to the unconditional, must address the metaphysics of the world-historical, political, not in the name of the energia or dunamis that converts nothingness into being, but a remnant which is always an *Eschaton*, being the last, not one last as 'this' particular last being but that which is not enough of being and not enough of nothing. For me it is always the question of time which is structured something like promise a remainder or a remnant that is an Eschaton of a future as an event. The name of this Eschaton is like a 'secret index' (Benjamin 1977, p. 251) that Benjamin speaks of which invisibly traverses through history as a reserve and donation at the same time and that while giving the world to us, subtracts itself and thereby keeping the world open once more, and once more.

I begin with the beginning of *The Star of Redemption* (Rosenzweig 2005) It begins with the task of opening up the indigestible remnant of philosophy once more, this nausea of the system of philosophy—that is death; and that reason why philosophy always needs to domesticate it and thereby include it in its fold as its immanent other. The violence of metaphysics lies, first of all, in this repression of death: 'only that singular can die, and everything that is mortal is solitary' (Rosenzweig 2005, p. 10). It is not, however, just the question of the repression of death but more that of opening up of death in still another manner the capitalization of death and capitalization of life that exists in language which never ceases inserting life and death into the force of law and into the vigilant gaze of history, intolerant of any secret that there may be in life and in death. Thus, Rosenzweig finds in the statement—and which is the philosophical statement—that 'all is water', spoken by one Thales of Miletus—a violence that gives to the 'brotherhood from Ionia to Jena' almost like the force of law or self-evident legitimacy of an imperative: that the world must be thinkable! Why should such an imperative be considered unconditional and self-evident as to the point of being considered sovereign? This question too, as old as philosophy itself, albeit repressed in its fold, is the question that emerges again, and has in fact never ceased to emerge. And we know that what is at stake here, once again, is none other than the fate of philosophy itself is, its possibility and its limit, but also the possibility of opening up the unconditionality which is the philosophical passion par excellence, the unconditionality in the name of which may there lie a critique of violence, an unconditionality which is so youthful that it must have been young always, immemorially for it has never passed by yet: it is a remnant, a remainder, a Rest, a reserve, and a donation, a 'waiting and wandering' (Rosenzweig 2005, p. 348), a secret and a language that alone gives us the gift of presence, a lack of the name for the Name and the overabundance of names that are made into prattle when the tower of the Babel was built.

There is always a possibility of violence in our act of our reading in reading of one's own writing or in reading of other's writing. There is, however, in reading, always a possibility of redemption from violence that momentarily advents without being controlled by the intentions of the reader. Such reading is not a reading of dead letters but a movement of remembrance that keeps alive what is threatened to be frozen in immanence, or that threatens to be coagulated into the decrees of fate or into the cages of the law. Such reading is not primarily oriented to cognition but to truth. Is not violence all about our attempt to arrest that seeks to fly with the speed of an arrow, or to coagulate the river of time that seeks to flow incessantly, or to imprison the immemorial promise into the frozen immanence of stagnant water? If reading, which I understand in Platonic manner as an act of *anamnesis*, keeps alive the promise in remembrance, this act of reading has always oriented itself towards the silence that marks the happiness of redemption. Such happiness or beatitude can be an unconditional limit of violence, a 'weak messianic reflection' (Benjamin 1977) to say in the Benjaminian manner. Such a reading, not primarily oriented by the ideals of cognition of what gives itself as latter, but rather as a remembrance of the spirit not yet damaged (by) the violence of cognition; such a reading alone gives a work its renewed breath and thereby leads the work again and again beyond the violence of cognition. Redemption hinges on the name and on silence, not the silence of the mute tragic hero in his frozen immanence transfixed by death and which he defies by refusing to speak; not, not that all, but a silence that is the fulfilment of all names, silence that the gift of presencing brings each of us to ourselves, to all of us but to each of us singularly and differently, each time newly and each time as immemorially old. Language recognizes each time and each one of us anew without enclosing us in the proprietorial claim of sovereignty of one name. The critique of violence must not forget to take into care of this enigma of the event of language's transcendence of itself beyond any proprietorial claims and beyond all sovereign appropriation of the world.

CRITIQUE OF VIOLENCE

A critique of violence must be an unconditional one. That in the name of which any critique of violence may happen at all must be the unconditional one: this exigency implies that the unconditional must not be consequent upon some other condition, nor should it be a result of a process like the synthesis of the dialectical movement. A *Yes* and again a *Yes* and so on: redemption is an affirmation of the before, a beginning before beginning, and only in that sense it can be called a 'result'. Only the immemorial is true *Eschaton*: this is the unconditional messianic sense of redemption, albeit not the only one. A critique always implies a judgement, but an unconditional critique must belong to an order wholly heterogeneous to the judgement nourished by and exhausted with law, for that to happen, that is, if the critique of violence is exhausted by an act of judgement nourished by law alone, then any critique of violence will be an act of violence anew. One can then never bring rupture to the circularity of the predicates, and since all predicates are conditioned, since it must presuppose that 'that' exists, a critique of violence as unconditional critique is not fulfilled. We are inserted in the infinitely growing—philosophers prefer the word 'becoming' process that forever approximates the end when the demand of the unconditionality will be fulfilled, for it already presupposes that the unconditionality is a result of a process, the goal reached at the end of a line constituted by points that are qualitatively indifferent to each other. So the line expands, and keeps on expanding: the unconditioned never arrives. It is indefinitely postponed though—an indefinitely long line of the conditioned forming an endless series, an eternity of a very long time. A critique of violence, if it be an unconditional one, can't, thus, be based on the exemplarity of an eternity of a very long time. At once awaiting and welcoming, the critique relates to the world with all the messianic impatience, as if the loss of a moment will be the loss of eternity itself—since eternity may arrive at any time; but also, the critique must open itself to an infinite patience at the same time, the infinity of patience that is nourished by hope that there always remains, and there will always remain a time for the Other to arrive so that we do not close the door too prematurely, and we do not end up speaking the immediate, what is the nearest, what is merely an epochal, relative manifestation—and that is the disaster—in the language of the Absolute. We may be helped by remembering Nietzsche's caution here—not to confuse 'big events' that emit lot of smoke and fire with the arrival of redemption, for what carries redemption comes on 'dove's feet' that guides the world and in 'stillest words' (Nietzsche 1995, p. 146), almost like a faint murmur or like the rustling of leaves, barely audible, in an autumn evening.

And he said, Go forth and stand upon the mount before the LORD. And, behold, the LORD passed by, and a great and strong wind rent the mountains and brake in pieces the rocks before the LORD; *but* the LORD *was* not in the wind: and after the wind an earthquake; *but* the LORD *was* not in the earthquake: and after the earthquake a fire; *but* the LORD *was* not in the fire: and after the fire a still small voice. And it was *so*, when Elijah heard *it*... (I Kings, 19: 11–13)

We must not jump over the nearest in the name of what lies afar or for the sake of the second nearest. However, we must also not consider that what merely immediately presents itself is the Other who is to come so that we do not absolutize what immediately presents itself with lot of smoke and fire. The messianic critique of violence, thus, allows itself to be thought in us only as *paradoxical*: one must wait patiently when there is no more time, for eternity that is to come today is not yet a 'today'; and also that one must not wait thinking that eternity is a very long time even though there remains a time to come, for at any time eternity may break through, since it is not a very long time. Paradox is always a breakthrough that sets the world apart from itself, an intensification of difference *in act*. A critique, even our critique of violence, is an act of setting the world apart from itself, a spacing open—or hallowing open, a *Kenosis*—from where, or from that which is 'nowhere' the voice of the critic cries out, as if from a wilderness. Paradox therefore always calls from us a double response born of double exigencies mentioned above, each incommensurable with the other: waiting for the not yet, and engage with the *here and now*, each time together and each time as separately as twice incommensurable affirmations.

METAPHYSICS AND DEATH

That death is its Musaget: this is the secret of philosophy Rosenzweig reports to us through the mouth of Schopenhauer. That each being is nourished by the abyss of non-being that constitutes its very dunamis or energia, being's potentiality *to be*, which is also the potentiality of *not to be*: does this brilliant discovery of philosophy take away from each existent, which is each time singular, the 'fear and trembling' before this nothing which is yet something called 'death'? That philosophy takes this brilliant discovery seriously, is nowhere as clear as in Hegel: the entire domain of the historical is moved—and mark, it is a 'movement'—by the energia or dunamis of potentiality that is nourished by the abyss of non-being, or better what we call by this strange name of 'death'. The energia or the dunamis of the non-being forces history forward in a march wherein an epoch passes into another epoch and still to another without ever looking back, drawing and gathering individuals into its fold who are now overwhelmed by its grandiose march of accumulative progression. This is the logic of world-historical politics in Hegel's phenomenological account of it: that the energia of the world-historical is the supreme work of death, a labour of non-being that never ceases to expose the existent to its nothingness for the sake of the epochal so that the 'fear and trembling' felt by the singular existent is felt no more. Death loses its 'poisonous sting' and its 'pestilential breath'. History, as Hegel grasped it metaphysically, is an exposure of each one of us to our death. In this exposure that history makes possible for each one us, we learn to die; but since there is a consolation in the universal march of the world-historical politics that elevates of our death to renewed universal life, our death becomes neutralized into mere work. 'The poisonous sting' of death is not felt anymore; or, better, it is better felt only as feigned death. That the neutralization of death from its 'poisonous sting' at once marks the triumph of the march of the world-historical politics is something remarkable here. Here occurs an exclusion in the inclusion that alone permits philosophy to close the other exit for the existent, the other gate, opening to revelation and redemption through religion. The theology of the world-historical politics ends up becoming an apology of the world. This is the price that Hegelian theodicy of history had to pay in the name of a truth of philosophy in the spirit of the utterance of Thales of Miletus, that 'All is Water', and in

Parmenides' 'Being and thinking are the same' whose violence has never been separable—and I am speaking in a certain spirit here—from the world-historical claims of the political. That philosophy is willing to become world-historical at the price of the apology of the world is not fortuitous. It lies in the very logic of origin upon which philosophy as its fundamental ground rests: being whose very dunamis or energia is an abyss, erupting without foundation and without ground, an ecstatic restlessness that never ceases converting nothing into being. That the theology of the world-historical politics in its apology of the world has something essential to do with philosophy in its fundamental constitution itself: this is quite a reason for Marx and Nietzsche's 'exit from philosophy' (Bensussan 2007). And this is also the reason for Rosenzweig's exit from philosophy, the reason that in all apology of the world there is violence implicitly inflicted upon the singulars in the name of anonymous world-historical politics. The ethics of messianism, if such a thing were possible, would consist it not being merely a gesture of receding, a retreating or withdrawing from such grand world-historical politics, for that would merely be a negative gesture and not at all unconditional and an affirmative one; it would also demand, and this we see in the case of Rosenzweig, a renewed opening of the other gate, and exit from the other gate that welcomes the other today and now, not a now that indifferently passes away like any other nows, but a *now* pregnant with eternity at not a very long time, for it must be nearer than the near—the *then*. The world-historical politics with its grand march of victory over time is also an eternity. It must seize the nearest so as to pass onto the next near and so and so forth. In this seizing lies there its violence. Time grows as its scale expands with the progressive accumulation of successive points, but the river of time congeals and its flowing water coagulates into stagnant water. It is in this forceful seizing of time and in this act of coagulation that the violence of the State consists in, and the tyranny of the world-historical politics founds upon it. Rosenzweig's critique of violence lies here.

THE MESSIANIC SUSPENSION OF LAW

In *The Star of Redemption,* Rosenzweig makes a fundamental distinction that is profoundly important for us in order to consider his critique of violence, the distinction between *Gebot* and *Gesetz,* commandment and law. The distinction lies not merely in that law is understood in its empty formality—and here Kant's notion of 'autonomy' in relation to moral law is the target for Rosenzweig—and that of the precision and clarity of the fullness of commandment on the other hand, but more importantly in the *event* character of commandment in a very essential sense that makes commandment wholly heterogeneous to the order of law. As event, commandment is not the order of goal and does not coagulate itself in the mythic frozenness of tragic time. It is rather otherwise: the event of commandment releases the being-in-existence from the violence of the mythic that freezes us into the cages of law. The mythic is the order of fate, *Moira*, that encloses being-in-creation. Upon this mythic foundation where it points nowhere points itself, rests the condition of law. The commandment in its two-fold events, revelation and redemption, releases being from the mythic cages of violence into the open process of radical historicity whose momentum is given by the eternity of redemption which is goalless and fateless. Occurring without destiny, it hurries near to us in the moment of sudden eruption in the midst of time, deconstituting the form of the temporal series made up of indifferent, accumulating instants dragging one after the other. Such arrival of redemption alone addresses the non-autarchy and non-autoch- thony of the mortal seized in the 'fear and trembling' before the pitiless death, and only for such a being is there given a radical historicity. Since there is nothing new as content here which is not already promised before, this non-content is nothing like the empty formality of law that forcefully and violently renews the old law into new law. The command- ment of love, thus—and Rosenzweig brings it to our attention without ambiguity—this commandment in its two fold events brings rupture into the mythic structure of the old becoming new law by an incalcula- ble eruption in an excess of knowledge and whose concept is not given to us in advance. Presupposing something other than freedom alone, the events of commandment open the-being-in-existence to an order het- erogeneous to the domain of law. The heterogeneity of *Gebot* from *Gesetz* lies in that unlike *Gesetz*, *Gebot* is not an ascertainment from what is established once in the past but an event in each *hic et nunc* that recoils from being inserted in the validity of general laws. Rosenzweigian critique of Kant and his followers down to the Idealists lies in his pro- found recognition that what makes an insertion of life into the law pos- sible, is its foundation in the mythic-tragic that constitutes the domain of Creation. Resonances of such concerns are to be found even in Benjamin's early works down to his work on *Trauerspiel*: the distinction between *Tragödie* which is mythic and *Trauerspiel* whose subject is history (Benjamin 2004, pp. 55–61). Therefore, a step beyond Creation is necessary, a step not possible within Kant and the Idealist philosophy of All, not as an accidental impossibility but that belongs to the constitutional failure and also constitutional success of philosophy itself. The philosophical proposition—'All is water'—asserts nothing other than a *Gewesenheit, an-already-having-been,* and not a *vérité a faire.* Therefore, the idealist philosophy always remains satisfied with a generic principle at its disposal that is the very principle of law which presupposes, as the condition of possibility of a new law, the old that a Gewesenheit. The metaphysics of this violence lies in the coagulation of the infinite fecundity of temporality into the mythic foundation of law where being—as existence that precedes thought is engaged in the tragic immanence, a false eternity it is, even if law never ceases renewing the old by means of an exceptional act. That existence precedes thought, an idea Rosenzweig borrows from Schelling, is always an exit from philosophy whose gate is already opened in the caesura that Schelling introduces between negative and positive philosophy. It is also the exit towards the event of revelation that Rosenzweig and Kierkegaard are to follow after Schelling. That the mythic-tragic foundation of the historical can never be the fulfilled time, because it can never redeem us from the violence of the past sufferings: messianic affirmation of remnant that Rosenzweig and Benjamin are to be concerned, in their singular ways, is born out of this crisis in the mythic foundation of the world-historical politics and its constitutional violence. Against the danger of Creation in its claim to autochthony and autarchy, Rosenzweig therefore calls forth a true notion of Creation whose secret word is not the force of law freezing and arresting being-in-death, but a/the commandment of love in its two fold eventive character that releases the being from its arrest in death to a remainder, an eternity to come, a 'to come' that is promised to it since the opening of the world. It is a promise of time that is tied to love as much as it is to death, or even more than death, for 'love is as strong as death'. It is this event of love which is as strong as death that alone, opening us to the world in the face of the neighbour redeems us from the violence of the immanence of self-consuming predicates. What then makes redemption irreducible to the mythic foundation of the world-historical politics is the fundamental incompletion of the world and its radical *Noch Nicht*, arising out of its unconditional and absolute, the *Unbedingt* insistence on the fact that 'the tears are not yet wiped away on all faces'.

God and man already are, the world is becoming. The world is not yet complete. Laughter and tears are still in it. And the tears are not wiped away on all faces. (Rosenzweig 2005, p. 235)

The *Noch Nicht* time of the tears is the tear of time which is not just another time of another world-historical politics but otherwise than time, for it does not occur *in* time. Rosenzweig calls this *Ewige*, an eternity which is an arrival (*l'avenir*) in the sense that it arrives from an extremity of time which is not a very long time. We can wait only for eternity; time passes away without waiting. The time of the world-historical politics does not have time to wait. Its 'warlike temporality' marches on triumphantly through the whole wide world with the banner and slogan of world-historical progress, for eternity for it is a very long time. But for the faces whose tears are not all wiped away, this impatience of time is violence because it justifies the unjustifiable past sufferings and thus turns out to be apologetic of the world as it is defined by the world-historical progress. If the waiting for eternity knows patience, it is not the patience of the concept that Hegel speaks of. It is rather a patience nourished by a remnant of time. Since such a remainder can only be awaited and cannot be violently seized by the State and by its power of law, it is the remainder that is of the one whose tears are not yet wiped away: 'in every inch therefore it is something that is coming, or rather a coming. It is that which must come' (Rosenzweig 2005, p. 236).

***

Therefore, for Rosenzweig, only that which withdraws its stake from the world-historical politics can be truly exemplary, not in the sense that it is a generic principle from which all cases can be deduced but a principle that is unique and singular in each case, withdrawn from any given form of abstract generality, and therefore is a true universality. Exemplarity is not a privilege of a people in terms of its territory and its power of world-historical expansion but rather is an infinite subtraction, a receding from all claims to autochthony and mythic immanence which is the essence of all violence. The notion of the 'holy' that Rosenzweig evokes here is always used conjoined with 'promise' which means precisely *that-which-is-set-apart-from-the-world,* that differs and differs from all self-foundation and self-presencing. Its fundamental mood (*Grundstimmung*) is not a triumphant joy of victory over time but a longing, tinged with melancholy for the downtrodden, for what is 'noch nicht', the 'not yet'. The holy is nothing but promise, from an immemorial inception: it is the promise given to whom who is set apart from the foundation of the world of mythic immanence. In that sense, the notion of 'holy' for Rosenzweig is 'atopic': strangeness from all that grows on earth, territory, and language that dies with the death of a people, and of people who stakes its life and death for the sake of soil on which it dwells. The holy language, on the other hand, is that which is disjoined from its time; banished from any homeland, it is the language of those mortals who have lost their 'tongue in the foreign land', as Hölderlin poetizes. By being out of *sync* from the synchrony with which the epochal orders march successively with their 'warlike temporality', it must open itself to the other eternity that since immemorial has never ceased opening the world. The holy interrupts the mythic foundation of community and separates itself equally from the past that congeals into myth and also from a future that renews itself as law which is a victory over time. The holy is that which is equally distant from twofold violence of the mythic law. As an infinite movement of distancing, the holy introduces separation between two times and two languages: on the one hand the messianic politics of the world-history founded upon the growth of time that only approximately moves towards its goal, and on the other hand, that which places itself beyond the oppositions between particularity and the anonymous universal history, and for which the arrival of eternity makes time a *nunc stans* that cannot be reckoned as the world-historical chronology. This notion of the holy makes 'war' into a purely political concept.

Rosenzweig thus makes the distinction between political war and war in the name of faith, a distinction that is blurred when Christianity, itself arising from messianic impulse, wants to be joined with the powers of the world-historical politics. It is from this conjunction that constitutes the theologico-political foundation of the messianic politics, that the violence of the world-history draws itself legitimacy. Rosenzweig's messianic critique of violence insists on the separation of *salus* and *fides,* a separation that is erased by the theodicy of history whose momentum is reached in utmost possibility in the Idealist philosophers like Hegel. The whole resistance to Hegel coming from Rosenzweig, who himself is one time Hegelian philosopher par excellence, lies precisely in this: that Hegelian theodicy of history that erases the distinction between *salus* and *fides,* between the domain of the religious and the political, is the inheritor of a metaphysics of history that turns out to be the apology of the world; it neglects, in the name of a *telos* that lies immanent in that auto-generative process, what remains to come and that, being the true *Eschaton*, may alone consummate history. Since the eternity to come does not come by in the incessant flow of time, the State in its impatient claim to sovereignty and being closed to the other opening, feels the necessity to force eternity to arrive by means of law. But since time cannot be stopped and the movement of life always triumphs, the only way the State must continuously insert life into law is by renewing the old law into new law. And this is, according to Rosenzweig, the meta-physical essence of all mythic violence that founds the State.

This is the meaning of all violence, that it founds new law… Law is, as regards its essence old law. Now it shows itself as what violence is: the renewer of old law. In the violent act law continuously turns into new law. And the State is therefore equally as much lawful and violent, refuge of the old law and source of the new; in this double shape as refuge of the old and source of new the State places itself above the mere flowing off of the life of the people in which custom unceasingly and non-violently multiplies and law changes.

And again,

To this natural allowing of the living moment to elapse…the State opposes its violent assertion of the moment…it masterfully seizes the moment, and every following moment, and forms it according to its will and its ability. At every moment the State violently settles the contradiction between preservation and renewal, old and new law. It is that continuous solution which the life course of the people constantly only postpones of its own accord through the flowing on of time; the State takes it in hand; in fact it is nothing other than this solving, resolved every moment, of the contradiction (Rosenzweig 2005, p. 353).

The messianic must therefore insist in the suspension of law, and must infinitely take to its task and as its imperative the irreducibility of life to law. The ethics of messianism would not, however, be limited only to that; it must also be able to open itself via another door, to another eternity which is not just victory over time and life but an eternity where time completely fulfils itself, where all 'things' enter the paradisiacal name given as pure gift of presence and where, the things in the world becoming all-soul, the world redeems itself from all violence arising from cognition and law. Before the world is gathered in the blazing landscape of redemption and everyone's tongue rests because language is fulfilled, the things of the worlds must be gathered by the name. As we can say of eternity that it is the fulfilment of time and neither a denial nor a congealment of time, so can we say of silence that it is the fulfilment of names and neither a denial nor a congealment of language. Rosenzweig names such thinking where language is nourished by the infinite fecundity of time and not a denial of it, as *Sprachdenken—language-thinking*. If philosophy is to take to its task as the redemptive fulfilment of life, then it must renounce its acts of metaphysical reduction of the fecundity of time nourishing language into mere categorical grasps of 'things' in the world at cognitive disposal. It is in this sense Rosenzweig speaks of idealist philosophy as the movement that is without language, because it does not know eternity as the true event of arrival (*l'avenir*) but eternity only in the form of law where 'every moment dams up in stagnant water' (Rosenzweig 2005, p. 353) without really flowing into the ocean of eternity. If eternity of redemption is to arrive today, it must bring rupture to the myth of law in its eternally recurring cycle of new law erupting to break the violence of the old and so and so forth. The true eternity as deformalization of the mythic cycle of law, this true eternity Rosenzweig does not find in the world-historical politics but in the domain of a liturgical recurrence, divorced from all world-historical calendar, where eternity is repeated without the force of law and is thus irreducible to the gaze of the power of the State. Here too occurs eternity as the renewal of the old in the new, but in different terms than the law of the State without which there exists no world-historical politics. It occurs in terms of allowing the river of time to flow into 'the ocean of eternity', each time as remembrance of the immemorial promise as a 'secret index' not wholly absorbed in the movement of world-historical progression. Against the monumental history of the world which marks each monument as a little station where time is arrested and which each time confuses 'the newest eternity as the true one' (Rosenzweig 2005, p. 354.), Rosenzweigian messianism evokes an eternity that arrives in midst of life without sword. And then tears will be wiped away from all faces.

References

Benjamin, Walter, 'Über den Begriff der Geschichte' in *Illuminationen* (Frankfurt/M: Suhrkamp, 1977).
————, *Selected Writings*, Vol 1, 1913–26, Marcus Bullock and Michael W. Jennings (eds.) (Cambridge: Belknap Press of Harvard University Press, 2004).
Bensussan, Gérard, *Marx le Sortant* (Paris: Hermann, 2007).
Nietzsche, Friedrich, *Thus Spoke Zarathustra*, tr. Walter Kaufmann (New York: The Modern Library, 1995).
Rosenzweig, Franz, *The Star of Redemption*, tr. Barbara Galli (Wisconsin: University of Wisconsin, 2005).

7 The Concrete Violence of History and the Apocalyptic Messianic Dwarf

Mike Grimshaw

How does one think about violence, especially within a frame of political theology? One possibility is through the relationship of Jacob Taubes and Carl Schmitt, for within their discussions and correspondence can be discerned, a gap between Taubes and Schmitt on violence that is to do with their apocalyptic trajectories. Yet both, in their opposition to liberalism, an opposition situated within a particular understanding of democracy, accept as a necessary part of human existence that which can be labelled 'real, concrete' violence.

But before I turn to the Taubes-Schmitt positions on violence, in order to begin thinking about concrete violence I wish to begin with three fragments from Walter Benjamin. These fragments, in their succinct impact, their theoretical sublime brutality, like the combinations of a great boxer like Ali in his prime, or the state-sponsored ideologically propelled brilliance of the magnificent Cuban Teofilo Stevenson, rattle our brains, concuss, bruise and stagger us. Singularly each is a blow to what we might hold as possible, as normative; experienced as a threefold combination they propel us to an encounter with the figure of concrete violence made manifest: the apocalyptic messianic dwarf.

The first fragment is that of Walter Benjamin's *Angel of History* who, arising from contemplation of Paul Klee's *Angelus Novus*, is propelled helplessly into the future while reviewing the singular catastrophe of history that we choose to view as a chain of events (Benjamin 1940, p. IX). To see history as a single catastrophe of existence challenges all our assumptions about liberal progress, for Benjamin's angel is hurtled backward into the future by the storm of progress that blows from Paradise, a Paradise to which we no longer have access. Instead, fallen humanity, exiled from the presence of God, undertakes progress amidst the wreckage of exile: exile within the concrete experience of time, watched helplessly by the Angel of History.

In the second fragment, from Benjamin's *First Thesis on the Philosophy of History*, we read of the dwarf of theology who while hidden, guides the puppet of historical materialism, a puppet that will always win if it enlists the services of theology, yet only if this is a theology kept hidden (Benjamin 1940, p. I). So what can we say of theology we *do* see, of theology that attempts to play the games of power and politics not hidden beneath historical materialism: is this theology destined to never win? Yet what of the violence that occurs? Is the violence of theology unstoppable when encased within historical materialism? Is this actually what the concrete violence of apocalyptic entails?

Third, we turn to Benjamin's *Theologico-Political Fragment* (Benjamin 1978, pp. 312–13). In this we are confronted with the claim that the catastrophe of history is finally consummated in the Messiah, wherein the Kingdom of God is the end of history, but not its goal, not its *Telos*. Profane history, while pointing against the direction of messianic intensity, in being profane enables the intensity of the counter-direction of the messianic coming of the kingdom. Politics, being in and of the world of the profane, is not to be confused with theocracy which has only religious meaning. Or if we 'short-circuit' (Zizek 2003, series foreword) Benjamin against himself: politics is the profane concrete world of history in which theology operates as a hidden dwarf, watched over by the angel of history who sees not events, only catastrophe.

The quest for human happiness, being a profane, concrete-world dynamic, leads us to undertake a chain of events which, contrary to a liberal belief and conception of progress, result not even in a profane Kingdom of God but rather leave a catastrophe of violence. But, if we become aware of the messianic as counter to the dynamic of profane progress, then we become aware of the challenge of messianic happiness which is a passing away of this world and is experienced here in the profane in an eternally transient worldly existence which is the task of nihilistic world politics.

Is this the real secret of concrete violence—that the return of the apocalyptic, messianic dwarf is the return of nihilism? Is the secret that nihilistic violence is perhaps the only true, real, historical—and meaningfully meaningless—violence; a violence created, encountered and undertaken within this profane world of history?

Benjamin's fragments remind us that any discussion of violence, if approached within the concrete world and the experience of profane history, can only be fragmentary, can only be encountered as a series of impacts that are sustained in combination but not in a singular event. For violence is a series of events, actions, episodes, assaults, and impacts; even sustained violence is never singular for it is undertaken by limited beings within the constraints of concrete world, time, and space. The only sustained violence would be the in-breaking of apocalyptic violence that causes an event within concrete time and space, an event so sustained in its impact to the extent of changing our experience of time and space, forcing a new time, forcing a new experience of space. Within Christianity, within the creation of Western history and time that for two millennia has existed under an angel of Christian-derived history, the violence, the apocalyptic in-breaking violence, is the violence of the death of God, a death that occurs within the crucifixion. And yet even then such apocalyptic violence, violence understood as to have been done within the body of God, results in a new time and space that is not recognized as such, because for almost all, the death occurs and nothing changes; rather profane, concrete life continues. In fact the death of God undertaken then and experienced still today, as heralded by Nietzsche and then yet again by what became known as the American death of God theology, was only ever a reminder of that which the first apocalyptic violence entailed: a new time and a new space for concrete life that we live without knowing, a profane world of historical materialism wherein theology, if it is to act, remains hidden.

Given that in a letter (9 December 1930), Benjamin acknowledged his gratitude to Carl Schmitt, thanking Schmitt for the influence on his own work of Schmitt's writing on sovereignty and the state; and then remembering that Taubes in mentioning this concludes by adding his esteem and devotion to that offered by Benjamin (Taubes 1986); we arrive at a position whereupon the question of concrete violence can begin to be addressed, always in reference to Benjamin, but more so in reference to the debates and discussions of Jacob Taubes and Carl Schmitt.

Concrete violence is *real* violence, not violence as abstract or theoretical nor is it violence discussed as that to be—or more so, as violence able to be—overcome. Concrete violence is the violence that is part of the catastrophe of history, a catastrophe of history that we undertake in the pursuit of progress, in the quest of happiness. It is violence that we undertake within the deliberate ignorance, the deliberate forgetting, the deliberate disavowal of the claim from within Christianity that the apocalyptic in-breaking has already occurred. Yet because such an in-breaking was not as and how we expected or wished, because it occurred within our profane world, because it did not take us out of this world, but rather located us ever more fully, ever more singularly within it, we act as if it has not, did not, and could not occur. In fact Christianity in so much of its institutional existence, an existence that sought to deny its internal claim of the apocalyptic in-breaking, in its pursuit of temporal power and influence, became the most vehement opponent to its event of origin, which is the death of God in an act of profane, concrete violence. Concrete violence is what happens in this world, happens because we live in this world, happens because we live in a profane word and yet attempt to pursue our own resolution of a profane Kingdom of God.

At this point I also want to introduce Terry Eagleton into this discussion or more specifically, a fragment from Eagleton's conversation with Graham Ward in which Eagleton makes the following observation:

It is interesting, isn't it, that in an era when religion is in one sense at its most obnoxious, all the way from Texas to the Taliban, theology in some guises is providing radical political resources for a world bereft of them… in a era of political downturn…a less euphoric left…appreciates that there are heterodox sources (theology amongst them) which it now doesn't have the luxury of looking in the mouth. (Eagleton 2008, pp. 91–92)

And a further fragment from Eagleton:

…the more I look at it, the more I see the sublime as a kind of secularized holy terror. It's one place where divine holy terror migrates once God has been gentrified by the Enlightenment, when he has become a super-watchmaker or Eminently Reasonable Being. You need a stand-in for divine terror, and the sublime is among other things just that. Most aesthetic concepts are theological ones in disguise. (Eagleton 2008, p. 94)

Here we can also hear echoes of the Futurists' religion of divine speed, the divine speed of violence, whereby violence is an act of purity, of cleansing, of being and becoming modern. Therefore to understand the siren call of concrete violence we also need to detour via the Futurists.

Founded by Filippo Tommaso Marinetti (1876–1944), the Futurists began as an aesthetic movement within literature and arts, but expanded to influence dada, surrealism, and Italian fascism. More widely, futurist ideas and themes have come to act as another hidden dwarf within modernity, residing and hiding as a secular, aestheticized dwarf fixated on redemptive, aesthetic violence. The Futurists were also a party of manifestos and while their manifestos have become, in many ways historical curiosities, the ideas expressed within them found their way into the thinking, politics, and actions of twentieth century society. A manifesto sets out an impassioned political and social argument, while traditionally the religious equivalent has been a creed. Yet writing from the position of a secular political theology, the historic and institutional nature of a creed acts as a barrier and limitation on political theology, reducing theology and especially political theology to sectarian disclosure and closures. A manifesto on the other hand, overtly political in nature and outlook, becomes the open call to possibility that sits at the heart of both secular and political theology. The Futurist manifestos were likewise calls to possibility, calls to a possibility that escaped from the sectarian discourse of futurism and became central to the modern engagement with the possibilities of technology, most strongly, but not limited by any means, to and with the aesthetics of Italian Fascism. The aestheticization of violence, which as Eagleton noted, is really a type of theological violence in disguise, is a central and troubling element of Futurism, because its appeal within Fascism has become part of the more widely engaged aestheticization of violence as event, as spectacle, and as action within late modernity. Fascism may have been defeated as a political ideology, but the aesthetics of Fascism have triumphed and make it difficult for us to reclaim the event of real, concrete violence without the aesthetics of the event turning our eyes from the event of the real. Central to this is the Futurist view of technology as 'not an ethically neutral vessel into which society *projects* values and uses but, rather, contains it own set of values embedded within it: speed, destruction, and orgiastic upheaval or violence' (Bowler, 1991, p. 772). The technology of violence has become central to the aestheticization of late-modern life: violence by ever-expanding technology and violence as technology, as a *techne*—something we as humans create. Combined with the Futurist/Fascist aesthetics and obsessions with speed, hygiene, the pageantry of power, and the overcoming of nature (Bowler, 1991, p. 776) we have reached a point whereby, in modern nihilism, as Eagleton notes: 'The self-alienation of humanity under fascism', writes Walter Benjamin, 'has reached such a degree that it can experience its own destruction as a pleasure of the first order' (Eagleton 2005, p. 119).

Central to this self-destruction is the triumph of the twin Futurist/ Fascist ideologies of 'the cult of irrational violence and aestheticization of violence', (Bowler 1991, p. 785), that get performed as spectacle and manifesto in the act of expressing the possibility of a new utopia to be achieved by the concrete violence of apocalypse. An apocalypse and violence that, beginning as abstract claim and idea, become technologi- cally expressed as the vanguard for the new messianic moment. Concrete violence is therefore also a type of manifesto, a manifesto to the aes- theticization of violence in late-modern life, an aestheticization that is simultaneously abstract hope, fear, and desire made concrete in its impact upon life, bodies, and existence. But this is also aestheticization as technology—as *techne*—as a way to give concrete violence its own Futurist/Fascist hygiene, by making it aesthetic and ideological. In this concrete violence as manifesto moment, is the expression of the Futurist aesthetics of simultaneity whereby in any single moment 'a potentially infinite and always changing multitude of events, noises, actions, and sensations may be experienced in concert' (Bowler 1991, p. 779).

The manifesto, as Mary Ann Caws observes, 'makes an art of excess', being 'a document of an ideology, crafted to convince and convert' (Caws 2001, p. xx, p. xvii). Central to the manifesto is what Caws terms 'the manifesto moment' which is its positioning 'between what has been done and what will be done, between the accomplished and the potential, in a radical and energizing division' a moment of crisis expressing 'what it wants to oppose, to leave, to defend, to change' (Caws 2001, p. xxi, p. xxiii).

In the *First Futurist Manifesto* (1909) Marinetti widely known as 'the caffeine of Europe', states that he wishes to institute a cult of 'synthetic' verbal violence, as well as proclaiming war as a 'hygiene' that will wipe away, in a very concrete way, all that is viewed as old, decayed, impure, and traditional. This is therefore a manifesto of apocalypse, an apocalypse that was to find tragic expressions in the destruction of the Great War, the inter-war rise of Fascism and then the wider concrete violence of World War Two wherein the technology of violence was to culminate in both genocide and atomic destruction. Helping to underpin such a secular, concrete apocalypse as the technology of humanity was Marinetti's Futurist Manifesto of 1916, *The New Religion-Morality of Speed*. In this, Speed is expressed as the new location and expression of divinity. Marinetti, viewing the Great War as one that is 'liberating', expresses a Futurist morality that: '…will defend man from the decay caused by slowness, by memory, by analysis, by repose, and habit. Human energy centupled by speed will master Time and Space' (Flint 1972, p. 94).

This creates a new religious response: 'If prayer means communication with the divinity, running at high speed is a prayer. Holiness of wheels and rails. One must kneel on the tracks to pray to the divine velocity' (Flint, 1972, p. 96). This also means that 'one must persecute, lash, torture all those who sin against speed' (Flint 1972, p. 95).

Out of this, Marinetti expresses as new Futurist-Purist doctrine of modernity:

Speed, having as its essence the intuitive synthesis of every force in movement, is naturally *pure*. Slowness, having, having as its essence the rational analysis of every exhaustion in repose, is naturally *unclean*. After the destruction of the antique good and the antique evil, we create a new good, speed, and a new evil, slowness. Speed = synthesis of every courage in action. Aggression and warlike. Slowness = analysis of every stagnant prudence. Passive and pacifistic. Speed = scorn of obstacles, desire for the new and unexplored. Modernity and hygiene. Slowness = arrest, ecstasy, immobile adoration of obstacles, nostalgia for the already seen, idealization of exhaustion and rest, pessimism about the unexplored. Rancid romanticism of the world, wandering poet and long-haired, bespectacled dirty philosopher' (Flint 1972, pp. 95–96).

Marinetti's linking of speed, destruction, modernity and war as hygiene against the unclean slowness of that seen to be in decay sits at the heart of both religious terror and the modern aestheticization of concrete violence more generally. Therefore this move, from 'art to be life' to a wider social and cultural politics of aesthetics of terror and violence as spectacles of the concrete event, is where that other hidden dwarf of Futurist/Fascist aesthetics resides. To insert another fragment: as Baudrillard notes of the 'immanence' of modernity,

The whole movement of modernity, its negative destiny, lies in the fact of transcribing all that was of the order of the imaginary, the dream, the ideal and utopia into technical and operational reality. (Baudrillard 1998, p. 50)

This is how we arrive at the figure of concrete violence made manifest: the apocalyptic messianic dwarf.

What then is apocalypse, how can it be understood? Here we turn to the debates of Jacob Taubes and Carl Schmitt for in their arguments, their conversations, their engagement as friend-enemy of each other occurs a central question of violence as the expression of human existence, violence as a central reminder of what it means to be human. This is not violence as we have been falsely led to believe by the Futurists, a violence that is redemptive and will enable us to master time and space. This is violence that reminds us of our limitation within time and space, violence we wilfully ignore and misread in our quest to become our own apocalyptic agents.

The relationship of the Jewish apocalyptic thinker Jacob Taubes and the German and Nazi jurist Carl Schmitt forces us to reconsider the central role of violence and its aftermaths in the twentieth century. Especially so given that Schmitt is the central figure of political theology, indeed in many ways he literally is the thinker who 'wrote the book'. What draws them together is a common engagement with history, a viewing and experiencing of history in which politics and theology are intertwined. For as Taubes states:

I don't think theologically. I work with theological materials, but I think in terms of intellectual history, of actual history. I ask after the political potentials in the theological metaphors, just as Schmitt asks after the theological potentials of legal concepts. (Taubes 2004, p. 69)

In many ways each was the dwarf to the other, that relationship within that drove the public expression of each. The theological metaphors, the theological potentials were in fact for Taubes the theological metaphors of Christianity and apocalypse in the political potentials that resulted in the Shoah. For Schmitt the theological potentials were those of the Jew, the friend-enemy who keeps the law in the face of a Christian society that now proclaims what could be viewed as the legality of grace. Central to both thinkers was the question of apocalypse, the forms of which Jan Assman (Gold 2006, p. 141) identifies as either an apocalypse from below central to constituting the identity of a community, which is Taubes' Jewish-focused apocalypse, or that apocalypse from above, an apocalypse from hierarchy and order, imposed from above, which is Schmitt's apocalypse. In the tension of the two, wherein these two forms of apocalypse encounter each other, is the political theology that unites Taubes and Schmitt.

We are reminded of that famous statement from the beginning of chapter three of *Political Theology*:

All significant concepts of the modern theory of the state are secularized theological concepts…The exception in jurisprudence is analogous to the miracle in theology. (Schmitt 2005, p. 36)

Here is the basis of the tension between a Taubean reading of apocalypse and the Schmittean: does the miracle and exception occur from above (Schmitt) or from below (Taubes); that is, does one proceed from state or community?

But then we must also consider the return of the miracle, which as Schmitt states, has been banished from the world by the modern constitutional state and deism (Schmitt 2005, p. 36). Does this mean that the return of the miracle has to be analogous to the sovereign wherein the exception is a form of miracle? For the exception is, like the miracle, an interruption to the normal order of things, an event that demands a response, a challenge to what is deemed possible—or even deemed acceptable. Perhaps this also raises the question Taubes asked under 'the price of messianism' whereby the question of messianism can also be seen to under sit such questions as that of the sovereign exception. Taubes asks: 'How else can redemption be defined after the Messiah has failed to redeem the external world except by turning inward' (Taubes 2010, p. 4).

The response is that this can also be seen to apply to the sovereign who fails to make the right choices—the redemptive choices for the exception. Therefore in the face of the failed sovereign does one also have to turn inward? Yet what if inward, in each of us, exists that messianic apocalyptic dwarf, a dwarf who is the driver of, and intoxicated with, the question and expression of violence, a violence that we may attempt to disguise and redeem by terming it apocalyptic, yet in its concrete expressions becomes the tragedy of history wept over the by the angel of history?

Therefore, as Joshua Robert Gold notes in his discussion of Taubes and Schmitt, the following points arise from the centrality of Taubes' issue with Schmitt regarding apocalypse:

…while apocalypse takes humanity out of the realm of necessity and nature and places it within the sphere of freedom and history, the apocalyptic quest for total liberation courts potential cataclysm. Consequently, Taubes argues that apocalypse must guard against its own destructive impulses without relinquishing its antagonism towards profane authority. (Gold 2006, p. 142)

Here we must note that the issue raised in the letters is how and why Schmitt effectively relinquished antagonism to profane authority in the quest for total liberation. Taubes' readings, therefore, ask questions of all who seek to use (and even mis-use Schmitt), for what occurs when apocalyptism surrenders antagonism? Does apocalyptism from above too easily facilitate the surrender to profane hierarchy? Gold further notes that:

...history for Taubes does not merely accumulate facts about the past; rather, it is an arena, a site of agon, 'the place upon which the substance of time and the substance of eternity, death and life cross paths.' [In Occidental Eschatology] Apocalypse is significant in the context of this struggle because it testifies to the triumph of eternity and the overcoming of time: it promises the passing away of transience. (Gold 2006, p. 143)

This is the attraction of the authoritarian apocalypse, the apocalypse from above. This is the attraction for all thinkers who, while aware of humanity are trapped as it were in time, seek the freeing of the exception from history, wherein the exception exists as the end, the fulfillment of history. The Fascist, totalitarian dream of a violent apocalypse freeing the redemptive exception has its roots here.

However, while this is the route taken tragically in the 1930s by Schmitt and Heidegger (to name the most troubling examples given their continuing influence), perhaps we can understand the Taubes-Schmitt relationship in light of Gold's next observation:

Yet the revolutionary aspect of apocalypse for Taubes not only has to do with the way that it breaks the hold of myth over humanity; by positing an end to time, it alsoconfers significance to the act of decision. (Gold 2006, p. 144)

This is why Schmitt's decision for Nazism is so important for Taubes. Does apocalypse from above explain his decision, and further, what do all similar decisions hold within them? Therefore unless we wish to inaugurate Fascism and a totalitarian sovereign, we must decide to reject apocalypse from above. This does not mean we must become liberals against Fascism and totalitarianism, for:

In contrast to official assurances that 'the situation is improving,' Benjamin and Taubes share the same militant pessimism that recognizes in history a legacy of cataclysm. For Taubes the crisis character of history means that the act of decision assumes an ethical character. (Gold 2006, p. 146)

What then if that act of decision includes the decision for and of actual, concrete violence? What if Benjamin, Schmitt, and Taubes are all in their own way just variations of the Futurist intoxication of redemptive violence, of an apocalypse that would sweep away the failings and failures of the liberal modernity that attempted a central violence against human nature? The central concrete violence of liberal modernity attempts to prise us out of history—and in prising us out of history also prising us from theology. For theology is that which reminds us, constantly, of the violence that sits at the heart of our historical experience and position of being human. History, without the internal dwarf of theology, becomes liberalism, history without apocalypse becomes liberal utopias, history without the messianic becomes the tragedy of the failed utopia that attempts to remake human nature and in the process undertakes horrific acts of concrete violence in the attempt to recreate, punish, and excise. The utopias of liberalism, the utopias of the pure society that as a sovereign makes the decision, that decides the exception of that or who must be removed in order for the society, the community to be whole and pure.

Violence is therefore that which occurs in real time, in real history. Violence is first and foremost a type of exception, for in deciding to undertake an act of violence we act as a type of immediate—even if fleeting—sovereign: for we decide on the act of real violence that is the exception to the everyday lived history. Every act of violence also holds within it an immediacy of the apocalyptic, of the end-time, its own possible end of the world for those involved. Yet such human violence stands in a difficult position to the claims of the redemptive, salvific violence of the apocalypse. For can humanity accomplish acts of redemption, acts of salvation that are also, in their event, for those involved, also acts of suffering, of suffering inflicted, of harm undertaken toward our fellow humans? Indeed, each act of real, concrete violence does end the world as we might know it, as we have known it and starts us in a new world whereby that act of violence is now a constant ongoing, repeatable possibility. Is not the claim of the final apocalyptic violence the claim that this singular act will end violence, will free us from violence, will free us from history whereby violence is the reminder of our limitations, of our humanity, of our creatureliness. Do we then also need to act as anti-apocalyptic agents against ourselves? Is this not the central claim of Christianity, that we must each, first and foremost, take up the role of *Katechon*, of restrainer? Is this perhaps even the dialectical tension within the apocalyptic, messianic dwarf, sitting within history attempting on the one hand to restrain the worst excesses of profane history, attempting to proclaim an exception against the recourses to violence, because it exists in the world of the fallible, fallen, historical humanity. Yet is the dwarf hidden precisely because when it attempted to be sovereign in this world of history, too often made the exception for violence, for violence that it decreed as within the possibilities of a sovereign.

Writing of his relationship with Schmitt, Taubes states, the drive of political theology is that of 'an apocalypse of the counter-revolution' (Taubes 1985). How then, in light of this, is political theology as a movement to be rethought? This counter-revolution is a revolution against liberalism, against claims of liberal progress, and all revolutions involve forms of violence, concrete violence, even when the violence is ideological, even when it is rhetorical, even when it occurs without the spilling of bloodshed. For all revolutions, counter and other wise, occur within human time and human history, all revolutions actually ask a central theological question: what time is it? Remember, as Graham Ward reminds us in *Cities of God* the question that theology 'does not handle', the question of 'what God is in relation to the world' does become addressed in the question of 'that relation and that world... [which]...is a question about history and salvation...the question becomes very specific; it becomes the question concerning 'what time it is'? (Ward 2002, p. 2). That it is a question implies, I want to state, the necessity of doubt to faith, of doubt to the encounter with grace, of doubt to the whole project of theology.

The apocalypse is the counter-revolution that asks what time is it and answers: the time that acts as violence to all that you have placed your hope and trust in; that which you believed would reconcile you to history by enabling you to self-transcend the limitations of history.

Taubes identifies concrete violence as sitting at the heart of the crisis confronting the apocalyptic drive of modern life. This crisis raising issues that philosophy does not want to have to deal with. Central to this crisis is the question, the problem, the reality and challenge of violence. Violence as a state of being exists as the act that can impose non-being that is impure, for violence is too tied into the actors and actions of impure history. Taubes identifies Schmitt as one of the few thinkers who will take the problem of violence seriously, whether from the viewpoint of law or from philosophy, because 'law does have a relationship to the problem of violence and power' (Taubes 1986). Here does *Nomos* sit in relation to *Chronos* to *Telos* to *Apocalypse?* For law is the attempt to act as *Katechon* to violence, yet law cannot act as Katechon to the apocalypse of the sacred, so law is always the human attempt to act as sovereign and Katechon to itself. In effect, abandoned by God to time and history until the apocalypse, violence is the constant reminder of this abandonment, a violence even effected by humanity upon God when God attempts to cross the divide of abandonment, to enter human history so fully that he is self-abandoned even to death by crucifixion.

To understand this we must return yet again to what has become the Schmittean cliché of political theology: 'All significant concepts of the modern theory of the state are secularized theological concepts… The exception in jurisprudence is analogous to the miracle in theology' (Schmitt 2005, p. 36). This needs to be read in tandem with the anti-liberal statement: '…all genuine political theories presuppose man to be evil, i.e., by no means an unproblematic but a dangerous and dynamic being' (Schmitt 2007, p. 61). For Schmitt this means:

Because the sphere of the political is in the final analysis determined by the real possibility of enmity, political conceptions and ideas cannot very well start with an anthropological optimism. This would dissolve the possibility of enmity and, thereby, every specific political consequence. (Shmitt 2007c, p. 64)

That opposition to a politics of optimism is further expressed by Schmitt's critique of liberalism:

Just as liberalism discusses and negotiates every political detail, so it wants to dissolve metaphysical truth in a discussion. The essence of liberalism is negotiation, a cautious half measure, in the hope that the definitive dispute, the decisive bloody battle, can be transformed into a parliamentary debate and permit the decision to be suspended forever in an everlasting discussion.

Dictatorship is the opposite of discussion it belongs to the decisionism…to assume the extreme case, to anticipate the Last Judgment. (Schmitt 2005, p. 116)

The tragedy of liberalism is that concrete violence becomes something which is allowed to happen to others while debates and discussions against it occur. The tragedy—and one could go further and state the crime of arrogance—is that liberals attempt to live outside history while they debate the problems of those who live within history.

This challenge to and rejection of liberalism is what has enabled the radical left to find common cause via Schmitt with what was once the anathema of the radical right. The rejection of the liberalism of Weimar is central to Schmitt's political theology, a rejection that Benjamin identified with, from the left, is a rejection that sees Schmitt as one of the very few prepared to take violence and power seriously in a way that takes account of the impurity of human history. The problem of concrete violence is therefore most amplified, most problematic in and for the liberal democracy seeking to make people, humans, time, and history *otherwise* than what they are. In doing so, liberal democracy attempts, through best intentions, to become a type of salvation drama. In the worst case, this is combined with a demand from the sovereign liberal state for humans to give up what gives them their identity; a sovereign liberal state that will always decide who is the exception; and that exception is those who are, who see themselves as, the expression and culmination of liberal history. This is a particular form of concrete violence, a violence of ontology, a particular type of liberal apocalypse from above, that is, from the state. For all others have to give up to become like liberals, to think like them, to believe and not believe, like them. In short, liberals seek to live, to exist, to govern, from, and as the sovereign imposing the state of exception, but a state of exception that proclaims a vantage point above and against history and identity.

Taubes and Schmitt share the recognition, grounded in the concrete experience of history that liberals and liberalism in effect wish to stop most humans from being time-located historical humans in the name of idealism and the self-interest of liberals. For the challenge to liberals is that when you are located in time, when you exist with an end point within a time with definite endings, then one is called upon to act. This means 'the problem of time is a moral problem' and liberals appear, all too often, to believe problems of time (in history) and morality can be handled by 'discussing without end' (Taubes 1986). In opposition to liberalism, anti-liberals, who position themselves as the ones who take humanity, history, time, and morals seriously, exist in a constant sense of the Katechon, knowing that there comes a point whereupon one must act, the parliament must act, the state must act, the sovereign must act. Against liberalism, the anti-liberals act as Katechon to restore the awareness that we are limited, impure humans who live in history, who live in time, who are confronted by moral problems that demand a decision, that we exist in a counter-web of identities that are finite as we are finite and so to put off the decision to a time yet to occur, in short to put the decision off to a time without present implication, is amoral. This is what we are constantly reminded of by the dwarf that liberals wish to believe does not exist.

Concrete violence is therefore the reminder that however we may have wished to exist in a world of liberals, a word of liberal utopias, a world of freedom from history, we are rather always flung back into history by fact of being human. The speed of the Futurists, the desire to increase history via a use of technology was, tellingly, always tied to an increase in violence; all that technology enables is more violence, faster, and more widespread: not the release from history but rather more for the angel of history to weep over. Schmitt and Taubes, coming at violence from differing perspectives, one from the side of those who used Fascist violence with the aim to achieving purity by technology, the other from the side of the victims of that violence, find themselves united as apocalyptic thinkers united against liberalism: as friend-enemy in the world of continuing concrete violence. Both further accept and can see that hidden dwarf of theology: a dwarf that speaks versus violence in the name of grace, yet a dwarf that for many sanctifies violence in the name of truth.

Is it only the continuation of the violence in history, undertaken as much by liberals as not, undertaken in our human attempts to inaugurate a secular utopia, a secular messianic age, that constantly reminds us that the messianic is only possible as an alternative perhaps because of the constant failures of the human attempt to inaugurate the messianic? Is the apocalyptic the position that is trapped in history as we are and we can only be released from history by the messianic in-breaking from outside, the final act of violence to end all concrete violence? Yet if the messiah has come—and if the messianic age has been inaugurated as claimed by the ultimate act of concrete violence, the death of God—are we ever fated to live under the *Angelus Novus* as long as we seek the final apocalypse, as long as we seek to inaugurate the new messianic? Or, perhaps, is concrete violence the reminder that being human has a permanent cost, a cost that Christianity proclaims wherein God becoming human suffered too from concrete violence? The messianic dwarf is therefore the constant reminder of the cost of being human, the reminder that there is no escape from being human, no escape from violence—and yet, to act against violence is whereby we truly attempt to become fully human— even unto death. The problem of liberalism is therefore not that it wants to end violence, but that it wants to stop us from being humans in history; it is perhaps the supreme act of concrete, ontological violence. Perhaps we also need to be reminded by Eagleton, reminded that is by a Catholic Marxist, that: 'at the centre of human history lies the image of a tortured and murdered political criminal' (Eagleton 2008, p. 95).

References

Baudrillard, Jean, *Paroxysm: Interviews with Phillipe Petit*, trans. Chris Turner (Verso: London & New York, 1998).

Benjamin, Walter, On the Concept of History (1940). Retrieved from http://
www.marxists.org/reference/archive/benjamin/1940/history.htm
———, *Reflections: Essays, Aphorisms, Autobiographical Writings* (New York:
New York, Harcourt Brace Jovanovich, Inc. 1978).
Bowler, Anne, 'Politics as Art: Italian Futurism and Fascism', *Theory & Society*,
vol. 20, no. 6 (Dec. 1991) 763–94.
Caws, Mary Ann. *Manifesto: A Century of Isms* (Lincoln: University of Nebraska
Press, 2001).
Eagleton, Terry, *Holy Terror* (Oxford: Oxford University Press, 2005).
———, 'Monotheism and Violence', in Graham Ward & Michael Hoelzl (ed),
The New Visibility of Religion. Studies in Religion and Cultural Hermeneutics
(London/New York: Continuum, 2008).
Gold, Joshua Robert, 'Jacob Taubes: Apocalypse From Below', *TELOS* Spring,
2006: 140–54.
Marinetti, Filippo, *The Founding and Manifesto of Futurism* (1909) http://www.
italianfuturism.org/manifestos/foundingmanifesto/
———, *The New Religion-Morality of Speed* [Futurist Manifesto, first number
of *L'Futalia Futurista* May 11 1916], in R.W. Flint, (ed), *Marinetti: Selected
Writings,* trans. R.W. Flint and Arthur A. Coppotelli (New York: Farrar,
Straus and Giroux, 1972).
Schmitt, Carl, *Political Theology: Four Chapters on the Concept of Sovereignty*,
trans. and with an introduction by George Schwab with a new foreword by
Tracy B. Strong(Chicago & London: University of Chicago Press, 2005).
——— *The Concept of the Political,* trans. and with an introduction by George
Schwab, with a foreword by Tracy B. Strong and Notes by Leo Strauss
(Chicago & London: University of Chicago Press, 2007).
Taubes, Jacob, 'Carl Schmitt. Apocalyptic Prophet of the Counter-revolution'
(1985) in Jacob Taubes, *Ad Carl Schmitt: Contested Concurrence*, introduction
by Mike Grimshaw, trans. Keith Tribe (New York, Columbia University
Press, 2014.
———, 'A Dispute about Carl Schmitt' (Paris, 1986) in Jacob Taubes, *Ad Carl
Schmitt: Contested Concurrence*, Introduction by Mike Grimshaw, trans.
Keith Tribe (New York: Columbia University Press, 2013).
———, *The Political Theology of Paul*, Aleida Assmann & Jan Assmann (eds), in
conjunction with Horst Folkers, Wolf-Daniel Hartwich and Christoph
Schulte, trans. Dana Hollander (Stanford: Stanford University Press, 2004).
———, *From Cult to Culture. Fragments Toward a Critique of Historical Reason,*
Charlotte Elisheva Fonrobert and Amir Engel (eds), with an Introduction
by Aleida Assman, Jan Assman, and Wolf-Daniel Hartwich (Stanford:
Stanford University Press, 2010).
Ward, Graham, *Cities of God* (London and New York: Routledge, 2000).
Zizek, Slavoj, *The Puppet and the Dwarf: The Perverse Core of Christianity*
(Cambridge, Mass.: MIT Press, 2003), Series foreword.

8 Kingdom-Come
Eschatology and Apocalypse

John Frow

This chapter starts with a discussion of the category of the sacred, and then discusses a particular mode of reading sacred time in the Christian exegetical tradition. My main case study is of a popular series of fundamentalist Christian novels which deploy this typological mode of reading to posit the ending of human history. I conclude by talking briefly about apocalyptic and messianic conceptions of historical time, and about the problems associated with the politics of the ruptural event.

THE SACRED

Does the sacred have a content, or is it a purely formal structure? In the classic Durkheimian formulation, the sacred is understood as an empty category defined structurally by nothing but its opposition to the profane (Durkheim 1915, p. 38). This opposition then comes to govern a series of further structural relations within the cosmos. Against the homogeneous, amorphous, undifferentiated space of the profane world is set the radical heterogeneity of sacred space, which—'saturated with being' and with significance (Eliade 1961, p. 12)—interrupts it, breaks its flow, opens out on to absolute otherness. Time is similarly heterogeneous: unlike profane time, sacred time is reversible, because 'every religious festival, any liturgical time, represents the actualization of a sacred event that took place in a mythical past, "in the beginning"' (Eliade 1961, pp. 68–9). But this sheer otherness of the sacred is itself a kind of content; and already in Durkheim it is possible to see the emergence of a positive characterization of the sacred as it divides internally to produce a distinctive ambivalence, an oscillation between repulsion and fascination, dread and desire, the *tremendum* and the *fascinans*.[1] For Durkheim this takes the form of a division between the pure and the impure, and between beneficence and malevolence, both of which are the object of interdiction: thus 'the pure and the impure are not two separate classes, but two varieties of the same class, which includes all sacred things' (Durkheim 1915, p. 411). The sacred, as evidenced in its ambiguous Latin root *sacer*, designates at once the accursed, the outcast, and the holy, a force which is above all dangerous, contagious, and compelling;[2] it is, in Roger Caillois's words, 'what one cannot approach without dying' (Caillois 1959, p. 21).

The sacred is thus a force or a presence, whether anthropomorphized or not, which is conceived non-naturalistically as a suspension or rupture of normal time and space by the uncontrollable outbreak of 'spots' of transcendence. Gods are positioned directly in relation to this force, as the force itself or as emanations of it. Within this framework it is 'normal' time which is aberrant, and the time of the sacred that carries the full weight of meaningfulness in a fallen world. Mundane history is subordinate to that other temporality which comprehends but surpasses human time.

FIGURA

The figural interpretation of the sacred Scriptures developed in the Christian patristic period is built around that subordination of mundane to sacred time, proceeding by the reading of one real historical event as the prefiguring of another, where the relation between them 'is revealed by an accord or similarity' (Auerbach 1984, p. 29). The term 'figure' originally designates a shape that emerges from a hollow mould (*forma*), although it then comes (by a transfer from instrument to effect) to mean form or shape in the sense of outline, a body that stands in relief against a ground. Erich Auerbach traces the development of a more abstract sense of the Latin *figura*, in part under the influence of the Greek *schema* (σχημα), so that 'side by side with the original plastic signification and overshadowing it, there appeared a far more general concept of grammatical, rhetorical, logical, mathematical—and later even of musical and choreographic—form' (Auerbach 1984, p. 15). Figure as shape moves in one direction towards the meanings of 'statue', 'image', and 'portrait', in another towards that of 'appearance' and of 'the deceptive likenesses that walk in dreams' (Auerbach 1984, p. 21), and in Lucretius it shifts from the form to its imitation, from model to copy. In Quintilian, it takes on the sense of rhetorical trope, and this lays the ground for the substantive hermeneutic meaning (as *figura rerum* rather than *figura verborum*) that it acquires with the Church Fathers: that of the prefiguring of one theologically significant historical event or personage by another.

Typically, an event in the Old Testament is taken to prefigure the person of Christ and is recast in terms of the fulfilment that is concealed within it. Paul's use of figural interpretation is strategically intended 'to strip the Old Testament of its normative character and show that it is merely the shadow of things to come' (Auerbach 1984, p. 50); with the advent of grace 'the old law is annulled; it is shadow and *typos*' (Auerbach 1984, p. 51), where the Greek *typos*—semantically close to the Latin *figura*—designates at once a rhetorical figure, a deeper level of meaning, and a deceptive semblance. In this schema, where a connection is established between two moments which are separate in time but which are both *within* time, the first 'signifies not only itself but also the second, while the second encompasses and fulfills the first' (Auerbach 1984, p. 53): Christ realizes the figure of David, for example, at once completing and transcending him. Figural interpretation is thus a kind of reverse prophecy, a back-projected teleology: what has happened was what was always destined to happen.

Both events—the *figura* and its fulfilment, the type and the antitype—are at once historical and yet in some sense 'provisional and incomplete', since 'they point to one another and both point to something in the future, something still to come, which will be the actual, real, and definitive event' (Auerbach 1984, p. 58): the advent of the Kingdom of Heaven, the end of historical time. Historical time is always shadowed by its atemporal other; it:

remains open and questionable, points to something still concealed, and the tentativeness of events in the figural interpretation is fundamentally different from the tentativeness of events in the modern view of historical development. In the modern view, the provisional event is treated as a step in an unbroken horizontal process; in the figural system the interpretation is always sought from above; events are considered not in their unbroken relation to one another, but torn apart, individually, each in relation to something other that is promised and not yet present. Whereas in the modern view the event is always self-sufficient and secure, while the interpretation is fundamentally incomplete, in the figural interpretation the fact is subordinated to an interpretation which is fully secured to begin with: the event is enacted according to an ideal model which is a prototype situated in the future and thus far only promised. (Auerbach 1984, pp. 58–9)

The figures are 'the tentative form of something eternal and time-less', and conversely 'every future model, though incomplete as history, is already fulfilled in God and has existed from all eternity in His provi-dence' (Auerbach 1984, p. 59).

To Auerbach's exposition we might add that the concept of *figura* has implications for the concept of person as it is understood in Christian theology. Christ is the archetype and fulfilment of human personhood, the redeemer in his own person of the fallen human nature of Adamic mankind. The essence of his being is that he is the incarnate form of God, consisting of two natures, human and divine, but having one person; and that person (the Greek term used at the First Council of Nicaea in 325 and again at the Council of Constantinople in 381 is *hypostasis*) is one of the three persons of the Trinity, distinct, co-equal, co-eternal, and consubstantial in the unity of substance of God (Boethius 1968, pp. 85, 87–9). Boethius, defining the person as embodied, ani-mate, rational, and particular, and thus as 'the individual substance of a rational nature', struggles to reconcile the Latin *persona*, derived from the mask which differentiates actors on the stage, with *hypostasis*: the former designates a substance, that which underlies accidental qualities; the latter designates the pure subsistence which is independent of acci-dental qualities, but corresponds to the former when it takes on a par-ticular form. Christ unites these two senses; he is, in brief, at once a fully human and suffering person (*persona*) and the promise of glorified per-sonhood in its reunion with the God from which it has been separated.

Dante's *Commedia* is Auerbach's key example of the working of fig-ural interpretation in a text in which 'the meaning of every life has its place in the providential history of the world' (Auerbach 1984, p. 71). Warren Ginsberg gives the more secular example of Gottfried's *Tristan*, where the hero is constructed as a typological realization of the Biblical David (who is more usually read in the exegetical tradition as a forerun-ner of Christ). Typology here works as 'a method that converts a theory of history into narrative structure, and rechannels a system of foreshad-owing and prefiguration into the formation of living character' (Ginsberg 1983, p. 78). I want to engage with a very different kind of text, how-ever, by looking at a more recent example of the fictional use of typo-logical interpretation.

PROPHECY

Mary Louise Pratt wrote some years ago of watching an evangelical preacher performing on television an exegesis of a passage from the Book of Ezekiel. She is struck by the receptiveness of his 'rapt audience of a couple of thousand', all of whom 'accompanied him, Bibles open in their hands, index fingers following the lines, lips moving as they weighed the powerful words' (Pratt 2005, p. 881); his work is charged with a sense of vital historical mission, which is enhanced by his charismatic use of the medium. In listening to the televangelist, Pratt is struck by the similarity of his work to her own as a teacher and an interpreter of texts; the exegesis she hears is 'spellbinding', combining the scholarly elucidation of allusions, etymologies, and historical references with an eloquent and morally informed ability to convey 'the depth and wisdom of the text, the plenitude of its meanings, the higher purposes to which it called them' (2005, p. 85). Yet what this interpretation is doing is reading the text—Chapter 38 of the Book of Ezekiel—as a prophetic anticipation of an apocalyptic war in the Middle East; the televangelist reads a coded text for its esoteric core of literal truth about a future event, and he no longer understands typology as applying only to the history of the Jewish people but extends it to all subsequent history, and specifically that of his own people.

This is in many ways a peculiarly American story. Although the combination of belief in the literal or coded truth of Scripture with the reach and power of the mass media can be found elsewhere—in the worlds of Islam and of Hinduism, in the mass-produced iconography of Catholicism, and spreading out from the evangelising Protestant churches of the United States to Central and South America and many other parts of the Western world—it works with particular intensity in that country which more than any other is the creature of Enlightenment reason and modernity, which understands itself as an exception among the nations, chosen by God to fulfil its manifest destiny, and where the tensions between secular and religious versions of the common weal have become pervasive.

During the late 1970s and the 1980s, the United States was swept by a cultural revolution at least as formative as that of the 1960s counter-culture, in which millions of Bible believers:

broke old taboos constraining their interactions with outsiders, claimed new cultural territory, and refashioned themselves in church services, Bible studies, books and pamphlets, classrooms, families, daily life, and the public arena. In the process, they altered what it meant to be a fundamentalist and reconfigured the large fellowship of born-again Christians, the rules of national public discourse, and the meaning of modernity. (Harding 2000, p. ix)

The movement had its origins in nineteenth-century revivalist movements (and in an eschatological tradition running through the whole history of Christianity), in the typological concordances of the widely disseminated *Scofield Reference Bible* (1909), in Billy Graham's crusades, and in Hal Lindsey's populist manual of prophetic belief *The Late Great Planet Earth* (1970), the single best-selling non-fiction title of the 1970s. Lindsey's manual drew together anxieties about communism, globalization, ecumenism, and the displacement of the nation state by supra-national governmental and monetary systems, all of which he read as indicators of 'the rise of the "Beast system", otherwise known as the ominous "New World Order", controlled by secret organizations such as the Council on Foreign Relations (CFR) and the Trilateral Commission' (Shuck 2005). The evangelical revolution of the 1970s and 1980s, appealing to the cultural anxieties of a white and largely working-class demographic 'left behind' by rapid social change, was guided and shaped by a number of evangelical preachers, most prominently Jerry Falwell and Pat Robertson, with a command of television that enabled them to reach well beyond their local congregations, seminaries and 'universities' to an audience of millions.

The significance of this movement outwards into public life lay in its challenge to the modern settlement in which religion is allotted a protected place outside of politics and the serious business of the state. As Susan Harding puts it, the huge 1980 'Washington for Jesus' rally tore up 'a tacit contract with modern America' which, 'fashioned in the wake of the 1925 Scopes trial, specifically proscribed the "mixing" of ostensibly premodern, that is, Bible-believing, Protestant rhetorics and routine politics. It thus rendered the public arena and the nation as a whole "modern" in the sense of secular' (Harding 2000, p. 21). Now, however, the assumption that a religious premodernity and a secular modernity are neatly separable into a 'before' and an 'after' is barely tenable; as the social landscape has changed, with religion and politics again forming a globally unstable mixture, we have come to realize that 'modernity is unthinkable without the constantly evolving, constantly renegotiated pact between religious and secular knowledge. What appears today as an "undoing of secularization" is a violent reworking of the pact, whose outcome we cannot foresee' (Pratt 2005, p. 882). The central assumptions of enlightened modernity—the primacy of scientific protocols of proof over faith, a non-transcendent understanding of history, value pluralism—are directly challenged by a discourse of Biblical certainty secure in its anchorage in the public sphere. It is not that an achieved modernity has been disrupted by an incursion of 'premodern' elements, but that the separation of religious and political spheres, which has been formative of the modern state since the late eighteenth century, has been replaced by a kind of fusion in which the force of the political is redefined: Jimmy Carter was elected in 1976 as a born-again Christian; Ronald Reagan built his foreign policy around millenarian beliefs, and his Secretary of the Interior, James Watt, refused to engage with environmental degradation because of his belief that the imminent return of Christ would make human intervention redundant (Shuck 2005, p. 63); George W. Bush proclaimed his rebirth and redemption as a Christian, and spoke in favour of the teaching of Creation Science in schools; and Jon Huntsman dropped out of the 2012 Republican primary race lamenting that he was the only one of the five leading candidates who believed in the reality of climate change and the theory of evolution. An estimated 70 million Americans call themselves evangelicals, and they gave George W. Bush 40 per cent of his vote. Each one of them wants to bring God into politics. Religion no longer knows, or accepts, its 'place'.

The exercise of biblical exegesis that Pratt witnessed is at the core of those fundamentalist modes of religious thought which understand the historical world not as an irreversible and linear unfolding of events, but as a concordance of sacred time with historical time within a closed (and therefore atemporal) order of the universe. Prophecy is what reads the sense of that closed order. The end days foretold in the Bible are always already inscribed in a patterning of the world which has the Biblical text as its encoded manifestation. Such a placing of the world within sacred time radically undermines non-transcendental forms of reading:

Current events and the daily news are not neutral, secular phenomena that exist independently and are subjected to religious interpretation by Christians. They are signs of the times. They are inside bible-based history. They are evidence that God and his enemy are coming to final blows over the fate of the Jews and of all mankind. (Harding 2000, p. 223)

Everything can be placed in relation to this interpretive schema. The historical time posited by fundamentalist Christians in the United States (and of course there are close negative parallels in fundamentalist Islamic and Jewish thought) draws a connection between Israel and America, the two covenanted nations: a Salomonic Golden Age flourishes in the US to the end of the Eisenhower presidency, then declines as the liberal-humanist enemies of religion (for which read in part the counter-culture of the 1960s) force through the 1962 decision banning school prayer and the case that legalizes abortion, Roe v Wade, in 1973. Then follows the presidency of Bill Clinton, the evil Zedekiah who ignores the admonitions of the prophets, and its culmination in the event that parallels the conquest and enslavement of the chosen people by Babylon, the attacks of September 11, 2001.

Biblical prophecy gives tens of millions of Americans a way of construing apparently secular events within a typological perspective; it gives them a line about

the AIDS crisis, the New Age Movement, satanic cults and demonic principalities, about the epidemic of abortion, pornography, homosexuality, divorce, crime, and drugs... about Israel, about what God has in store for Israel... about the Persian Gulf war, or the Middle East peace treaty... [about] what the election and reelection of Bill Clinton meant for America... about the North American [Free] Trade Agreement, [the] General Agreement on Tariffs and Trade, the European Economic Community, about borderless travel between nations, the Internet, transnational business and finance, and UFOs and alien abductions. (Harding 2000, p. 223)

The dominant interpretive framework amongst American fundamentalists—the doctrine of dispensational premillenarianism—posits that 'God at the beginning of time determined a *specific, detailed* plan for history's last days—a plan revealed in the Bible with minute particularity, though in symbolic language and veiled images' (Boyer 1992, pp. ix-x). In this plan, history culminates in the 'rapture' of the saints or chosen ones, who ascend with Christ to Heaven and dwell there for seven years while those left behind suffer terrible tribulations culminating in Israel in the battle of Armageddon between the forces of Christ and the Antichrist; the chosen ones then return with Christ to rule with him on earth during the Kingdom Age of 1000 years. The schema is enunciated in Tim LaHaye and Jerry Jenkins's best-selling end-time novel, *Left Behind* (later expanded to a series, as well as to a number of franchised movies, graphic novels, children's novels, a television series, digital games, and merchandising spin-offs; cf. Shuck 2005, pp. 10–11), in which the initial moment of rapture is followed by the story of those church members who were not truly saved, and to whom the divine order of things is explained in a DVD left behind for them by their raptured pastor. Dozens of other novels, and untold numbers of populist doctrinal texts, expound some version of this pattern (cf. Robertson 1996; Myers 1999; Gillette 2003; Beauseigneur 2003a, 2003b, 2004).

LEFT BEHIND

As it happens, it is Ezekiel 38 that forms the basis for much of the underlying pattern of *Left Behind*; an appendix to the novel, 'The Truth Behind the Fiction', reads Ezekiel 38 and 39 as prefiguring the role of Russia in attacking Israel in the end times (LaHaye and Jenkins 1995, pp. 479–80). The identification of Ezekiel's 'Gog, the land of Magog' (an unspecific power from the north) with Russia is here merely stated, but it draws on a long history of exegesis deriving in part from the much later identification of Gog with the land of the Scythians (Boyer 1992, pp. 153–54), and from the identification made by the nineteenth-century philologist Wilhelm Gesenius of the Hebrew noun *rosh*, meaning prince ('the chief prince of Meschech and Tubal'), with the Nordic Rus people (Price 2007, p. 148). The authors also note that Saddam Hussein began the rebuilding of Babylon, and that his 'removal' will facilitate this revival of Babylon (LaHaye and Jenkins 1995, p. 484). In a later novel in the series, *Tribulation Force: The Continuing Drama of the Left Behind*, the figural hermeneutics which establishes the concordance of the Old and New Testaments receives narrative embodiment in the person of the orthodox Rabbi Tsion Ben-Judah, who is commissioned by the state of Israel to examine the scriptures for their prophetic truth and discovers that Jesus is indeed the predicted Messiah (LaHaye and Jenkins 1996, p. 391ff). In Robert Price's analysis, this mode of allegorical exegesis represents a shift from treating the New Testament (as the earliest gospel, Matthew, does) as representing actions undertaken in order to bring about a fulfilment of the words of the prophets, to the appeal by Luke and later exegetes to the Old Testament texts as anachronistic anticipations of a future to which they are merely the prelude (Price 2007, p. 63). That future is at once the coming and the second coming (*parousia*) of Christ, two distinct times within a closed order of temporal recurrence.

Left Behind begins with Captain Rayford Steele piloting a Boeing 747 across the Atlantic, thinking lustful thoughts about his 'drop-dead gorgeous' flight attendant Hattie Durham (LaHaye and Jenkins 1995, p. 2), and then suddenly finding out that a number of passengers are missing, leaving behind their clothes and their loved ones. The plane returns to Chicago to find widespread devastation: cars and planes have crashed, and millions of people—including babies in the womb and corpses on their way to a funeral—have vanished into thin air; video footage shows people instantaneously dematerializing. Steele returns to his home to find that his wife and young son are amongst those who have disappeared (for numerous earlier examples of these themes, cf. Boyer 1992, p. 255ff).

From this point the novel follows two parallel and interwoven narrative strands. One is the story of Steele's private moral quest, which involves a rejection of his adulterous self, a recognition of the truth of his wife's religious beliefs, and the decoding (with the help of the DVD left behind by the pastor of her congregation and of the spiritual leadership of that pastor's replacement, a man who has recognized his own previous lack of true faith) of Biblical prophecies in Revelations and Ezekiel, which tell of the rapture of the faithful followed by a seven-year period of worsening warfare, famine, and plague, ending in the Great Tribulation which precedes the millennial rule of Christ. It becomes clear to Steele that 'God had tried to warn his people by putting his Word in written form centuries before' (LaHaye and Jenkins 1995, p. 316); he is born again as a believer, and persuades his daughter Chloe to convert to his newly-found faith.

The other narrative strand follows the more public quest of the ace reporter 'Buck' Williams to uncover a conspiracy on the part of a cabal of powerful, ruthless, and very wealthy men to install a young and charismatic politician, Nicolae Carpathia ('a stunningly handsome blond who looked not unlike a young Brad Pitt'; LaHaye and Jenkins 1995, p. 116) as the leader of a world government, technically the United Nations, with its headquarters in the renovated city of Babylon, with a single currency, a single language, a single world religion headquartered in Rome, and with the United Nations having a monopoly of weapons in a world that has disarmed. Carpathia is Romanian but (the implication is: therefore) of Roman stock. Together with Buck we learn to read the clues: a series of men who have got in the way of Carpathia's rise have been murdered, including Buck's English contact who tipped him off to the conspiracy and the Scotland Yard detective who revealed the extent of the power of the financiers backing Carpathia. Talking to the born-again pastor, Bruce Barnes, Buck realizes that all the signs point to Carpathia's being the Antichrist; he himself undergoes a spiritual conversion, which gives him the power to resist Carpathia as he exercises his evil powers over a gathering of his inner circle, executing his two most powerful backers and hypnotising everyone except Buck—protected by his newfound ally, Jesus—into seeing a double suicide instead of a murder. The novel finishes with an annunciation of the challenge that awaits the three male protagonists:

Steele, Buck Williams, and Bruce Barnes faced the gravest danger anyone could face, and they knew their mission.

The task of the Tribulation Force was clear and their goal nothing less than to stand and fight the enemies of God during the seven most chaotic years the planet would ever see. (LaHaye and Jenkins 1995, p. 472)

The text quoted in the DVD left behind by the raptured pastor is 1 Corinthians 51–7, proclaiming the Resurrection and the raising up of the dead to their incorruptible bodies. This is the event the novel narrates: 'Bible prophecy', we are told, 'is history written in advance' (LaHaye and Jenkins 1995, LaHaye and Jenkins 1995, p. 219). In this instance; in another story told at the beginning of the novel about the invasion of Israel by Russia in alliance with Libya and Ethiopia, where the invading planes and rockets are mysteriously destroyed in mid-air; and in another concerning the apparently supernatural powers of two Jewish prophets proclaiming that Christ was the messiah, the laws of the physical universe are suspended, and this (fictional) suspension is then adduced as proof of the power of Biblical prophecy.

Generically, *Left Behind* has elements of a number of popular genres. Buck at one point feels 'as if he were living in a science fiction thriller' (LaHaye and Jenkins 1995, p. 399), and there are components too of the fantasy epic. Thematically the novel is close to such movie genres as the catastrophe movie and the alien invasion movie. And although it predates *The Da Vinci Code* (2003) by eight years, the central role given to the decoding of Biblical texts and the political melodrama of the conspiracy plot mark it as a close relative. At its core, *Left Behind* is a proselytising novel written for a nonsecular interpretive community that already accepts its underlying assumptions. It has no common ground with those who believe in the principles of scientific or historical method, or in the provisionality of literary response. And its primary mechanism is that of identification with the process of spiritual conversion on the part of its central characters—Rayford Steele, Buck Williams, Chloe Steele, Bruce Barnes—as they repeat the figural archetype of Christ and the biblical pattern of the redemption of sin.

ESCHATOLOGY

One reason why the abstruse theology of dispensational premillenarianism matters to those of us outside this interpretive community is that—because of the central role played in such eschatological narratives by Israel and its chosen people—the typological account of the shape and direction of contemporary history has had real effects on US foreign policy. At a dinner speech given to Californian legislators in 1971, Ronald Reagan was explicit about his commitment to an eschatological view of history:

Ezekiel tells us that Gog, the nation that will lead all of the other powers of darkness against Israel, will come out of the north. Biblical scholars have been saying for generations that Gog must be Russia. What other powerful nation is to the north of Israel? None. But it didn't seem to make sense before the Russian revolution, when Russia was a Christian country. Now it does, now that Russia has become communistic and atheistic, now that Russia has set itself against God. Now it fits the description of Gog perfectly... For the first time ever, everything is in place for the battle of Armageddon and the second coming of Christ. (cited in Boyer 1992, p. 162)

Many years later, in a kind of deranged parody of political commentary, Mark Hitchcock wrote of the 2006 Hamas victory in the Palestinian elections:

These recent events seem to confirm there will be no lasting peace in the Middle East until the Antichrist arrives on the world scene. According to Daniel 9:27, the seven-year tribulation will begin when the final world rulers make some kind of treaty with Israel that guarantees her security and access to the temple mount in Jerusalem. This peaceful condition for Israel is further described in Ezekiel 38:8 and 11... While world leaders should continue to do whatever they can to limit violence and bloodshed in the Middle East, I don't believe any lasting results will be achieved until the Antichrist arrives on the scene. (cited in Hitchcock 2012)

This discourse is embedded in institutions which are culturally mainstream, including much of the American political establishment. The novel *Left Behind* is one small component of a complex apparatus made up of movies, graphic novels, digital games, sermons, prayer meetings, study groups, television and radio stations, websites, parts of the music industry, bible colleges and seminaries, Christian bookshops, political pressure groups—all working to shape the persons of the faithful as the bearers of a particular view of the world, a particular kind of worldly force: to position them as the freely self-positioning subjects of its discourse. The immense power that this assemblage, this *dispositif*, wields in the United States threatens the notion on which this Enlightenment state was founded, that there should be separate spheres of responsibility and truth for religion and politics; the prospect half-glimpsed before us is of the fusion (or 'de-differentiation') again of those relatively distinct spheres and the end of a secular order based in principles—however inadequately they may operate in practice—of consensual rationality. Although the role of religion in US politics is largely restricted to the relatively peripheral areas of the control of fertility and sexuality and a single field of foreign policy, the Middle East, the guidance of American evangelical thought by eschatological principles is entirely ominous. Islamist and Hindutva ideals of theocratic governance are shared—*mutatis mutandis*—by the American religious right, whose goal is a fully Christian state promoting Christian ethical and cultural norms, and whose 'wilfully mad rhetoric... is a political act, a constant dissent, disruption, and critique of modern thought, specifically of the modern theories of history that shape prevailing knowledge about world events, past and present, in America' (Harding 2000, p. 238).

VIOLENCE AND THE SACRED

Apocalypse is the event of transcendental violence that marks and effects the end of sacred time, or rather the end of the temporal dimension of the sacred; it announces and effects the advent (to use a necessary paradox) of eternity, the *pleroma* in which time ceases to exist. In the fundamentalist vision enunciated in the *Left Behind* texts this event is above all a spectacle: the witnessing by those who are saved of the torment of the sinful masses. The certainty that one will partake of this joyous spectacle is guaranteed in advance by the sure knowledge that the elect have of their salvation: 'If you have already trusted Christ for your salvation, you have the mark of the seal of God on your forehead, visible only to other believers… this decision, mark, seal is also irrevocable, so you need never fear losing your standing with him' (LaHaye and Jenkins 1999, p. 327; cited in Price 2007, p. 275). The decision and the mark are equivalent: to trust Christ is to be marked as one of the elect, to choose is to be chosen—and conversely, it is those who are not chosen who will choose to be marked with the mark of the Beast. The spectacle of torment is one of the signs by which the chosen ones will recognize their election to grace.

Violence is at the heart of this version of the sacred, just as, in Benjamin's 'Critique of Violence', it is at the heart of the law, taking the form of the originary act of violence that founds any juridical system (the 'lawmaking' [*rechtsetzend*] moment) and of the ongoing violence that preserves it (the *rechtserhaltend* moment). If the sacred is 'what one cannot approach without dying' (Caillois), it is, for Benjamin, above all in 'the exercise of violence over life and death'— that is, in capital punishment—that the law is most fully affirmed (Benjamin 1996, p. 242). Conversely, 'When the consciousness of the latent presence of violence in a legal institution disappears, the institution falls into decay' (Benjamin 1996, p. 244). The violence of the law corresponds to what Benjamin calls mythic lawmaking, whose end is power; it is, in its archetypal form, 'a mere manifestation of the gods' (Benjamin 1996, p. 248), being governed by fate, or pure contingency. It is contrasted with divine violence, whose end is justice and whose action is law-destroying.

How are we to understand this divine violence? In Benjamin's later writings, oriented equally to Marxism and to the Kabbalah, it takes the form of the messianic event which ruptures the continuity of homogeneous empty time. That event is at once the transcendental Revolution which overturns all previously existing structures, and the advent of the Messiah, who 'comes not only as the redeemer; he comes as the victor over the Antichrist' (Benjamin 2003, p. 391). Revolutionary violence, as 'pure immediate violence', is 'the highest manifestation of unalloyed violence by man' (Benjamin 1996, p. 252). It corresponds to that absolute event which in Sorel, taking the form of the general strike, has 'a character of *infinity*, because it puts on one side all discussion of definite reforms and confronts men with a catastrophe' (Sorel 1961, p. 46), and in Badiou is the ruptural initiation of truth (Badiou 2005).

On the theological ground that Benjamin shares with Carl Schmitt, then, the transcendental critique of violence is resolved by appeal to the Sorelian mysticism of a pure and apocalyptic violence which is its own end. Here, just as in the Girardian understanding of violence as a mimetic contagion which affects language and representation, violence is conceived as a unitary category with a constant relation to law and the sacred. Let me conclude this chapter by briefly opening up a directly contrary line of argument. I posit that, just as the discourse of figural history must be understood, in both its actions and its effects, in terms of the *dispositif*—the heterogeneous assemblage of texts, institutions, doctrines, polemics, money, and actions—through which it exercises its persuasive power, so too the category of violence must be disassembled into its constitutive parts, the particular historical arrangements (including specific sets of laws and legal systems and the particular workings of capitalism) within which it takes on a differential form and is distributed between unequally empowered social protagonists. Neither in Rapture nor in Revolution will there be an end to the complexity of mundane politics, or to the complexity of the structural violence of neoliberal capitalism and of whatever will succeed it.

Notes

1. These are the two adjectives—the awe-inspiring and the uncannily attractive—with which Rudolf Otto characterizes the *mysterium*, the absolute otherness, which is at the heart of the numinous (Otto 1958).

2. Agamben's critique of the notion of the ambivalence of the sacred seems to me not to dislodge it (Agamben 1998, pp. 75–80).

References

Agamben, Giorgio, *Homo Sacer: Sovereign Power and Bare Life*, trans. Daniel Heller-Roazen (Stanford: Stanford University Press, 1998).

Auerbach, Erich, 'Figura', trans. Ralph Manheim, *Scenes from the Drama of European Literature* (1959; rpt. Minneapolis: University of Minnesota Press, 1984).

Badiou, Alain, *Being and Event*, trans. Oliver Feltham (New York: Continuum, 2005).

Beauseigneur, James, *The Christ Clone Trilogy* (*In His Image*, 2003a; *Birth of an Age*, 2003b; *Acts of God*, 2004) (New York: Warner Faith, 2003–4).

Benjamin, Walter, 'On the Concept of History', *Selected Writings, Vol. 4: 1938–1940*, trans. Edmund Jephcott and others, Marcus Bullock and Michael W. Jennings (eds.) (Cambridge, MA: Harvard University Press, 2003).

Benjamin, Walter, 'Critique of Violence', trans. Edmund Jephcott, *Selected Writings, Vol. 1: 1913–1926*, Marcus Bullock and Michael W. Jennings (eds.) (Cambridge, MA: Harvard University Press, 1996).

Boethius, Anicius Manlius Severinus, 'A Treatise Against Eutyches and Nestorius', *Boethius: The Theological Tractates and The Consolation of Philosophy*, trans. H.F. Stewart and E.K. R and, Loeb Classical Library (Cambridge, MA: Harvard University Press, 1968).

Boyer, Paul, *When Time Shall Be No More: Prophecy Belief in Modern American Culture* (Cambridge, MA: Harvard University Press, 1992).

Caillois, Roger, *Man and the Sacred*, trans. Meyer Barash (Glencoe, IL: The Free Press, 1959).

Durkheim, Emile, *The Elementary Forms of the Religious Life*, trans. Joseph Ward Swain (London: George Allen and Unwin, 1915).

Eliade, Mircea, *The Sacred and the Profane*, trans. Willard R. Trask (1959; rpt. New York: Harper and Row, 1961).

Gillette, Britt, *Conquest of Paradise: An End-times Nano-Thriller* (Lincoln, NE: Writers' Club Press, 2003).

Ginsberg, Warren, *The Cast of Character: The Representation of Personality in Ancient and Medieval Literature* (Toronto: University of Toronto Press, 1983).

Harding, Susan Friend, *The Book of Jerry Falwell: Fundamentalist Language and Politics* (Princeton: Princeton University Press, 2000).

Hitchcock, Mark, cited in http://www.calvaryprophecy.com/q597.html, February 2006; last accessed 20/03/2012.

LaHaye, Tim and Jerry B. Jenkins, *Assassins: Assignment: Jerusalem, Target: Antichrist* (Wheaton, IL: Tyndale House, 1999).

———, *Tribulation Force: The Continuing Drama of the Left Behind* (Wheaton, IL: Tyndale House, 1996).

———, *Left Behind: A Novel of the Earth's Last Days* (Carol Stream, IL: Tyndale Publishers, 1995).

Myers, Bill, *Fire of Heaven* (Grand Rapids, MI: Zondervan, 1999),

Otto, Rudolph, *The Idea of the Holy*, trans. John W. Harvey (1923; rpt. Oxford: Oxford University Press, 1958).

Pratt, Mary Louise, 'Subjects and Predicators', *PMLA* 120: 3, (2005).

Price, Robert M. *The Paperback Apocalypse: How the Christian Church was Left Behind* (Amherst, NY: Prometheus Books, 2007).

Robertson, Pat, *The End of the Age* (Nashville: Thomas Nelson, 1996).

Shuck, Glenn W., *Marks of the Beast: The Left Behind Novels and the Struggle for Evangelical Identity* (New York: New York University Press, 2005).

Sorel, Georges, 'Introduction: Letter to Daniel Halévy', *Reflections on Violence*, trans. T. E. Hulme and J. Roth (New York: Collier Books, 1961).

9 Capital Violence

Clayton Crockett

> There are blows in life, so powerful...I don't know! Blows as from God's hatred.
>
> César Vallejo, *The Black Heralds*

What are the questions of violence today? How does religion affect, respond to, or produce violence? We live in a violent world, and the spectacle of religious violence captures our attention. Some intellectuals argue that if we could free human beings from religion then we could pursue a predominantly peaceful co-existence. But what if the violence of our world has less to do with religion as a cause and more to do with the workings of corporate capitalism? How can we compare the relative violence produced by religious institutions and adherents to the violence generated by our economic and political forms of life?

In an essay from 1921, Walter Benjamin provides an important 'Critique of Violence.' This critique plays on the semantic ambiguity between the words force and violence contained in the German word *Gewalt*. Benjamin suggests that it is not easy to separate an ordinary force from an extraordinary violence, and both constitute a morally justifiable means to a just end. Benjamin surveys both natural law and positive law traditions, and characterizes the law-making and law-preserving forces of each as saturated in violence. He claims that 'all violence as a means is either lawmaking or law-preserving' (Benjamin 1996, p. 243). Even though language exists as a sphere of non-violent discourse, 'it is never reason that decides on the justification of means and the justness of ends.' (Benjamin 1996, p. 247). For Benjamin, all of our executive, lawmaking power, as well as our administrative law-preserving forces that serve them, are 'pernicious' insofar as they are necessarily implicated in positive violence (Benjamin 1996, p. 252).

In the essay, Benjamin contrasts mythic and divine violence, where mythic violence is also a positive and instituting power. Benjamin gives the example of the myth of Niobe, and claims that 'this immediate violence in mythic manifestations' is identical 'to lawmaking violence' (Benjamin 1996, p. 248). In the myth, Niobe brags about her fourteen children to Leto, who sends her two children, Apollo and Artemis, to kill them all in a brutal and horrific display of violence. Benjamin argues that Niobe's situation is not simply a punishment, but illustrates the law of fate. The punishment of Niobe's arrogance illustrates 'a violence [that] establishes a law far more than it punishes the infringement of a law that already exists,' (Benjamin 1996, p. 248).

Divine violence, on the other hand, is a purely destructive force in a more profound way. It is 'lethal without spilling blood.' Benjamin claims that this divine power, which he affirms and sets against mythic violence, is found not only in religious traditions but also in present day life as an educative power (1996, p. 250). Divine violence is a revolutionary and expiatory form of violence, because it brings to an end mythic violence as such. Divine power exposes and weakens mythic violence by separating out the mythic aspect from its instantiation in contemporary law. Benjamin claims that while power is 'the principle of all mythic lawmaking,' 'justice is the principle of all divine endmaking' (1996, p. 248).

Benjamin's essay has proved extremely influential, informing Jacques Derrida's famous 'turn' or pivot to explicitly address issues of ethics, politics, and religion in his later work that begins with his 1989 article 'Force of Law: "The Mystical Foundation of Authority" '. In this essay, Derrida following Benjamin distinguishes between law, which is always complicit with violence and always susceptible to deconstruction, and justice, which is not deconstructible. Derrida does not follow Benjamin's exact distinction, but claims that there is an unforeseeable and impossible appeal to justice in any establishment of law, or lawmaking power. That is why there is always a 'mystical foundation' for any authority, because any law-making power is both violent in terms of establishing a determinate law, and non-violent in its appeal to justice. According to Derrida, 'deconstruction takes place in the interval that separates the undeconstructibility of justice from the deconstructibility of *droit* [French for law and right] (authority, legitimacy, and so on). It is possible as an experience of the impossible, there where, even it if does not exist (or does not yet exist, or never does exist), *there is justice*' (Derrida 1992, p. 15). Justice, which Benjamin associates with divine violence, becomes the mystical limit within law itself for Derrida.

In another, more phenomenological sense, the Italian philosopher Gianni Vattimo suggests that we can draw a connection between Benjamin's 1921 reflections on violence and his powerful 1936 essay on 'The Work of Art in an Age of Mechanical Reproduction.' In the latter essay, Benjamin claims that the effect of modern art is that it offers a shock to its viewer. In cinema, for example, the rapid succession of projection of images on a viewer's consciousness disrupts human experience of the world. According to Vattimo, 'Benjamin's comments open the way for a reflection on the new *Wesen* of art in late-industrial society that overcomes the traditional metaphysical definition of art as a place of harmony' (Vattimo 1992, p. 47).

Vattimo associates Benjamin's notion of shock with Martin Heidegger's claim in his 1936 essay on 'The Origin of the Work of Art' that the work of art is a "setting-into-work of truth" arising in the strife between the work's two constitutive elements: the setting up of the world and the setting forth of the earth' 1992). The strife between earth and world delivers a blow to the observer of such a work, in German *Stoss*. By bringing together Heidegger's *Stoss* with Benjamin's shock, we can 'assemble the essential features of a new "essence" of art in late-industrial society,' which is consonant with modern capitalism (Vattimo, 1992). Instead of producing harmony or accord between modern human beings and the world, this new understanding of art in the twentieth century is concerned with disorientation; it consists of a low-level form of violence in consciousness that 'is directed toward keeping the disorientation alive' (Vattimo 1992, p. 51). Vattimo does not fully draw out the implications of this violence at the level of human consciousness, and he appears ambivalent about its consequences, but we can observe how Benjamin's theorization of violence is significant for an understanding of aesthetics. Furthermore, by focusing on aesthetics we can connect his critique of violence more directly to a type of modern historical experience rather than a more timeless, universal experience[1].

In his book *The Transparent Society*, Vattimo draws attention to the modes of aesthetic disorientation unleashed by technological innovations in the twentieth century, and these disorienting effects are further explored by the architect and theorist Paul Virilio in *The Vision Machine, The Art of the Motor*, and other works. In *The Art of the Motor*, Virilio claims that 'technology is no longer exploding a long way away from the body, it is exploding inside the body,' specifically in the form of miniaturization or nanotechnology (Virilio 1995, p. 113). Industrial and post-industrial capitalist technologies invade the body, transforming our physiology, altering our perception and self-perception in dramatic ways. We are experiencing 'the motorization of the living being,' which involves the breakdown of the distinction between organic and machinic (Virilio 1995, p. 111).

The motorization of humanity involves the production and intensification of images designed for the representation and control of complex processes. Virilio emphasizes the negative, dystopian aspects of these processes, particularly the interaction of military and information technology and their complicity in war. From the 'simultaneous invention of gunpowder and printer's ink', he affirms to a similar connection between the machine gun and the camera, nitrocellulose and film, radar and video—but also between the *trick effects* of the depiction of actual events in graphic illustration, photography, film, and television, and good old fashioned camouflage...[we are] no longer able to tell *where reality begins or leaves off* (Virilio 1995, p. 54).

Virilio argues that the technical creation of images screens us from reality, and screens us from ourselves, and this is both an aesthetic and a military project. The most important aspect of this aesthetic image is the speed of its motor, a speed that approaches the speed of light and overwhelms critical or self-conscious thought and reflection. Authoritarian forces benefit from the proliferation of images that confuse and disorient thinking. As Virilio explains in *Desert Screen*, his reflections on the first Gulf War of 1991, 'no politics is possible at the scale of the speed of light. Politics depends upon having time for reflection' (Virilio 2002, p. 43).

Paradoxically, the proliferation of images induces a breakdown in perception, and brings about blindness, a blindness caused by the overwhelming intensity of the speed of light. The vision machine is an autonomic, inhuman entity that bypasses thought and reflection. Human reflection is cut out of the loop, in order to perfect and extend authoritarian control, which is the thesis of Manuel De Landa's book, *War in an Age of Intelligent Machines* (1991).

In addition to the blows inflicted by aesthetic, economic, and military weapons, or perhaps even as an example of the extremely sophisticated weaponization of our global culture, we currently exist under a near-constant barrage of images. In this hyper-visual culture, how are these technological effects related to the resurgence of seemingly traditional but in fact postmodern forms of religiosity and their spectacular instances of violence? Are we perpetually disoriented, are we reeling under the blows of these images, and what are the possibilities for either making sense or for fighting back?

In another essay from 1921, an unpublished fragment entitled 'Capitalism as Religion', Benjamin analyses capitalism itself as a kind of religion. He claims that we can discern a religion in capitalism because 'capitalism serves essentially to allay the same anxieties, torments, and disturbances to which the so-called religions offered answers' (Benjamin 1996, p. 288). Furthermore, Benjamin states that the earliest forms of all religious traditions were entirely practical and worldly affairs, rather than other-worldly pursuits. We cannot view capitalism's full religious import from inside it, but we can distinguish three main aspects of its religious structure. First, capitalism is a purely cultic religion, which means that has no dogma or theology. I would qualify somewhat Benjamin's assertion that capitalism lacks any theology, however, since there are many people who espouse faith in capitalism, in liberal democracy, and in free markets. The point is that even if you don't believe in capitalism as a creed, you can still participate in its cult by buying and selling.

The second aspect of capitalism is that it is a cult without any 'weekdays.' It is totally sacred as well as completely profane, at least in temporal terms, because there is no time at which is does not function.

'There is no day that is not a feast day, in the terrible sense that all its sacred pomp is unfolded before us,' Benjamin proclaims; 'each day commands the utter fealty of the worshipper' (Benjamin 1996). Markets, financial transactions, and consumption operate twenty-four hours a day, seven days a week, and this constant feature of capitalism has only intensified since Benjamin's time. Finally, the third element of capitalism as religion is that instead of atoning for or alleviating guilt, 'the cult makes guilt pervasive' (Benjamin 1996). Again, I would qualify Benjamin's analysis here, and suggest that if guilt becomes pervasive, it is perhaps better named as anxiety. Anxiety becomes the affective mode of capitalism, precisely because it cannot be eliminated, only buried or forgotten for a short time by means of consuming. And this consumption later generates more anxiety.

Max Weber's thesis about the religion of Protestant Calvinism favouring the rise of capitalism does not go far enough. According to Benjamin, 'the Christianity of the Reformation did not favour the growth of capitalism; instead it transformed into capitalism' (Benjamin 1996, p. 290). Capitalism is the outcome of Christianity itself, which then becomes universal, turning against its own and other determinate religious forms. That is why Christianity is always privileged in capitalist modernity. Furthermore, capitalism means that 'God's transcendence is at an end. But he is not dead; he has been incorporated into human existence' (Benjamin 1996, p. 289). Capitalism incorporates God into human existence at the level of everyday life and practice, which is at once completely sacred and absolutely profane. Or to put it another way, we could say that the capitalist religion is entirely secular without thereby ceasing to be a kind of religion.

Is it necessary to provincialize capitalism? How could we do so? In his influential book *Provincializing Europe*, Dipesh Chakrabarty suggests that one way to combat the legacy of colonialism in the modern world is to attend to a more careful reading of Marx on Capital. According to Chakrabarty, we should think about two distinct forms of History, History 1 and History 2. History 1 is the universal history that is the retrospective effect of a number of History 2s, which are contingent and local histories. The global history of capital is constructed out of particular and contingent local forms. 'No historical form of capital, however global its reach, can ever be universal,' write Chakrabarty

(2000, p. 70). This means that the universal 'can only exist as a place holder, its place always usurped by a historical particular seeking to present itself as universal' (Chakrabarty 2000, p. 70). The fact that these local History 2s always exist and disrupt the accomplishment of a universal History 1 means that historical differences always disrupt and defer 'capital's self-realization' (Chakrabarty 2000, pp. 70–71). In Chakrabarty's terms, History 1 would be the history of capital itself, whereas History 2 would be a religious history of capital as what succeeds Christianity, whether or not it is still Christian.

Even if this self-realization of capital is never seamless or fully realized, however, it still works because we cannot eliminate the fantasy of History 1, which is based on the universal sovereignty of money. According to the British philosopher of religion Philip Goodchild, money's weak force always triumphs over any other value, because it provides the notion of value itself. In his book *A Theology of Money*, Goodchild claims that 'money exercises a spectral power that exceeds all merely human power' because it creates and shapes desire itself (Goodchild 2007, p. 12). While capital is the means of production of any human or non-human power, capitalism is 'the social system in which capital is measured as an accumulative quantity in terms of exchange value' (Goodchild 2003, p. 84). This accumulative quantity is profit, and today it is more profitable in the short term to consume the means of production of capital itself than to preserve them for the production of future capital. I will return to our current situation of corporate capitalism, but first I want to consider money in broader historical terms.

In his important book *Debt: The First 5000 Years*, David Graeber provides something like a provincialization of money. Graeber, an anthropologist, explains that the notion that money and economic exchange developed out of an original social situation of barter is a myth, because barter did not exist until after money came into use. He says that 'we did not begin with barter, discover money, and then eventually develop credit systems. It happened precisely the other way around' (Graeber 2011, p. 40). Credit develops out of complex moral and social relations, which then produces physical money in the form of metal and coin. Graeber shows how many economic and religious explanations posit human society as founded upon an original debt, but this is not how debt came into existence historically. Debt assumes a universal position as History 1, but it is in fact the product of various History 2s.

We think that debt is universal, and that the primary moral obligation is to pay one's debts, which are then enforced with state military power. But debt is founded instead upon prior social relations. Graeber says that 'there are three main moral principles on which economic relations can be founded, all of which occur in any human society, and which I will call communism, hierarchy, and exchange' (Graeber 2011, p. 94). Communism is not the actual existing state communism of the USSR or China, but a basic foundation of moral relations that relies on the principle 'from each according to their abilities, to each according to their needs' (Graeber 2011, p. 94). While Graeber is being provocative in naming this situation communism, he is suggesting that every human society behaves in this way at the primary level. We find ways to work together, based on whatever talents and skills people have, and taking care of those who need to be taken care of without any external economic considerations. Graeber gives the example of how people pull together in the face of natural disasters, as well as small courtesies like borrowing a cigarette or helping a child in need. He claims that for any person identified as 'one of us,' this 'communism is the foundation of all human morality' (Graeber 2011, p. 96). This communism is about sharing, about mutuality, and it relies on 'a recognition of our ultimate interdependence that is the ultimate substance of social peace' (Graeber 2011, p. 96, 99).

What happens when human groups become larger and more settled geographically? Hierarchy is the second moral principle of economic relations, and it involves that recognition of social differences. Graeber says that hierarchy 'tends to work by a logic of precedent,' and is most pronounced in heroic societies that emphasize the great deeds of great men. Hierarchy creates a continuum of one-sided social relations ranging from benevolent to cruel, and these relations are super-imposed upon communist social relations. Hierarchy is based on a concept of social, political, and even religious identity, and one example is that of caste. He says that 'it is only when certain people are placed above others, or where everyone is being ranked in relation to the king, or the high priest, or Founding Fathers, that one begins to speak of people

bound by their essential nature' (Graeber 2011, p. 111). Hierarchy orga-
nizes the equality of basic social relations into the inequality necessary
for a state. A small group of people in a community become aristocrats,
and then once the element of war and plunder is added, you can have
the creation of ancient states, 'where rulers almost invariably represented
themselves as the protectors of the helpless, supporters of widows and
orphans, and champions of the poor' (Graeber 2011, p. 113.). The
point is that this benevolent charity presupposes a fundamental hierarchical inequality, with the ruler or king at the top. Graeber concludes
that 'the genealogy of the modern redistributive state—with its notori-
ous tendency to foster identity politics—can be traced back not to any
sort of primitive communism, but ultimately to violence and war'
(Graeber 2011, p. 113).

One last element is needed, which is the constructed equality of
exchange. Exchange is 'a constant process of interaction tending toward
equivalence.' This exchange can take the form of gift-giving, where each
side tries to equalize the situation by returning a gift of slightly higher or
lower worth, until the situation appears close enough to even and the
two sides can break it off. The point is that equivalence games only work
between people who are relatively equal, and do not make sense in terms
of hierarchy. Exchange technically precedes hierarchy, but once hierarchical relations appear, then the equivalence of exchange creates debt,
which is a violent process. Graeber attends to the violence that is necessary 'to make a human being an object of exchange,' in contrast with a
human economy in which 'each person is unique, and of incomparable
value, because each is a unique nexus of relations with others' (Graeber
2011, p. 158). Violence is necessary to create a market economy, where
human beings themselves becomes objects of monetary value and are
able to be exchanged—their labour, their property, and their lives. And
something like a state is necessary to sanction, threaten, and carry out
this violence, on its own or other states' peoples, to allow this to occur.
'It is only by the threat of sticks, ropes, spears, and guns,' Graeber argues,
'that one can tear people out of the endlessly complicated webs of relationships with others…that render them unique, and thus reduce them
to something that can be traded' (Graeber 2011, p. 208). We tend to
overlook and ignore this constitutive lawmaking violence, to use
Benjamin's terms.

Graeber gives a sweeping survey of human history to show where and how money develops out of the nexus of hierarchy and exchange, and shows the violence it produces. Interestingly enough, the middle ages, a time when hierarchy prevailed without so much monetary exchange because so much of the world's physical money was locked up in religious artefacts and institutions, is seen as less violent than the ancient and the modern world, where money has been circulated much more freely. We tend to think that debt is universal, even if physical money is not, but that is a myth that has caused a tremendous amount of violence. Today our entire civilization runs by debt, the servicing of debt and the forcing of people, companies, and nations into debt. But what is debt? According to Graeber, 'A debt is just the perversion of a promise. It is a promise corrupted by both math and violence' (Graeber 2011, p. 391).

While Graeber offers a tremendously powerful historical genealogy of money, he does not explicitly treat the issue of energy resources. The current economic situation is that capitalism is reaching real limits to growth, which forces it to consume the means of production of capital in ever-shorter and more desperate cycles of short-term growth. As Graeber shows, modern capitalism is a tremendously violent and inequalitarian process, despite the ideology of liberty and democracy. Even so, during the last four decades we have seen an unprecedented concentration of wealth, as the global economy has run up against real limits to growth in terms of finite amounts of natural resources, including water, oil, rare metals, arable land, and atmospheric absorption capacity.

Neo-liberalism serves as a name for this the economic transformation. In response to a situation of growing physical scarcity, neo-liberalism, led by the United States, largely generates financial wealth as profit and redistributes most of this remaining wealth and potentialities for growth from the poor and less well-off materially to the rich corporate elites. This process takes place both within and across nation-states, in conjunction with the creation of enormous speculative bubbles, the largest of which was the real estate bubble that popped in 2008, setting off a global recession. This concentration of wealth accompanies the financialization of the economy, which means that economic growth involves buying and trading securities and other financial assets more than 'real' products. According to Christian Marazzi, finance capitalism emerged at the end of the 1970s, and today, 'finance permeates from the beginning to the end of the circulation of capital' (Marazzi 2011, p. 107). This financialization in turn produced the global financial crisis beginning in 2007 and continuing today, most acutely in Europe.

Capitalism is a kind of faith in free markets, as well as the practices of production and consumption of goods and services in an unevenly globalized world. Capitalism is based on the premise of indefinite if not infinite growth. But growth is not possible on a global scale any longer in real terms, which means that the only way for corporations, nations, and economies to growth is in relative terms, at the expense of others. Despite the shining allure of globalization, the reality is that we are creating what Mike Davis calls a 'planet of slums.' For the first time in human history, 'the urban population will outnumber the rural' in the first decade of the twenty-first century (Davis 2006, p. 1).

The book *Planet of Slums*, published in 2006 and based mainly on 2003 data, claims that 'there are probably more than 200,000 slums on earth, ranging in population from a few hundred to more than a million people. The five great metropolises of South Asia (Karachi, Mumbai, Delhi, Kolkata, and Dhaka) alone contain about 15,000 distinct slum communities whose total population exceeds 20 million' (Davis 2006, p. 26)[2]. A more recent report from UN-Habitat claims that while 227 million people have moved out of slum living conditions, the 'absolute number' of slum dwellers has actually increased from 776.7 million in 2000 to some 827.6 million in 2010.'[3]

In the United States, the slums are created as inner-city ghettoes as wealthy and middle-class people flee to the suburbs, while in many other cities, especially in the Third World, slums expand outward at the edges of the cities. Davis claims that 'the principal function of the Third World urban edge remains as a human dump' (Davis 2006, p. 47). Why have these slums been created at such a fast pace? He explains that neo-liberal 'policies of agricultural deregulation and financial discipline enforced by the IMF and World Bank continued to generate an exodus of surplus rural labor to urban slums even as cities ceased to be job machines' (Davis 2006, p. 15). Economic liberalization in the wake of the green revolution of the 1960s left rural populations without any means of feeding their communities and themselves, due to the economics of industrial agriculture. As more and more countries succumbed to austere conditions placed on them to service and restructure their debts, more and more local peasants became unable to scratch out an existence and relocated to cities in search of jobs and economic opportunities. But these opportunities for the most part no longer exist.

Capitalism is reaching real limits to growth, and the only growth possible is in relative terms. The impoverishment of millions of people is less spectacular than fanatical religious violence, but it is no less devastating, and perhaps one purpose of the latter is to hide the former, or at least to distract us from this pauperization of many of the people on the planet. Or perhaps what passes for religious violence is often more accurately understood as a protest against this predominant state of affairs. The neo-liberal ideology frequently focuses on religious violence as the irrational protest of uncivilized peoples who are the main obstacles to prosperous globalization. In addition, the subjects of this violence are often racialized, especially if they are members of Third World nation-states. How can and should we compare and contrast the more obvious violence perpetrated in the name of religion with the less obvious but more insidious violence generated in the cause of capitalism?

As already mentioned, one response is the attempt, following Chakrabarty (2000) and Graeber (2011), to provincialize capital. And as part of this process, it is helpful to think of capitalism itself as a form of religion, following Benjamin. Finally, however, what does it mean to think of religion, or at least to think beyond the limits of secularism as an ideology of liberal capitalism?

POLITICAL THEOLOGY IN A POSTSECULARIST CONTEXT.

In the United States and other parts of the first world, postmodernism came to name a political neutralization of ideas and actions, which were subsumed under the blanket term culture. Postmodernism became a form of literary and cultural criticism. Despite this conservative usage, I understand the term postmodern more as a way to open up questions about the nature and stakes of the modern world, of what we call modernity, which in large part is determined by European colonialism and the West. Postmodernism does not overcome or replace modernity, but names either a condition of late modernity or a method of intervention that is willing to question the principal values and concepts of modernism.

Modern liberal capitalism emerges by instituting a secular public sphere that is imagined as non-religious; religion is relegated to a realm of private belief. Secularism as the strict demarcation of religious and non-religious spheres is part of the ideology of modernity (Asad 2003, pp. 181–201). For me, post-secularism suggests that we understand that this project is impossible; an absolute distinction between public and private, secular and religious, cannot be sustained or maintained. It deconstructs. Post-secularism provides a context to understand and evaluate this 'return' of religion at the level of politics, philosophy, and culture. We cannot simply champion or eliminate religion; it must remain a fundamental object of critique. As Marx says, all critique begins with the critique of religion.[4]

For this reason, I resist the label post-secular as used in some contemporary forms of theology, because it tends to suggest that we can overcome and dispense with the secular and restore an earlier or more traditional form of religion.[5] At the same time, in a postmodern and a post-colonial world we cannot completely divorce the religious and the secular, or the public realm of civil and political law from the private sphere of religious belief, so we cannot simply shore up the public realm by pushing religion back to the private where it belongs. Whether we believe or practice this or that religion, whether we see religion more as a saving power or as a danger, if religion is always implicated in political forms and vice versa, then we cannot rigorously separate political philosophy from political theology.[6] This is why the issue of political theology is so urgent today, in both theoretical and practical terms. I think we don't just need a political theology of religion, although we do need that, but we also desperately need a political theology of capitalism itself, and an understanding of how capitalism functions in religious and non-religious ways.

Chakrabarty states that his project of *Provincializing Europe* must ground itself philosophically 'in a radical critique and transcendence of liberalism…a ground that late Marx shares with certain moments in both poststructuralist thought and feminist philosophy' (Chakrabarty

2000, p. 42). The ideology of capitalism and liberalism, has degenerated into an invidious economic neo-liberalism and a cynical political neo-conservatism. At the same time, the so-called return of religion at the level of thought and culture testifies to the re-emergence of neo-traditionalist and neo-fundamentalist religious discourses and practices in the public sphere. This return of religion, with its sometimes spectacular violence, is the penumbra that accompanies capitalism's discontents. Although this resurgence of religious violence is disturbing and dangerous, it may also harbor under-appreciated potentialities for a radical political thinking and practice dedicated to combating the 'worst' violence of corporate capitalism and creeping fascism. A radical political theology that avoids the either/or of traditionalist religion and triumphalist secularism offers theoretical tools for developing what Benjamin calls our contemporary form of divine violence, which is the 'educative power' to disarm without killing, to be lethal without spilling blood, at least potentially.[7] This educative power is a power of thinking and of language. In a world that is saturated with violence, this not nothing.

Notes

1. Vattimo (1988) follows Heidegger in identifying violence with metaphysics, and he develops the notion of 'weak thought' precisely to weaken metaphysics and overcome its violence, and this critique is also consonant with Benjamin's. Rather than being apolitical, this project of weakening metaphysics possesses a strong political component (Vattimo and Zabala, 2011) For a similar approach to Vattimo's that grounds a critique of violence in the overcoming of metaphysics based on a reading of Schelling via Heidegger and Benjamin, see Das: 'This is one way to conceive of a new critique of violence, not merely of the violence that manifests every now and then as 'this' or 'that' violent act, but of this metaphysical violence on the basis of which alone the violence of man can be understood' (Das 2011, p. 83). I think that the best historical designation of modern metaphysics is capitalism, and we must come to terms with the underlying, metaphysical violence of capitalism, rather than being distracted by 'this' or 'that' violent act.

2. Davis says that in India, while a million new millionaires have been created, this 'growth has been tremendously lop-sided, with enormous speculative investment in the information technology sector leaving agriculture to stagnate and infrastructure to decay' (2006, p. 171).

3. UN-Habitat, 'Urban Trends: 227 Million Escape Slums,' available at http://www.unhabitat.org/documents/SOWC10/R1.pdf (accessed 25 March 2012).

4. The exact quote is 'The criticism of religion is the prerequisite of all criticism' (Marx 1975, p. 243).

5. See the works of British Radical Orthodoxy, including sets the agenda for this movement (Milbank 1990).

6. Talal Asad says that 'if the secularization thesis no longer carries the conviction it once did, this is because the categories of 'politics' and 'religion' turn out to implicate each other more profoundly than we thought, a discovery that has accompanied our growing understanding of the powers of the modern nation-state. The concept of the secular cannot do without the idea of religion' (Asad 2003, p. 200).

7. For a more fully developed account of what is necessarily compressed here in the conclusion, see my work, *Radical Political Theology: Religion and Politics after Liberalism* (Crockett 2011).

References

Asad, Talal, *Formations of the Secular: Christianity, Islam, Modernity* (Stanford: Stanford University Press, 2003).

Benjamin, Walter, 'Critique of Violence', 'Capitalism as Religion', trans. Edmund Jephcott, in *Walter Benjamin: Selected Writings, Volume 1, 1913–1926*. ed. Marcus Bullock and Michael W. Jennings (Cambridge: Harvard University Press, 1996).

Chakrabarty, Dipesh, *Provincializing Europe: Postcolonial Thought and Historical Difference* (Princeton: Princeton University Press, 2000).

Crockett, Clayton, *Radical Political Theology: Religion and Politics After Liberalism* (New York: Columbia University Press, 2011).

Das, Saitya Brata, *The Promise of Time: Towards a Phenomenology of Promise* (Shimla: Indian Institute of Advanced Study, 2011).

Davis, Mike, *Planet of Slums* (London: Verso, 2006).

De Landa, Manuel, *War in an Age of Intelligent Machines* (New York: Zone Books, 1991).

Derrida, Jacques, 'Force of Law: 'The Mystical Foundation of Authority' trans. Mary Quaintance, in *Deconstruction and the Possibility of Justice*, ed. Drucilla Cornell, et. al. (Routledge: London and New York, 1992).

Goodchild, Philip, *A Theology of Money* (London: SCM Press, 2007).

Graeber, David, *Debt: The First 5,000 Years* (Brooklyn, Melville House Publishing, 2011).

Marazzi, Christian, *The Violence of Financial Capitalism*, trans. Kristina Lededeva and Jason Francis McGimsey (Los Angeles: Semiotext(e), 2011).

Marx, Karl, 'A Contribution to the Critique of Hegel's Philosophy of Right. Introduction,' in *Karl Marx: Early Writings*, trans. Rodney Livingstone and Gregor Benton (New York: Penguin, 1975).

Milbank, John, *Theology and Social Theory: Beyond Secular Reason* (Oxford: Blackwell, 1990).

Vattimo Gianni., *The Transparent Society*, trans. David Webb (Baltimore: The Johns Hopkins University Press, 1992).

————, *The End of Modernity*, trans. Jon R. Snyder (Baltimore: Johns Hopkins University Press, 1988).

Vattimo, Gianni and Santiago Zabala, *Hermeneutic Communism: From Heidegger to Marx* (New York: Columbia University Press, 2011).

Virilio, Paul, *Desert Screen: War at the Speed of Light*, trans. M. Degener (London: Continuum, 2002).

————, *The Art of the Motor*, trans. Julie Rose (Minneapolis: University of Minnesota Press, 1995).

10 St. Paul, Gabriel Naudé, Antonin Artaud
Three Violent and Delicate Exceptions to Law and Liturgy

Soumyabrata Choudhury

St. Paul arrives to make a departure from the Graeco-Roman sense of *nomos* and its corresponding liturgical obligations; he departs as well, in significant ways, from Judaic law and the liturgy of the Jewish congregation. In the seventeenth century Gabriel Naudé praises and challenges what could be called the 'secular' liturgy of Machiavelli, a liturgy in the service of the Prince's survival and power. In the period roughly between 1930 and 1935, Antonin Artaud shatters the overall liturgical logic of western theatre and its Law of the Text in a series of essays and manifestos that might be seen to have an errant historical origin in the creative 'auto-mockeries' of Alfrel Jarry towards the end of the 19th century. Vast differences in their contexts and visions notwithstanding, these three figures exemplify the rare and precarious point of separation, of cutting-off, not only from an external inheritance we might call 'culture' but from the continuity and development of their *own* path and passion, their path of passion. I will use a word from the Bible to name this point of division and cutting off, and the name, in its general appropriation by language, will reveal its great violence and 'monstrosity', especially when directed towards the very self who uses it: The word used by Paul in the *Letter to the Romans* (9–11), is 'anathema'.

In *Romans* (9–11), Paul says:

I am speaking the truth in Christ—and I am not lying; my conscience confirms it by the Holy Spirit—I have great sorrow and unceasing anguish in my heart.

For I could wish that I myself were accused and cut-off [*anathema*] from Christ (Taubes 2004, p. 27).

Paul would make himself *anathema* of Christ. I will not ask the specific question, why Paul wants to cut himself off from Christ's love— it is a complicated and fascinating investigation Jacob Taubes conducts—but make the more general enquiry as to what does it mean to make oneself *anathema* in the moment, and at the conjuncture, of one's *decision* to affiliate (*Pistis*) oneself to that very 'event' of which one makes oneself anathema. What are the stakes of the affiliation and the self-anathematization? Of the faith and the abandonment? And if, going back to Paul, the decision is one unto a new 'power' and sovereignty— the power of weakness against the imperial sovereignty of Rome—then can such sovereignty further exceed and disfigure its traditional (liturgical) stakes to reach across to the side of anathema and abandonment? Is this possible?

PAUL: 1 CORINTHIAN. 7:29–32

Now to read the following passage from a *Letter to the Corinthians*:

But this I say, Brethren, Time contracted itself, the rest is, that even those having wives may be as not [*hōs mō*] having, and those weeping as not weeping, and those rejoicing as not rejoicing, and those buying as not possessing, and those using the world as not using it up. For passing away is the figure of this world. But I wish you to be without care. (Agamben 2005, p. 23)

What has this passage to do with the paradoxical stakes of anathema and a new power? Well, clearly the connection has something to do with politico-philosophical thinking since Carl Schmitt frequently calls the fundamental status of the 'exception' as an impasse *and* as a passage vis-à-vis the pre-givenness of the sovereign apparatus (*dispositive*). And surely everything also hinges on the access of the above 'and' to any consistent if a 'forcing' thinking.[1]

Now it seems that Paul, in the *Letter to the Romans*, makes himself the accused or anathema of Christ under the terrible pressure of the circumstances of the *congregation* from which he comes—and from which he never ceases departing. This is the congregation of a people which has sinned. Now for a sinful people God has undertaken the most vengeful and punishing oaths. But, as Taubes points out, the real task for Paul is not to *continue* the history of enforcement of oaths and laws within the liturgical discipline of the community (Taubes 2004, pp. 37–40). Between Moses and Paul, the real point of ruptured transformation that is being created is the wagering of what could be called 'counter-circumstances' or an 'event', if you will, which will make possible the 'un-doing' of sovereign oaths, their ineffectuation as the ciphers of sovereign performativity. The self-avowal of 'anathema' is a step in that direction—but it is a complicated point which I am only hinting at here for its broad implications.

I think it is important to repeat the paradoxical stakes that come out in Paul: On the one hand they express a decisive intervention in the structure of divine commandment and its opaque obverse contained in the prescription 'obey!'; at the same time the stakes are not only incounter or ineffectuating sovereignty, they also pertain to the eventative basis for the creation of a *new people*. And to that extent, sovereignty—whether gnomically compressed into the 'power of weakness' formula or not—must go over to the side of this post-abyssal 'people. To the daunting question, how such a thing is possible, let us pick up a few leads in the terrain of Graeco-Roman or *Hellenist* law and liturgy that Paul seems to arrest *and* pass in the <u>hōs mē</u> part of the *Letter to Corinthians* quoted earlier.

Giorgio Agamben has interpreted the passage (and impasse) as the messianic revocation of all vocations (Agamben 2005, pp. 23–25). Indeed it can be shown from a brief genealogy of Greek and Roman *civic* practices that the subjective association of a 'vocation' is deeply entrenched in a *liturgical* and *incorporeal* (Stoic) logic of public debt and civic obligation. The so-called Hellenist and sovereign subject—distributed between its early democratic locus of 5th century B.C. Athens and its later personification of Roman legal *potestas*—can be shown to be subject to a certain undifferentiated sovereign capture (*nexum*) and a subject of a certain attenuated 'credibility' (Adam Smith's word which can be substituted for a certain 'credit worthiness') and civic solvency. The Romans, in the context of law and attenuated payment of debts in installments, called the late moment of subjectification, '*mutuum*' (Dumézil 1988, pp. 99–104). These technical references apart, the basic point is that the subject's 'vocations' which are several worldly instrumentalities (having wives, owning property, utilizing possessions, etc.), are rooted in a logic, or should one say axiomatic, of debts that prescribes an *incorporeal* subjective payment by civic and political participation, of the liturgical pecuniary credits advanced to the Greek and Roman 'congregation'. In the case of the 5th century Athenian democracy, the credit is liturgical and cultural; in the Hellenist Roman era the credit has a liturgical-legal modality. In Paul's 'revocation of all vocations', the revocation applies to both the Greek and Roman groundings of worldly vocations. In the two cases taken separately and together, we are witness to Paul's declaration of a *defaulting* on both these powers and obligations of the debt[2].

But what is the logic of defaulting then, if it is not simply a willful declaration? However, we cannot assume that this logic simply *passes* from an earlier history to the event of revocation, *even if* at the end of the citation Paul joyfully declares the passing of this world. The whole question of anathema must return here though there is no apparent connection. 'Anathema' represents the invention and wager of Paul's 'divine violence' (Benjamin 1986, pp. 277–300) as response to the messianic impasse brought upon Graeco-Roman *nomos* and liturgy, to 'force' a passage through this impasse.

This is a crucial stage of the argument: at the exact precipitation of the messianic 'exception'—the announcement of the Messiah upon the resurrection—we can either be launched into the *return* of the old (imperial) sovereignty in all its juridical, legal, mythic, and liturgical insistences to hold back (*kat-echon*) the imminence of a new messianic people (Schmitt 2005, p. xxxii); or we can be absolutely and unconditionally *abandoned* to the expiration of this imminence such that the wager becomes that the name of this infinitely imminent abandonment will be 'a new people'. In that sense the new people will not be sovereign, will not be a liturgical congregation, will not have a unified nomos or Torah—will not be a people (*laos*). The 'divine violence' thesis applied to Paul attaches to this strange, impassible yet joyously passing and ecstatic thought of a messianic 'non-people.'[3]

If we are to think the meaning of 'divine violence' as a recessive passion unto, not a futural horizon, but a void-point where stakes are unconditionally withdrawn and defaulting on debt is as much on behalf of the *creditor* as that of the debtor, then we must not confuse the above event of a 'non-people' with what a constitutionalist like Polybius and Stoic philosophers of incorporeal congregations, called the *Ochlos*.[4] *Ochlos*, translated popularly as 'multitude', stands for a *violent* notion in that the multitude are supposed to be an uncongregated mass of violent virtualities, whose exigency demands a legal and liturgical—that is, sovereign—*constitution*, and so, congregation. Despite the intervention of the strange, and divine, violence of the anathema Paul directs at himself vis-a-vis Christ in the wake of an earlier people who have sinned, this is not the event of a passage from one people or one state-of-the-people to another. The event is the declaration of an 'impasse' of a non-people which is not the initial and virulent virtuality waiting for sovereign and constitutional capture but the culminating and imminent 'dis-figure' of an *actual* intervention.

Very briefly, even elliptically, let us state this mode of actuality in the light of the hōs mē passage from the Corinthians. I suggest, the antinomic pressure, generated by the *synchrony,* of a world-in-passage maintains that synchrony and that passage in the mode of the 'as not' (hōs mē). The same pressure is contained in the meaning of 'imminence', in an imminent passage to come, which passes along the contour of a void and impasse, a meaning which can also be expressed in the mutilated term 'monstration'. A term used by Jacques Lacan once in a mathematical mood and equally useful for several phenomenologies of 'inappearance' and abandonment, 'monstration' is the self-showing of the passage in its imminent maintenance. That is its existential actuality.[5]

But the main question concerning us remains that how such a *monstrum* or 'monster' abandoned to the ineffectual element of existence relends itself, in that abandonment, to sovereign capture (*nexum*) and the installation of sovereign debt (*mutuum*)? Because without such capture and installation the Pauline inauguration of an *oikonomia* yielding a 'new people' will forever stay in messianic suspension. Indeed that is not only an aporia and impasse of 'thought' that encounters the 'event', it is also the forced opening onto a certain global history of the Pauline *oikonomia* (Mondzain 2005). I think the real problem, which is also a singular opportunity for a wager of thought, is the following: How is it that the violent, delicate, almost *child-like*, in its self-anathematization, messianic annulment, and re-vocation, played out so effectively and actively in the history of the Pauline oikonomia and its attendant sovereign *dispositifs*? How is the 'infancy' of the messianic passage characterized by abandoned 'play' of use-less, 'illiturgical', and scintillating gestures, play out as the history of the most adult economy of strategy and tactics, sovereignty and power? Instead of offering any hypothesis by way of solution(s) to this problem—though such hypotheses are not unthinkable—let us look at its articulation at another level and position of history—which are definitely not 'messianic'.

GABRIEL NAUDÉ: EXCERPTS FROM *CONSIDERATIONS POLITIQUES SUR LES COUPS D'ETAT*, CITED IN MICHEL FOUCAULT'S *SECURITY, TERRITORY, POPULATION*

Gabriel Naudé (1600–1653), at one place in his text, with regard to the *coups d'Etat* writes—

with *coups d'Etat*, we see the thunderbolt before we hear it rumbling in the clouds...Matins are said before the bells are rung, the execution precedes the sentence; everything becomes Jewish;—who thought to strike receives the blow, who thought himself safe dies, another suffers what he never dreamed of, everything is done at night, in the dark, in the fog and shadows. (Foucault 2007, p. 266)

Admittedly, these reversals of the *coups d'Etat* do not have the 'child-like' non-orientation and suspension of Paul's declaration. The *coups d'Etat* is surely a reversal of gestures and indices unfolding in time, born of a disorientation of predicates that compose a 'world'. But the crucial point is that Naudé's definition of *coups d'Etat* is included in the *raison d'Etat*, the Reason of the State that in the 17th century is emerging as a possibility of thinking the question of power which escapes the dominant discourse of sovereignty at that time, that is, the discourse under the sign of Machiavelli (Foucault 2007, pp. 242–248).

Two aspects of the above proposition need to be highlighted. First is the Machiavellian background: It has to be understood that Machiavelli, though through a tortuous and elusive passage which is nothing but the passage(s) forced out of a historical and theoretical impasse, ended up creating the prescription of a kind of 'secular liturgy' to subjectify and enforce debts of sovereignty.[6] This means that the relationship of the Prince and the people is prescribed to be mediated by a structure of free and public obligation of the citizen to participate in the affairs of sovereignty and law that taken together, comprises the space of the state. This 'liturgical' obligation of the citizen, which is always (at least in the best case scenario) by *right*, not coercion, is exemplified by such free and obligatory practices as defending one's country as a solider does during war or performingjury-service in public litigation. The military liturgy is particularly illustrative because its practice, which is born of public obligation and public *love*, is conducted in the situation of the exception, which is war.[7]

This brings up the second aspect of our earlier proposition. Gabriel Naudé's vivification of the *coups d'Etat* is *not* the table of reversals during a war or a seizure of power by a pretender against the sovereign, etc. It is the self-showing of the state itself, the point of intensification of the Reason of the State so as to vivify it as a splendour and a theatre. The exceptionality of the *coup d'Etat* is not one which is either an external provocation to law and liturgy or an exigency already subsumed by the foresight of sovereign wisdom; it is the constitutive exceptionality of the *state itself*. How is that possible? How to pass this thought which is a thought come upon an impasse? I think it might be an interesting risk to take to articulate this self-showing or 'monstration' of the state during the *coup d'Etat* with the wounding self-abandonment of the Pauline anathema. What this might mean in the context of the irreducible exigency of 'everything becomes Jew...' is that the becoming-Jew is the point of immanent and self-anathematizing exception of the *raison d'Etat*. The 'Jew' is not outside the thought of the state but is the included remainder and exception. And it is not even the 'figure' of the Jew that is in question but the naming of a *torsion* cutting of the self of the subject from the very 'love' which constitutes it—for the sake of that very love's exceptional splendour indiscernible from its greatest distress. The name given to the 'torsion' is 'Jew' in Naudé's text.

The above analysis has a specific bearing on the status of western theatre. The theatrical and gestural localization of the *raison d'Etat* in the *coup d'Etat* when refracted back through the political theatre of these times, or through the theatre of sovereignty of which Shakespeare, Racine, Corneille, etc. provide exemplary texts, show lines of escape from liturgical as well as Baroque theatre.[8] We are not witness to some *other* theatre here—let that be clear—but what we encounter are a series of irreducible exigencies, immemorial monstrations that taken together, in their emergent escapes, escape the *debt* of theatre-participation and the *mourning* of Baroque lamentation. At the level of the emergence of the theatre as well as the state, what emerges is a kind of *new immemorial* which configures this theatre and this state as belonging to an infinite imminence—which is the same thing as the 'world' with no eschatology envisagable but with every moment of this worldly infinity containing an eschatological exigency. The name for that exigency contained in the immanence of the world is the *coup d'Etat* in political terms—and in theatrical terms, the *coup d'Etat* is the intensive self-showing of a potentially *useless* sovereignty, a 'Jewish' one, in all its shame and splendour. In Shakespeare's history plays, the uselessness is either given the shape of a Richard II crumbling under the weight of 'mortal' delicacy in the face of the enforced immortality of sovereign power, or gifted the words of absolute exigency on the edge of defaulting on sovereignty itself, as in Richard III's ' A horse, a horse, my kingdom for a horse!' Really, there is no liturgical audience for this theatre; for such a theatre, which is one of the *coups d'Etat* and not of sovereignty *as such,* the audience is included in the violent and delicate logic of the immanent exception. In seeing the state's self-anathematization in the wounding scintillations of the *coups d'Etat* in the theatre, the audience, to form itself, must anathematize itself.

ANTONIN ARTAUD: *THEATRE AND THE PLAGUE*

Once the plague is established in a city, normal social order collapses. There is no more refuse collection, no more army, police or municipality. Pyres are lit to burn the dead whenever men are available...too many corpses...the houses are thrown open and raving plague victims disperse through the streets, their minds full of horrible visions...plague victims who, without bubos or delirium, pain or rashes, examine themselves proudly in the mirror, feeling in splendid health, only to fall dead with their shaking dishes in their hands, full of scorn for other victims...The scum of the populace...enter the open houses and help themselves to riches they know will serve no purpose or profit. At this point theatre establishes itself. Theatre, that is to say the momentary pointlessness which drives them to useless acts without immediate profit...The remaining survivors go berserk; the virtuous and obedient son kills his father, the continent sodomise their kin. The lewd became chaste. The miser chucks handful of his gold out of the windows, the Soldier Hero sets fire to the town he had formerly risked his life to save. Dandies deck themselves out and stroll among the charnel houses... (Artaud 1993, pp. 14–15)

Can one speak of a messianic plague in light of the long citation? Possibly not but one can risk a Stoic plague because according to Antonin Artaud, the subtle origin and point of irreducible localization of the plague is not organic and gnosological but *incorporeal* and *spiritual.* If the plague is a revocation of all vocations, a forfeiture and defaulting on liturgical debts, obligations, and 'uses', it is not so by the in-effectuating procedures of the Pauline hōs mē that the declaration holds in suspensive non-orientation. Clearly the incorporeal dis-orientation (as varying from non-orientation and simple functional or temporal reversal) of the plague is the disease of uncontrolled *incorporeal transformations*. That in Stoic terms means, that during the plague the subjective delirium consists in an incorporeal and spiritual activation beyond the limits of civic and cultural participation. 'Theatre' is the event of the spiritual gesture of this excess over liturgy and its sovereign virtuality of the theatre text ('No more masterpieces!', Artaud's slogan. Artaud 1938/1993, pp. 55–64). Gilles Deleuze has taught the art of this Stoic delirium, this counter-effectuated theatre of the plague that mobilizes the violence and distress of the miasmic illness into the delicacy of the mime's gestures that return the disorientation of the state of the plague into the abstract and self-showing non-orientation of the monstrative exception.[9]

I suggest that Antonin Artaud's fantastication of the plague follows the logic of anathema at a *world-historical* level—and in that shifts from both the subjective intervention of Paul that is the self-abandoning condition of messianic neutralization (or non-orientation) and the *raison d'Etat's* self-showing in the objective intensifications of the *coups d'Etat*. At the level of the self-anathematization of the world itself, the incorporeal-objective correlative of this anathema is the natural historical motif of the plague. For the paradoxical function of in-effectuation performed by the plague, we have the virulent undoings of the Indo-European 'scourges' that undo oaths, pledges, sacraments—and which scourges these performative acts return to seize and rebind—as structural homologues (so well analysed by Georges Dumezil; also see Agamben 2010, pp. 6–8). But that is not the trajectory I want to develop here. What, in Artaud's incorporeal scenarios of theatre and the plague, theatre *of* and *as* plague, stirs the most ineluctable response from us, is the *repudiation* of the overall world-historical context of both the subjective option of a local and enigmatic fidelity (*Pistis*) to the impasse *and* passage of a 'new' (non) people' and the option of objectively 'conserving' the necessary *and* exigent self-abandonment of the state to the intensifications of the *coups d'Etat*.

Surely the name of this world-historical context is 'Europe'. While, I think, in the aspects of reversal, inoperativity and immemorial exigency, Artaud does share with Paul and Gabriel Naudé the declaration of a 'defaulting' on liturgical and sovereign debt(s), the former still essentially repudiates the imminent passage of *this* world in Paul and the infinite impasse of *this* world encoded in the *raison d'Etat* of Naudé—both of which passage and impasse describe the potentiality and stagnant crisis of *this* Europe, according to Artaud. A Europe, where, as he says speaking as an actor and audience of its age-old liturgy and law, no one knows how to scream anymore.[10]

In the last part of the nineteenth century Alfred Jarry, in his play *Ubu Roi* and other scenarios which he used to call 'pataphysical' and 'auto-mockeries—pataphysical auto-mockeries—had shown the destiny of sovereignty in a situation of extreme self-anathematization and self-abandonment—which simply means a situation of near-total withdrawal of the stakes of legitimacy—to be one of 'grotesque sovereignty' (Foucault 2004, pp. 11–2; Jarry 1968). Abandoning the juridical and liturgical axiom of apodeictic, self-showing legitimation, the grotesque sovereign, enacted in the dis-figure of Ubu the King, becomes that much more effective and powerful as he gets further and further useless as a self-legitimator of his actions. This is the grotesque limit of the structural violence that once exposed in the theatre of the west, which is dominantly liturgical and statist, exposes that very liturgy and law to historical and metaphysical ruin. In the first half of the 20th century, Antonin Artaud's declaration of theatre as an event of plague declares, violently and delicately, the absolute repudiation of the structural violence of the Europeanist induction of a global debt of sovereignty. This repudiation on a world-scale, and implemented in the vital tissue of European culture, is the 'call' (again a word from Paul!) to wager a new immemorial giving birth to and affirming, along with a non-people and a non-audience, a non-Europe. A Europe as not (hōs mē) Europe...

A Brief Excursus on Plato, Patočka, and the Training of Guardians

A brief excursus in conclusion: Jan Patočka, a thinker abandoned to the streets and rooms of Prague at a certain stage of history, which the stage itself lies abandoned today in a state of strange monstration, practiced a thought joined in 'faith'(*Pistis?*) to the heritage of Europe. But what is that heritage? For Patočka, it is a heritage of sovereignty *and* abandonment, of faith, love, hope...*and* anathema—and the wandering heritage of the thought of that violent and delicate 'and'.... In any case, Patočka says to his interlocutors in a 'non-public' philosophy discussion in Prague that Plato prescribes something for those youths who will be trained as the guardians of the city that is of paradoxical interest: In the *Republic* it is said that the guardians should be given nothing by the community who they are being trained to rule, except basic nutrition (Patočka 2002, pp. 106–108). Now this is an anti-liturgical prescription. Because in the 5th century democratic Athens—of which Plato is a derisive opponent—public procurement of grains along with other modes of collective existence are part of the liturgical funding of the city's citizens. By that logic, the guardians are *not* to be treated as citizens in their period of education since the nutrition they get is only to sustain their 'natural' (*zoe*) lives in a situation of studied abandonment.

But this wouldn't be so extraordinary because it could be treated in line with a strategy of training through deprivation and isolation that carries on upto the modern military liturgy. Patočka's point becomes extraordinary—and self-anathematizing from the point of view of a 'proud' European sovereignty to which the world today is as if *indebted* for the very idea of sovereignty!—because he says the guardians are taught, in their isolation, to risk their lives and to think... for the sake of what? Not simply for the sake of society's functioning, its primitive circuit of exchanges, and communicative-civic actions, etc. but for the sake of society's endemic 'injustice', its capacity for error, its defaulting capacities, which is to say, its generic in-capacity. But what are the guardians to do in the 'event' of error? Correct, punish, play juridical sovereign? No. their primary role is to treat the crisis as a battle, to be ready to be anytime on the battlefield and at war in a 'crisis'. A war to be fought neither against the defaulters (which would be playing a juridical, legal, and punitive role) nor on their behalf (which would either be to 'privatize' their roles as mercenaries aiding insolvents or to participate in revolutionary civil war, *stasis*)—but this is an education towards the readiness to be on battlefield on the 'neutral' behalf of the extreme partisan possibility of defaulting or in-capacity in society.

Very clearly, Patočka is already diagnosing in Plato's prescriptions in the *Republic,* a slippage from the guardians' sovereignty-function to their government-function for whose preparedness 'war' and 'crises' are the paradigms, not liturgy and law. This implies that the topology of the guardians' place of education (*Paideia*) is the fringe (*Eschaton*) of the city, not its *agora* or *meson* (centre). The guardians are made ready not on behalf of a centered community but on behalf of the generic emergence of a kind of an 'a-common' in the order of the common.

At the same time, the guardians are not some sort of a military society—or crisis management group—trained to recognize and act upon the *signs* of a crisis, a war, an exception. The guardians are a 'people', a kind of 'cultivated' (from *Paideia*) throw of dice which yields decisions on the exception when there exists no 'signs' to go by and interpret. The 'decision' of the guardian is fundamentally a decision of 'any-one' indiscernible from anyone else. Is it possible that an indiscernible anyone among any-ones, violently manifest as an instance of insupportable and decisive self-showing, is who Plato calls 'the philosopher-sovereign'?

Notes

1. 'Forcing' is Alain Badiou's extraction from Paul Cohen's theorem on 'forcing' of the real existence of generic sets into a new language for that type of set, which otherwise is strictly indiscernible from any other sub-set. In our very approximate use, 'forcing' is an act of thought crossing the threshold of 'laws' of thought which carry a legitimate violent potential for enforcing these laws in propositions of knowledge. Hence 'forcing' here must be distinguished from 'enforcement'.

2. Is there a contradiction between the proposition on Paul's declaration of defaulting and Jesus's exhortation to pay unto Tiberius-Caesar what is due to Tiberius Caesar? It is a precarious enquiry and requires extremely sure-footed mobility between the *historical* submission to authorized debts and the *generic* defaulting on the very 'value' of the credit advanced.

3. In this context, Agamben's technical point on the *hōs mē* as 'tensor' can be applied to the 'new people' as the name of an imminence maintained in its infinite passage and expiration by the work of the tensor. The 'tensor' maintains the revocative structure not by opposing one concept to another but by intensifying a concept to the point of its revocation. The question Paul–and Agamben—lead us to ask is, can this revocation apply to the concept 'people' and can the threshold of revocation be the threshold of the 'new'? (Agamben 2005, p. 24).

4. For sections from Polybius *Universal History* in relation to constitutional forms including mob-rule or *ocholocracy*, see Polybius (1959, pp. 103–124). In the introduction to this section (Polybious 1959, pp. 103–105), there is a very interesting comparison of the Greek and Hebraic (based on Book of Daniel) views of history.

5. Apart from the mathematical examples of non-oriented, monstrative figures—mobeius strip, torus, etc.—that Lacan was so attached to, it is

important to refer to the use of *monstration* in the much-debated discourse and 'style' of a phenomenological theology. See, for example, Michel Henry (2003, p. 14).

6. The tortures of 'thinking alone' that Machiavelli experienced have been brought out with the force of articulated parallels of his own 'tortures', *anathemas*, by Louis Althusser in his interpretation of Machiavelli.

7. Machiavelli, in more than one place, particularly in his *Discourses,* counsels the cultivation of 'good' soldiers to fight and win wars—where 'good' means the *public* capacity for active patriotic love and sacrifice. To this he opposes the mercenary-client relation on a kind of contractual basis.

8. While the departures from the liturgical and congregational model of western theatre have been part of the present argument on the theatre of exigencies in the *raison d'Etat,* the role of the baroque exception is another level of complication which is not really dealt with here. But Walter Benjamin's incomparable work remains at the tremulous centre of our construction (Benjamin 1998).

9. Gilles Deleuze brings a certain weightless beatitude, a pure pleasure of 'surfaces' to the Stoic linguistic events which produce incorporeal abstract 'objects' in the world to transform the world's contour every time anew. The paradigm for this art of surfaces is the mime. Antonin Artaud, who localizes the origin of the plague in some incorporeal region, still plumbs that region in the *depth* of crazened bodies. In this he does radicalize Augustine's suspicion of the theatre as acting on the morals as pestilence acts on the bodies, congregations and nations. But doesn't Artaud, in his *manifest* affirmation of another theatre as such, seek to redeem this suspicion by affirming its reality? Theatre does not act on the spirits of people and nations–and in the perpetration of the event of theatre, 'spirit' is produced as the 'incorporeal' of bodies. This is Artaud's great repudiation of a *Christian* and *European* metaphysics of dualistic suspicion (Deleuze 1990, pp. 148–153; Artaud 1993, p. 17).

10. Yet the 'scream' is not an expressionist climax in a logic of cathartic and mythic (from *muthos)* development of the theatre-plot virtualized in the 'text' The scream is the strict alphabet of a world-historical *and* metaphysical necessity in respect of which European (or Western) theatre is illiterate. From his own 'illiterate' position then Artaud risks the name for a so-called truly 'literate theatre', without the Law of the Text and devoted to the creation of an Alphabet of the Theatre-Body—the name 'orient', 'oriental theatre' (of which Balinese performance is an empirical instance).

References

Agamben, Giorgio, *The Sacrament of Language: An Archaeology of the Oath, Homo Sacer II, 3,* tran. Adam Kotsko (Cambridge: Polity Press, 2010).

——, *The Time that Remains: A Commentary on the Letter to the Romans,* tran. Patricia Daily (Stanford, California: Stanford University Press, 2005).

Artaud, Antonin, 'Theatre and the Plague' in *The Theatre and its Double*, trans. Victor Corti (London : Calder Publications, 1993).

Benjamin, Walter, *The Origin Of German Tragic Drama*, trans. John Osborne (London and New York: Verso 1998).

——, 'Critique of Violence', in *Reflections*, ed. Peter Demetz, trans. Edmund Jephcott (New York: Schocken Books, 1986).

Deleuze, Gilles, *Logic of Sense* trans. Mark Lester with Charles Stivale (New York : Columbia University Press, 1990).

Dumézil, Georges, *Mitra-Varuna: An Essay on Two Indo-European Representations of Sovereignty*, tran. Derek Coltman (New York: Zone Books, 1988).

Foucault, Michel, *Abnormal: Lectures at the College de France, 1974–1975*, trans. Graham Burchell (New York : Picador, 2004).

——, *Security Territory, Population: Lectures at the College De France, 1977–1978*, trans. Graham Burchell (Hampshire, New York: Palgrave, 2007).

Henry, Michel, *I am the Truth: Towards a Philosophy of Christianity* trans. Susan Emanuel (Stanford, California : Stanford University Press, 2003).

Jarry, Alfred, *The Ubu Plays*, trans. Curil Carnolly and Simon Watson Taylor (London: Methuen, 1968).

Mondzain, Marie-Jose, *Image, Icon, Economy: The Byzantine Origins of the Contemporary Imaginary*, trans. Rico Franses (Stanford, California: Stanford University Press, 2005).

Patočka, Jan, *Plato and Europe*, trans. Petr Lom (Stanford, California: Stanford University Press, 2002).

Polybius, *From Alexander to Constantine : Passages and Documents & Illustrating the History of Social and Political Ideas 336 B.C to A. D 337*, trans. with notes, essays, and introductions by Ernest Barker (Oxford: Clarendon Press, 1959).

Schmitt, Carl, *Political Theology: Four Chapters on the Concept of Sovereignty* trans. George Schwab, Foreword by Tracy B. Strong (Chicago and London: University of Chicago Press, 2005).

Taubes, Jacob, *The Political Theology of Paul*, trans. Dana Hollander (Stanford, California: Stanford University Press, 2004).

Part II

11 Roots of Violence
Jīva, Life, and Other Things

Rustam Singh

The roots of violence go into the nature of *jīva*.[1] What is jīva? Jīva is that which lives, that which is alive. But what is the nature of jīva? Being alive, jīva tries to prolong its life. In order to do that, jīva eats and consumes other jīvas, or it kills them trying to defend itself. By doing one or both of these things, jīva keeps itself alive. However, by doing these things jīva extinguishes the life of other jīvas.

What does this analysis show us?

Firstly, what we call life is found in jīva, or it is jīva that carries life. Secondly, jīva and life are inextricably bound up with each other: there is no jīva without life, and there is no life without jīva. Thirdly, in order to remain what it is (in one jīva)—that is, *life*—life tries to extinguish life (in another jīva).[2]

This latter observation reveals, in turn, a frightening fact about life, a fact that needs to be underlined. Namely that it is not just (one) jīva that tries to kill or consume (another) jīva; it is also life that tries to extinguish life. But is this not a strange thing to happen—that life itself should try to extinguish life? It *is* a strange thing, and in fact this is the most common feature of life, but one which is most commonly forgotten. But, if we do not forget this feature and remain focussed on it, then it leads us on to see that life is not that *One* entity that we often take it to be: there are pieces of what we call life and they are as many as there are jīvas. Further, the nature of these pieces is such that they cannot come together and become one entity. As such, there is no such entity as Life, with a capital L, and it is this that makes it possible for life in one jīva to extinguish life in another jīva.

And here, we should modify our initial statement and say that more than the nature of jīva, it is the nature of life itself in which the roots of violence lie. For, the nature of jīva comes from the nature of life. In a way, jīva is only a vehicle through which life manifests its nature. By doing that, it also gives its own nature to jīva. But this does not mean that jīva is secondary to life, or that life is a supernatural entity that chooses or creates jīva to manifest itself. It only means that life as it is manifested in jīva—and that is the only way it manifests itself or the only way we see it manifested—manifests its own nature and in the process gives its nature to jīva.

What, then, is the nature of life? We have had a glimpse of this nature in what we have said above. But we will elaborate it here a bit further. We have seen that it is life which makes jīva alive and then also keeps it alive. At the same time, life itself is something which tries to keep itself alive. And this is a trait that it shares with jīva. However, since life can keep itself alive only in jīva, it propels jīva to kill or consume other jīvas. The aim here is not simply that jīva should kill or consume other jīvas; rather the aim is to make sure that this particular piece of life keeps itself alive or is not decimated by the life in another jīva. This is how the life in a jīva is able to prolong itself. This is how, too, a jīva goes on killing or consuming other jīvas so long as it is alive—so long as it itself is not killed or consumed by another jīva, or so long as the *life* in it can no longer prolong itself, that is, keep itself alive.

When it can no longer prolong itself, life comes to an end, dies. And this again is a trait it shares with jīva. What is significant, however, is that—and this is what follows from these observations—what we know and revere as life cannot keep itself be alive *without causing death*, which is the death of jīvas. Life, as such, is a harbinger of death, the only one apart from the other natural or unnatural causes which, too, may extinguish the life of a jīva.

Clearly, life is not that benign entity which it is held forth as being. On the contrary, it is the most demonic thing around. And it is more demonic than any demon we can imagine. Its demonicity lies in this: as an entity which is alive and has to keep itself alive, it constantly extinguishes other lives. This is how an unimaginable number of deaths take place on the earth every day. These deaths are not caused by a force that we cannot know anything about. They are caused by a thing which is right here among us, and in fact is within us: they are caused by life.

WHO ARE THE JIVAS?

But who are jīvas? What are the examples of jīvas?

Jīvas include animals and humans, insects and birds, and beings which are smaller than insects. They also include plants and trees. Do they all belong to the same category? In one sense, yes: they all try to kill and/or consume other jīvas.[3]

HUMANS AND OTHER JIVAS

Yet humans think that they are different from other jīvas. They often compare themselves with animals and take pride in saying that they are superior to them.[4] The thing that humans have often mentioned to show their superiority to other jīvas is their 'superior' ability to think, and language, as it has been developed by them, is regarded as part of it.

But has this ability made humans different from other jīvas in such a way that they no longer kill or eat jīvas? They have definitely stopped eating other humans. This was certainly a result of thinking: they began to feel that it was disgusting to eat their own kind. But this disgust has not been commonly extended to include other jīvas. Moreover, although they have stopped *eating* other humans, they have not stopped *killing* them—and *hurting them and other jīvas* in all those innumerable ways which humans have invented. We can see that there are two sides to this thinking. One side shows humans the direction which leads them away from killing and hurting. The other side turns them into ever more sophisticated killers and torturers. It will not be wrong to say that humans have made progress in both these directions. Nevertheless, they seem to have gone further in the *latter* direction.

Hence, the question that we should ask here is this: Is it enough to have the ability to think?

THE ABILITY TO THIN

One can think about thinking in various ways but we should keep in view here the context in which we are trying to talk about thinking. And the context is this: There is a claim by humans that they are superior to other jīvas and that what makes them superior is their superior ability to think. They are claiming, in other words, that jīvas other than humans do not have this ability to the same degree as humans and because of this lack they are inferior to them. But there is another thing that is being said here, namely that non-human jīvas perform their functions more or less without thinking.[5]

Now, if we presume this view to be true for the moment, then what is the main function that nonhuman jīvas perform? In order to keep themselves alive, they try to kill or consume other jīvas. Thus killing or consuming other jīvas and keeping themselves alive are activities that are natural to them: it does not require much thinking. However, we have seen that killing and consuming other jīvas is an activity that is also performed by humans. Therefore we can say that like the jīvas other than humans, this activity is natural to humans as well, and that in their case either, it does not require much thinking. Thinking, as such, is not something that humans require in order to kill and consume other jīvas. This activity belongs to a realm where they do things quite *unthinkingly*, and this is the realm that they share with other jīvas which supposedly do little thinking.

But what about activities in which humans kill and hurt other jīvas—including human jīvas—for purposes *other than* killing and consuming them? Can we say that these activities too require little thinking; that little thinking goes into them? Clearly we cannot take such a position, for these are activities which have been consciously and carefully *thought of* by humans. In fact, they have been thinking about them and trying to devise them for a long time.

There are two things that follow here. Firstly, even though humans are able to think, thinking is not involved in all their actions. There is an activity that they do quite unthinkingly and this is one of the main activities they perform as jīvas, namely killing and consuming other jīvas. Secondly, not all of their activities that *involve* thinking are such that they would meet the approval of a different kind of thinking. This latter kind of thinking too is found among humans and it believes that humans should not kill and hurt other jīvas, including their own kind.

As such, it is really not enough to have the ability to think; what is important is also the *kind* of thinking we do and the direction in which this thinking takes us.

HUMANS AS MONSTERS

And here we should ask one more question: Why have humans gone further in the direction that we have pointed out above—the direction that makes them even more sophisticated killers and torturers? What are the roots of the thinking that has led them to this direction?

It is quite probable that the roots of this thinking lie in the same drive[6] that makes humans—and other jīvas—kill and/or consume jīvas other than themselves. This is so because this drive is the only factor we have seen so far that has made humans kill and consume other jīvas. The sophistication they have acquired over a period as killers and torturers, and the kind of thinking that has gone into this acquisition could only have been the result of either a gradual refinement of this drive or a transformation of a part of it in such a way that the thinking retains somewhat the character of the drive.

Nevertheless, there are differences between this thinking and the drive it seems to have come from. These differences are the following.

Firstly, the drive was and continues to be natural; it is something that jīvas *have* when they come to life. It is something that they *receive* as jīvas; it is part of the *life* which is there in them. The thinking under focus, on the other hand, has at least partly been *acquired*; partly because even though it might have been the result of a gradual transformation of a part of the drive, the human agency itself seems to have played a role in it, for it looks like a transformation that must have, after a point, been desired. Secondly, whereas the drive makes humans kill and consume other jīvas in order to prolong their own lives, the thinking leads to killing and/or torture for more complex purposes. These purposes are not always connected with that basic purpose which is the purpose of the drive, namely prolonging life, but sometimes they are. For example, when animals are tortured in the process of testing medicines, it is primarily that basic purpose the testers have in mind, for medicines are manufactured essentially for prolonging life.[7] However, animals and humans are killed, maimed, and tortured for a number of other purposes and these purposes have no connection with prolonging human life.

Given these differences, it would be logical to say that the thinking which leads to such complex acts of violence has, to a large degree, become disconnected from our life as jīva. And that to the same degree, humans are no longer jīvas—as the non-human forms of jīva still are—but have become something other than jīva, something which is much more complex than jīva but is also much more vicious and cruel. In other words, some of the transformation that has taken place in the jīva represented in the human form is such that it marks a *degradation*, rather than upliftment, in the basic nature of jīva. At the same time, this transformation also marks a *distance* from the human jīva found in nature and this distance takes place in such a way that the 'human' in the human jīvas no longer remains human but rather becomes a monster—still retaining the human form.[8]

LISTING THE MONSTROSITIES

However, not all humans, at a given moment, have undergone this transformation and turned into monsters. Nevertheless, a majority of them carry this potential. Although we believe that we are all the time surrounded by humans in our daily life, yet—strictly speaking—that is an illusion. Quite a few people around us, at any time of the day—and this could include us as well—are no longer fully human, and at least some of them are full-fledged monsters. If we start counting all the ways in which humans behave in a monstrous fashion, we might end up with a long list. But I should mention a few examples.

It is monstrous, I think, to eat the flesh of animals and fowl which are reared only for this purpose. It is monstrous especially when they are reared in inhuman conditions and by eating their flesh we sanction this treatment.

It is monstrous to use deodorants and perfumes which are poured into the eyes of animals to see how safe they are for humans.

It is monstrous to test chemical and bacterial agents (and medical drugs) on unsuspecting human populations. It is monstrous, firstly, to *make* such agents.

It is monstrous to set up plants to produce nuclear energy and industries to produce gases knowing that if they burst, they will frightfully harm humans, animals, and other jīvas for decades or may be centuries to come.

Are not all motor vehicles small, little monsters moving around on the surface of the earth and polluting it? Aeroplanes are definitely monsters and so are rockets and satellites. It is monstrous to make bombs and weapons which will kill and damage not only humans but also nature. It is monstrous to *use* such weapons.

Killing people in the name of religion, caste, creed, race, and language, etc. is the height of monstrosity.

Human trafficking is monstrous. So also is animal trafficking and killing animals for their skin.

Aborting female foetuses because they are female is sheer monstrousness.

Animals performing in circuses is a monstrous sight as well as animals in zoos, cabins, and cages.

Making huge profits by making and/or selling *anything* is monstrous.

It is monstrous to coerce people to buy new things—such as computer software—when the old are still serviceable.

Computer hardware itself is monstrous, if it is immune to decay. It follows that producing anything which cannot be degraded by the elements is monstrousness.

It is monstrous to turn rivers away from their natural course or link them up in an unnatural way.

It is monstrous to build large dams and artificial lakes which inundate and submerge villages, forests, and myriad forms of life and leave people and animals homeless and without means to sustain themselves.

Forcing people and animals out of their habitats for setting up industries and digging mines is monstrous.

Industries and enterprises that pollute water, air, and other natural elements are monstrosities. It is monstrous to allow them to do that.

Spraying pesticides and insecticides on crops and fruit and making people eat such food is nothing short of monstrousness.

VIOLENCE AS CONSUMPTION

This list shows in brief that humans in general have emerged as a big monster on the face of the earth. What has exacerbated the effect of their monstrousness is the *increase in their population* in the last few centuries. The size of their population has pushed up enormously the amount of violence they perpetrate. And this includes the violence caused by the increase in the amount of living and nonliving things they use and consume.

It is true that the growth in population is not the only factor that has pushed up consumption. That is how levels of consumption in the richer countries are much higher than those in the poorer ones, or they are higher among the middle and upper classes everywhere than among the lower ones. Nevertheless, the poorer countries and the lower classes seem to be taking the same path that the richer countries and the middle and upper classes had taken, or at least they wish to do that. Secondly, in my opinion, one should no longer feel ashamed of saying that now there are too many humans on the earth.

Whatever the case, a simple increase in the levels of consumption is not the only fact about consumption. There is also the fact that, whenever they are in a position to do so, humans tend to use and consume almost everything *in excess*, and it is *this* fact that I think is the most crucial in any discussion of consumption in connection with violence.[9] For, in the present-day context of the life on earth, the human tendency to consume in excess is a central reason for violence in the world. It is also, as such, a central element in the monstrosity of humans. In fact, it is probably the central feature to emerge in human nature after the drive that makes humans—along with other jīvas—kill and consume other jīvas. At the same time, it is a feature whose emergence makes humans different from other jīvas *in as fundamental a way* as the so-called ability to think. Actually, I wish to regard the emergence of this tendency in human nature—namely, the tendency to consume in excess—as the most fundamental event in the evolution of human nature, an event that—*much more than their ability to think*—marks the deviation of humans from their nature as jīva and their assumption of the typically monstrous in their nature.[10]

When we delve into the nature of this tendency, we find that it has *little connection with thinking*. Depending upon how much money people have—and this is true of all the classes—they buy and use things fairly indiscriminately, that is, *without thinking*. If we were to ask them, they would of course tell us the reason for buying each thing and they would convince us quite easily that they need that thing. And there is a thinking involved in this. But surely, that is not the level of the thinking we are discussing. What we are discussing is this: Do people really need *all* the things that they think they need? And we need to remember here that these things are part of a list that has been getting longer for quite a few centuries. When we keep in mind this level of thinking, we discover that people buy and use things almost blindly, and sometimes they buy things that they do not even use. Also, they buy things for the fun of it or just because these things are there and are available, or even because other people are buying them. And so if we look at this phenomenon carefully, we can see that this tendency is almost like a drive.

PURSUIT OF KNOWLEDGE

But there is another thing that humans do quite blindly, *and this is the way they pursue what is called knowledge*, trying to acquire as much of it as possible. As we know, humans as a body are busy pursuing knowledge all the time and they have been doing it since ancient times. What kind of knowledge do they try to acquire? It is the knowledge about the world and about things in general, both living and nonliving; knowledge about themselves, their mind and body; knowledge about histories, economies, and societies. What has been the aim of acquiring such knowledge? Purportedly the aim has been to increase the well-being of humans, but this answer is not accurate. It would be difficult to say that *all* those people who are actively engaged in the pursuit of knowledge of different types at any given time or are in any way or at any level associated with it are motivated by this aim or that they are motivated by it *all the time*. In this connection, what seems closer to the truth is this: many of these people are driven by curiosity; many others wish to devise new things or generate new ideas; the interest of many is to make profit; and there are others—a large number—who are engaged in it simply because it provides a job. Finally, there are quite a few people who involve themselves in this pursuit of knowledge because by using it they would be able to kill and destroy other people. This is the kind of knowledge that is pursued, for example, for the so-called strategic purposes.

Now, it needs hardly be said that not all the ways and means used during this pursuit of knowledge are benign. In fact, some of them are distinctly and dangerously harmful to the human and other jīvas.

Further, and as we have seen in the list above, the use of a lot of this knowledge has played a major role in damaging the earth and nature and in killing and harming the human and other jīvas, and it is still playing this role. As such, the desire to acquire knowledge *incessantly and indiscriminately*, which has turned into a habit and already looks like a drive, is one more thing that holds a central place in the monstrosity of humans.

But let us take note of two more things about this desire. Firstly, most of the knowledge that humans now acquire under the influence of this desire is *artificial*. And by this I mean that, unlike most of the knowledge acquired by other jīvas, this knowledge is no longer acquired with the use of senses while living a life in nature. Rather, it is acquired by using a faculty which seems to be getting largely disconnected from both the senses and nature, namely, thinking. Second, this knowledge is *excessive*, that is, a lot of human knowledge now is such that it is *not required*. One can mention a few examples here: (1) the knowledge that tells humans how to make nuclear and chemical weapons; (2) the knowledge that enables them to clone animals and will possibly enable them to also clone humans; (3) the knowledge that reveals to them the sex of a foetus; (4) the knowledge that allows them to genetically modify crops and vegetables, and possibly in the future also humans; (5) even the knowledge of the inner structure of a plant, tree, or flower.

But these are not the only examples.

And I am reminded here of Yājñavalkya and Gotama, the Buddha. Both of them forbade excessive or misplaced curiosity, by which they probably meant pursuing knowledge for its own sake or pursuing purposeless knowledge.[11]

Now, I have pointed out these two features of human knowledge because they have implications for our discussion here and also in general. For example, a substantial way of remaining sensitive to the life in nature, that is, to jīvas other than humans, is to keep in touch with them through senses. But when the life of the senses is pushed to the background, is kept in abeyance, or is distanced from nature, or, in other words, when humans no longer look at themselves as jīvas who too are located in nature, but rather as beings who are away from it and in fact more or less superior to it, and when what is called nature is reduced to being just an object of curiosity or just a source of exploitation for consumption—then, the knowledge that is thus acquired is likely to become insensitive or at least indifferent to the life in nature, and, ultimately, *in fact*, to the life of humans. Secondly, it is also then likely to lose sight of its limits or boundaries, because in such a situation, namely, by losing touch with the life in nature, it loses its direction. And perhaps it is no longer an exaggeration to say that the human pursuit of knowledge, at least in the last few centuries, *has*, to a degree, lost its direction.

Meanwhile, isn't it ironic that humans have dissected an endless number of plants and flowers, animals and insects, but they still do not know how to live with them? Actually, they do not even know how to live with other humans. What is perhaps even truer is that they know how to do this but do not care to follow such knowledge.

Some of this latter kind of knowledge, too, humans have evolved by thinking. For example, the knowledge that tells humans how to live and conduct themselves in such ways that the least possible violence is done to the world. Saints, sages, and philosophers have many times come up with the knowledge of this kind and it is available in a variety of forms.

USELESS PHILOSOPHY

Yet, such knowledge is rarely put into practice. In fact, it is not valued very highly and is often held to be unusable. Which reminds me of Adeimantus who in *The Republic*, more than two thousand years ago, tells Socrates that 'people who study philosophy for too long', namely philosophers, become completely useless as members of society. And it is instructive to listen to Socrates' answer to Adeimantus here. He says that 'it's quite true that the best of the philosophers are of no use to their fellows'; however, it is not philosophers who should be blamed for this, 'but those who fail to make use of them' (Plato 1955, pp. 248–50).

JĪVA AS SUCH

I will end this essay by pointing out some crucial differences between jīva *as such* and the human-as-a-monster: (1) Jīva kills (or plucks or picks) little more than it needs to eat at a given moment or time. It rarely wastes. (2) The things that jīva needs for a purpose other than eating and filling its belly are minimal. And it manages to make them or forage for them without causing much damage to the earth or nature. (3) Jīva rarely stores. When it does, it does so in limited quantities and for brief periods. (4) Jīva does not produce things that are not found in nature. As such, it does not produce things that cannot be degraded by the elements. (5) It follows that jīva does not produce weapons other than those given to it by nature. (6) It also follows that jīva does not pollute the earth, the air, and water. (7) Jīva does not try to acquire artificial and excessive knowledge. And, (8) Jīva tries to cure itself only by using as medicine, things that are available in nature.

It should be clear from what we have seen earlier in this essay that none of these things apply to humans-as-monsters.

Notes

1. *Jīva* is a Sanskrit word which has been used in many senses. Monier Monier-Williams, in his *A Sanskrit-English Dictionary* (Monier-Williams 2002) mentions the following senses of the word: living, existing, alive; any living

being, anything living; life, existence; the principle of life, vital breath, the living or personal soul, etc. However, we are concerned here only with the sense that is retained in this essay and is then given a particular elaboration. In the rest of this essay, this word will appear without italics.

2. The *Encarta World English Dictionary* (1999) defines life as 'the quality that makes living animals and plants different from dead organisms and inorganic matter. Its functions include the ability to take in food, adapt to the environment, grow, and reproduce.' Similarly, according to *The Concise Oxford English Dictionary* (1999), life is 'the condition that distinguishes animals and plants from inorganic matter, including the capacity for growth, functional activity, and continual change preceding death.' However, life is not just a quality or condition, for if we look at it carefully life seems to have an agency which is independent of the agency of the jīva that carries life.

3. For the knowledge of the behaviour of plants and trees especially, it is still helpful to read Charles Darwin (1859). According to Darwin, they actively try to deny food to other plants and trees, including those belonging to their own species, in order to ensure their death.

4. This tendency goes to ancient times, and it has been a general tendency in human thought, including in religious and scientific thought, and continues into our own times.

5. I should note here that biological theory (perhaps you could specify the theory) has supported this view for a long time and, in fact, this still seems to be the dominant view in that theory, even though recent research in the behaviour of animals and birds shows that this is not altogether true. Animals and birds such as chimpanzees, elephants, whales, dogs, parrots, and crows, etc. have shown remarkable ability for abstract thinking and I suspect that researchers do not know at this moment the actual depth and reach of their thinking. At the same time, whether some more jīvas also have this kind of ability is not clear yet to people investigating non-human jīvas.

6. *The Concise Oxford English Dictionary* (1999) defines a drive as 'an innate, biologically determined urge'. *Encarta World English Dictionary* (1999) defines it as 'a powerful need or instinct, e.g., hunger or sex, that motivates behaviour'. We may add that a drive may also be acquired over a period of time, and may gradually disappear under changed conditions.

7. As we know, medicines are manufactured not only for prolonging the life of the patients; making money is always a strong motivation. That is how there are so many spurious medicines around. We also know that the testing of medicines on animals has been questioned on moral grounds. Clearly, I am not defending that practice here.

8. *The Concise Oxford English Dictionary* (1999) defines a monster as 'a large, ugly, and frightening imaginary creature'; also as 'an inhumanly cruel or wicked person'. According to *Encarta World English Dictionary* (1999), a

monster is 'any large, ugly, terrifying animal or person found in mythology or created by the imagination, especially [something] fierce that kills people'; also somebody 'whose inhumanity or vicious behaviour terrifies and disgusts people'. We can see that there is no monster to be found in nature. At the same time, however, a monster is also not a person or even a jīva any more. A monster, as we have here defined it, is to be found only in the so-called human world and has the shape and appearance of a human jīva.

9. I am aware that large numbers of humans are denied access to even the basic things they need in order to survive. But that is only another facet of the violence we are talking about.

10. We can see this tendency going back to the ancient times. There were always people in history who placed little check on what and how much they would consume. However, as we look back into history such people seem to be fewer in number. The relative lack of the variety of things to be used also reduced the volume of consumption in earlier periods. But in the last few centuries humans seem to have gone berserk in this matter. There is no end to the number of things they need in order to use them in various ways including putting them into their stomachs. And this tendency cuts across modes of production and types of societies. Thus it is not just the capitalist mode of production and the liberal societies which have shown this tendency. Nor is it linked very closely with modern advertising (which certainly is one of the most violent and most crude and obnoxious ways of persuading people to buy and consume things), for advertising has only used this tendency. In other words, the tendency was already there to be exploited by forces like the 'advertisement industry'.

But the people who belong to this 'industry' were not the only ones who exploited this tendency. In fact, they came much later. Those who were among the first to exploit it were the manufacturers, who later developed into the industrialists and business people of the modern period. These were the peo-ple—and they continue to do so—who, with the help of the 'inventors' and 'innovators', began to fill the marketplace with a dazzling variety of things. Meanwhile, an increasing number of people had money to spare and this money gave a boost to the desire to purchase. It is true that not all people could buy many things but there were always some who could and they did it with gusto and excitement. Their number has grown over the recent centuries and has, of late, become huge. Simultaneously, the tendency to buy, use, and consume things has developed into a mania, a disease.

11. In the Sixth Brahmaṇam of the Third Chapter of Bṛhad-araṇyaka Upaniṣad, Yājñavalkya, who is responding to the questions posed by Gārgi, tells her, after a particular question, not to 'question further' because any further question would be an 'over-question' and if she asks it, her head might 'burst' (Deussen 1997, pp. 456–57). In a somewhat similar context, the Buddha, while replying to the questions asked by Mālunkyāputta, chides him for asking

misplaced questions which, being misplaced, amount to being useless or purposeless (Gethin 2008, pp. 168–72).

References

Darwin, Charles, *On the Origin of Species* (London: John Murray, 1859).

Deussen, Paul, *Sixty Upaniṣads of the Veda*, translated from the German by V. M. Bedekar and G. B. Palsule, Volume I (Delhi: Motilal Banarsidass Publishers Private Limited, 1997).

Gethin, Rupert, *Sayings of the Buddha: A Selection of Sutras from the Pali Nikāyas* (Oxford: Oxford University Press, 2008).

Monier-Williams, Monier, *A Sanskrit-English Dictionary* (Delhi: Motilal Banarsidass Publishers Private Limited, 2002).

Plato, *The Republic* (Harmondsworth: Penguin Books, 1955).

12 Violence of/on Languages
The Political Topography of Linguistic Nationalism

Asha Sarangi

The relationship between religion, language, and violence has been much debated and analysed in the discipline of social sciences through various conceptual and methodological approaches. In a non-reductive and non-exclusive manner, the three terms pose before us the scales of hierarchies and inequalities which often result in extreme forms of violence at the state-societal levels. In this essay, I take the category of language in a conceptually nuanced way to reflect further on this relationship, and its imbricative association with religion along with the specific forms of violence endemic to their internal constitution as social categories of community and national identity formation. I consider here language and religion as unique forms of culture in a mutually reconstitutive fashion and habitus of practices and power. As distinct forms of life inhabiting certain belief-system and world-views, language and religion have remained central to human life across civilizations. As a primary human resource, language is sustained through social recognition and difference but one which is collectively constituted. Language is both a divider and unifier based on an inter-subjective dialogical interaction among the individuals. Due to its communicative agentive force, it is based on the social practices which are relational, interactive, collectively drawn from heterogeneous ideologies, histories, and cultures. Zizek argues that language and its symbolic order is primarily reconciliatory and has a non-aggressive element in its interactive mode with individuals, and therefore any kind of violence of and on language is intrinsically pathological and inhuman. He suggests that because of the inegalitarian and asymmetrical relationship among individuals, this reconciliatory character of language is lost out, and language, a medium of non-violence, becomes the extreme and most brutal force of violence. In this context, verbal and written violence perpetrated through linguistic means becomes the most inhuman exercise in the performance of a language loyalty in a society. In this regard, then, there is some kind of relationship between ontological and social violence, one defining the other in a democratic political society. For Zizek, 'the wall of language' is what separates us from each other but not without various modes and forms of violence in it (Zizek 2009, p. 10–12).

Since the late 19th century onwards, South Asia has witnessed numerous political struggles over the (un)making of specific linguistic, religious, and cultural identities. The political process from colonial to post-colonial making of the nation-states in most of the countries of this region was entangled within the seamless web and circuits of violence in its multiple forms—linguistic, religious, political, cultural, and social, etc. The partition historiography has shown the trajectory of violence at multiple levels. In this essay, I examine the *nation-form* of one particular kind of violence, that is, linguistic violence, and its genocidal effects over numerous language communities and their cultural habitus through various state-society directed strategies and programs culminating in the language decay and language decline or even death. In addition to it, the religion based violence has continued to inter-penetrate the linguistic-cultural modes of social life in South Asia. In this context, it is necessary to situate the historical locatedness of these overlapping hierarchies of linguistic-cultural and religious identities, and their subsequent encompassment into the territorial boundaries of specific nation-states in order to understand the logic and reasons of this form of violence in this linguistically dense and culturally diverse part of the world. In case of South Asia, it is significant to note how languages create boundaries of belonging, affinity, devotion, and passion which are deeply associated with notions of (the) mother tongue. In recent years, scholars have tried to examine the intense emotive entrenchments of language communities with Telugu, Tamil, Urdu, Hindi, Punjabi, and Oriya, among others, as their mother tongues.[1] The questions central to my inquiry in this chapter are the following. Are there clearly visible forms of linguistic violence or are they enclosed into much deeper and denser forms of violence that a particular society inhabits? How do we conceptualize the notions of language rights and language recognition in linguistically heterogeneous societies? How do these societies negotiate with linguistic loyalties and capabilities within dominant linguistic inequalities and hierarchies of various kinds, and finally to what extent does the state power resolve or manage the linguistic crisis through a number of legislations and laws? This is further complicated in the phenomenon of linguistic nationalism which gets intertwined with the demands for territorial demarcation, and boundedness of nation-states, and their distinctive ethnological attributes based on language, religion, caste, and region predominantly. For example, the phenomenon of partition in 1947 in this region along with the brutal form of violence suggests, to say with Zizek, three dominant strands—subjective, objective, and symbolic. This dense interpellation of the violence is both a reality and real since the former is more in terms of its subjective articulation and the latter a more abstract form that determines what manifests in the social and political reality. Similarly, Balibar takes this interdependence further and distinguishes two opposite but complementary modes of excessive violence, which are, the 'ultra-objective' or systemic violence inherent in the social conditions of global capitalism resulting in the displacement and homelessness of human beings and the 'ultra-subjective' violence of newly emerging ethnic and/or religious and racist violence. There are numerous such cases in South Asia to illustrate this point. When a few languages are identified as languages of nation-states of particular political territories, they get cultural and political patronage and protection more than other languages. For example, Urdu becomes the official language of Pakistan ignoring Punjabi, Balochi, Sindhi, Siraiki, and Pushto. Similarly, the elevation of Hindi as the national language in independent India marginalized numerous languages and in particular Urdu language. Alyssa Ayres draws attention to this kind of linguistic nationalism of the Pakistani state after the partition (Ayres 2009). Urdu's dominance over Bengali in East Bengal of undivided Pakistan, and over Kashmiri in Kashmir has not been without unleashing excruciating forms of violence and oppression over people and communities of other languages. Sri Lanka has been subjected to decades of linguistic genocide over Tamil vs Sinhalese. All these cases in South Asia reveal a close nexus between religion and language. For example, conflict over Hindi and Urdu in India since the early twentieth century is closely tied up with contestations over

Hinduism and Islam, and over Buddhism and Hinduism, in case of Sri Lankan strife over Sinhalese and Tamil languages respectively. This larger religio-linguistic identity is invoked violently and enforced to institutionalize the lingua franca of the newly created nation-states of India, Pakistan, and Sri Lanka. Who could be the true claimant for this status has at times precipitated the territorial division of the geo-cultural space of the new states which began to carve their linguistic, religious, and cultural identities along with major re-articulation of the Indo-Persian, Indo-Dravidian, and Indo-Buddhist literary histories, and their territorial topographies. The historical trajectory of linguistic national-ism in each of these cases is woven through narratives of woes and trag-edies over the loss of languages and mother tongues considered to be equivalent to the cultural dislocation and loss of their users and territo-rial spaces. In all of this, a certain degree of violence over the sense of martyrdom and sacrifice remains central to the ideology of linguistic nationalism. Similarly, language began to provide a 'new foundational category' for understanding the cultural and political mobilization in the Indian society during the late 19th and early 20th centuries when significant changes occurred in the principles and methods of instruc-tion in terms of grammar, translation, and pedagogy.[2]

18 April 1900 marked a crucial point of departure in the historiog-raphy of Indian nationalism. On this day, Hindi language in the Nagari script was recognized officially as the language of court and administra-tion in the United Provinces of colonial north India. This recognition of Hindi language led to (and still continues) a long drawn struggle between Hindi and Urdu language communities in North India. The conflict around linguistic differences took various forms of cultural, political, and ideological differences, and gave rise to distinct forms of linguistic nationalism in twentieth century colonial north India. It is in this regard that I would like to suggest that the complex relationship between language, identity, community, and nation is mutually re-con-stitutive and re-producible. I analyse this relationship through three dis-tinctive modes by considering language as discourse, practice, and an identity, and how each of these three modes is affected and internally constituted by in/visible forms of violence at times disguised in the name of community and/or nation. In doing so, I characterize language as a category of *social collectivity*. I contend that the understanding of language both as a 'dialectical productive activity' (Marx) and a 'verbal-ideological sign-system' (Voloshinov) points to the processes through

which language is socially mediated, politically mobilized, and ideologically structured on the one hand, and represented as identity, community, state or nation on the other (Marx 1972; Voloshinov 1986). It is within this duality of language as structure and practice, as sign-system and activity that we need to situate the historical, social, cultural, and political formations within which various language movements emerged in colonial South Asia. For instance, if we take Hindi-Urdu linguistic movement in the late 19th century colonial north India, we see how it aimed at the political mobilization and cultural collectivization of Hindi and Urdu languages and their (Hindu and/or Muslim) communities. Similarly, linguistic nationalism in this part of the world culminated in the formation of national linguistic identity of Hindu/Hindi and Muslim/Urdu, and in the most violent slogans of 'Hindi, Hindu and Hindustan' or 'Urdu, Muslim and Pakistan' that gave a clarion call for the partition of India into India and Pakistan as two separate nation-states. I contend that these three modes of language as discourse, practice, and identity are closely intertwined with identical modes of culture and cultural system such as defined through its material-symbolic system of religious order of social communities at the given historical junctures.

LANGUAGE AS DISCOURSE

By analyzing language as discourse, I point out the ideological and political modes of representation used in defining the category of language in both colonial and nationalist discourses. This entails examining the nature and form of colonial and nationalist discourses, their structures of formation, and impact on the discursive, political, and institutional reframing of the language question in early twentieth century South Asia. The colonial state followed an ideology of *language as culture* and linguistic differences as cultural differences to characterize the nature and form of linguistic diversity and cultural geography of this region. The ideology of 'language as culture' remained predominantly visible in various forms of intervention that the British colonial state made in spheres of education, administration, law, politics, and culture. It is within this context that we can locate the historicity of various language movements, and show how the colonial-official intervention on the language question had discursive and institutional effects on the larger public spheres of these societies. It is important to note how the ideological-political differences were played out in defining the languages of different groups and communities with specific roles assigned to different Indian languages. Within this ideological framework, 'languages come to be identified with mentalities, ethnicities and identities of the colonized' (Turner 1991; Marx and Engels 1972). Fabian suggests that to establish communication with the colonized is one of the requirements for the colonial regime to sustain itself. It is through a 'shared communicative praxis that use and control of verbal means of communication are needed to maintain regimes, military, religious, ideological and economic' (Fabian 1986). Fabian shows how in case of Uganda, Swahili was eliminated from schools, and English was made a language of people so much so that those who wrote in their mother tongue were tortured and those who wrote in English were awarded prizes. Similarly, the colonial state in India recognized some languages as languages of governmental-administrative rationality more than others resulting in the enclaves of inclusion and exclusion of social communities from seats of power and politics. Farina Mir shows as to how the elevation of Urdu and suppression of Punjabi at the hands of colonial administrators and missionaries could make the latter more and more invisible and unrecognized from the domains of education, law, administration, and production of print and pedagogy (Mir 2010). All of this entails, to say with Sheldon Pollock, the un/making of 'socio-textual community' particularly at the high noon of nationalism (Pollock 2004, p. 27).

On the other hand, the Indian nationalists defined the representational identity of Indian languages radically differently than the colonialists. Nationalists used *language as an ideology* and tried to embody in it the 'nation-form' or 'nation-ness' of India. For them, the communicability of language with the nation establishes, as Benjamin would say, 'a social existence without which the relationship to language is an idea only, and not a communication because there is no relationship between mental being and communication' (Benjamin 1986, p. 314).

The representation of *language as collectivity* having an organic bond and intimacy with the nation is remarkably explicit in the nationalist discourse. The nationalist discourse as a form of political discourse engages with the language question as a deep political-ideological concern for the making of the nation. The nationalist discourse represents language as a social collectivity idealized in the form of linguistic communities and their formations as cultural-political collectivities being significant for the processes of nation-formation. In other words, nationalists argued that the dual processes of linguistic formation and political formation would go together in the making of a nation. This ideological-political understanding of the category of language remained central in their participation of numerous regional linguistic movements. It would be important to track the nationalist discourse at three levels; in its engagement with the English language, in its cultural and political representation of various languages and their communities within the nation, and with the making of a national or state language as a possible common/national language. It is in their attempts of creating a common (possibly national) language as a 'unitary language' that, to say with Bakhtin, reveals 'forces working toward concrete verbal and ideological unification and centralization developing in vital connection with the processes of socio-political and cultural centralization' that the nationalist discourse and its structure points to (Bakhtin 1981, p. 271).

It is important to analyse how a particular language and its community of users is considered equal to realizing the nation-ness of the nation, and, often times, for nationalists holding the two together becomes a political project. The process of discursive and institutional formation of the nation is also a process of linguistically consolidating the state. Thus, the linguistic reconstruction is carried out simultaneously with the cultural and political restructuring of the given social order. For nationalists, the natural and innate bond between language and nation entails the possibility of creating linguistically bounded borders, which can be geographically unifying and culturally consolidating. These borders, as Fichte said, could act as 'internal borders' to delimit the boundaries of the nation-state. Fichte suggested that communities bound by these internal borders would be more communicable and morally stronger. He pointed out in his famous address to the German nation in 1807 in the following manner:

The first, original and truly natural borders of states are beyond doubt their internal borders. Those who speak the same language are joined to each other by a multitude of invisible bonds by nature herself, long before any human art begins; they understand each other and have the power of continuing to make themselves understood more and more clearly; they belong together and are by nature one and an inseparable whole (Fichte 1994, p. 64).

For the nationalists, the idea of a nation as a *collective communicative community* remained central to their project of nation-formation.

This also meant that nation-formation was a particular form of social as well as political formation. It is within the nationalist discourse that each language is imagined to have a distinctive *Weltanschaunng* (world-view). The ideal of a common/national language within the nationalist discourse is symbolized with the linguistic-cultural consciousness leading to the gradual transformation of a particular linguistic community as a nation. The discourse considers language as a form of *mentality*, national *character*[3], and 'collective treasure' which encloses the discrete and specific identities of individuals, groups, and nations.[4] Nationalists see how 'linguistic ideologies and linguistic differences interpenetrate each other, reinforce each other and people have to act in relation to ideologically constructed representations of linguistic differences.'[5] (Gal and Judith 1985). In this regard, the efforts of the Indian nationalists' to create a national language was an ideological project symbolizing the struggle for cultural hegemony over the role of the colonizers' language, i.e., English (and its expanding ruling class).[6] The colonial and nationalist discourses interrogated both the existing and newly established various forms of linguistic practices aimed at producing particular kinds of social identities and communities.

LANGUAGE AS PRACTICE

Language is not simply an abstract grammar or set of rules but also an activity and practice. To consider language as practice is to see its forms of social constitution and production, its duality of producing subject and object, structure and agency.[7] A set of linguistic practices helps reformulate and reconstitute a particular form of language, its identity and community. I suggest that in order to conceptualize this mode of language, we can consider, among others, the three distinct forms of practices. They can be broadly defined as enumerative, print, and pedagogical practices. It is through these practices that a particular language can be viewed historically as a socially constructive, constitutive, and agentive category embedded within the larger communicative social realms. These practices create and consolidate specific social-political formations within which language as a collectivity is produced and institutionalized. Language as practice entails the possibility of a dialectical relationship between individual and collective, and between social and political.[8]

By considering language as practice, I suggest that specific historical and socio-political conditions establish a set of linguistic practices as

dominant and socially legitimate. These practices, however, do not necessarily create a completely homogeneous linguistic community. Instead,
these practices create *linguistic habitus* (Bourdieu 1977) which, as
Bourdieu argues, is 'not simply an instrument of communication' but
'contains the *potentiality* of an act of power' (Bourdieu and Wacquant
1992, p. 145). They create a 'socially regenerative character of linguistic
habitus' on the one hand, and establish 'language as a form of symbolic
capital' on the other (Bourdieu 1991; Duranti 1997). Furthermore, it is
in these practices that the larger processes of state rationalization of linguistic social order, collectivization of linguistic identities, and the institutionalization of linguistic-cultural practices are carried out.

Language as practice creates social-cultural sites where the processes
of social mediation, production, and construction of particular linguistic ideologies and identities are produced and contested. These sites
could be legal, administrative, cultural, educational, ideological, and
religious. There seems to be a reciprocal relationship between specific
linguistic practices and their sites during particular historical and social
conditions. It is within this context that the enumerative discourses and
practices through census records, gazetteers writings, and linguistic
survey reports initiated and gradually consolidated a far more complex
process of classification, categorization, and collectivization of languages
and their communities. The enumerative practices intricately affected
the politics of linguistic identity and community formation. It was
through these enumerative practices that narratives about social, cultural, geographical, and philological representation of languages and
communities were produced. These enumerative practices acted upon
the given linguistic social order, and produced processes of social mobilization and collectivization of linguistic identities leading to the process
of codification and quantification that opened up the possibilities for
representational politics and its forms of collectivization.

A set of print practices become intrinsic to the mobilization and
institutionalization of particular linguistic identities of social communities. It is through the mediation of print that particular linguistic practices are collectively publicized and socially legitimized. The print
practices provide *literary public sphere* to the contesting language communities over their struggles for linguistic recognition and identity. The
politics of print creates politics of recognition and its violence through
numerous institutional practices and their manipulation. Ceremonies
and rituals of linguistic-cultural communities publicized and recognized

through print and pedagogical practices become part of the school curricula. It is important to see how print practices establish *dialogical communicative public space* for otherwise spatially segregated speech and language communities to interact and engage with one another. Print provides language communities with discursive space to collectivize their dialogical interactive acts. Print as a collective social practice helps formulate social and political formation of languages into collective, heterogeneous, and public identities. The textual and scribal histories and their narratives fix the quest for the past with its symbolic repertoires and memories for their communities.

In my analysis of the print practices, I make a significant departure from the Benedict Anderson's theory of 'print capitalism' (Anderson 1991). In Anderson's account, print capitalism is preceded by the desacralization of Latin by the English language combined with processes of in the form of standardization of languages and the growth of literacy. The 'imagined community' in Anderson's analysis is literate and vernacularized but is an undifferentiated homogeneous public mass. Anderson's imagined community is a nationalized community, a communicable community but may not necessarily be a communicative community. A degree of communicative rationality, however undefined in his account, seems to characterize this imagined community that symbolizes the nation and its representational modes.

The two dominant characteristics that go into the making of imagined community in Anderson's analysis are—religion and language. The 'desacralization of Latin' (a religious change) and the inception of print language/s (linguistic change) define the uniqueness of this imagined community. However, despite such a powerful theory of print capitalism and nationalism in 19th century Europe and parts of Latin America that Anderson provides, it does not explain adequately as to how such a world historical change—desacralization and print—is simultaneously intertwined with a much larger process of changes occurring violently in several other spheres of the society. The forms of violence endemic to this change aim at creating new modes of hierarchies and differentiations in the everyday domains of human life. However, for Anderson, print capitalism erases these linguistic social hierarchies, undermines their diversification, and promotes unification in a rather less violent manner. Print capitalism encourages vernacularization followed by an ascendancy of one language over others as the former is made the language of court and administration. Anderson's analysis does not point to the complex socio-historical processes within which communities and nation-states are linguistically and religiously embedded and deliberately unified. More often, it is a much more turbulent and intensely violent process marked by practices of social and political demarcations and fragmentations. The process within which a community becomes an 'imagined community' is a specific historical social formation which restructures linguistic social order and establishes the dominance of one language as close to becoming a political community.

Anderson accepts the linguistic diversity and its social and historical locatedness in a society as an inevitable fact. However, he does not account for the violent structures and practices which enable the print capitalism to shrink this linguistic diversity and allow the development of an exclusive and limited reading public to grow into an imagined community. In his analysis, the print practices (newspapers, books, periodicals) bind the modern imagined communities through the communicative role of language which, he says, 'is not like a flag, costume, folk dance but its most important role is the capacity for generating imagined communities, building in effect particular solidarities because language is not an instrument of exclusion' (Anderson 1991; p. 122). On the other hand, I suggest that the logic of print capitalism works through the principle of selectivity and particularity within the larger processes of homogenization and vernacularization of languages, and works as a site of discrimination too. Language is not simply a metaphor of national unity and symbol of solidarity but also a sign of social and cultural exclusivism, and political dominance. However, for Anderson, 'language is not an instrument of exclusion…in principle, anyone can learn any language…print language is what invents nationalism, not a particular language per se' (Anderson 1991, p. 122). For him, vocabularies, words, phrases, and their meanings are naturally given entities for creating an 'imagined community'. He does not recognize the processes through which linguistic signs and signifiers are constructed and manipulated socially and politically to stimulate the sense of an *imagined-ness* of the community. Print affects the social life of languages and their communities in several different ways. It creates new modes of socio-cultural and political hierarchies as well as unities. They are further carried forward through a set of pedagogical-linguistic practices in the form of school

textbooks produced to institutionalize linguistic identity, and to reformulate the boundaries of the linguistic community and its production
and consumption. I argue that the pedagogical linguistic practices such
as textbooks' writing, compilation of dictionaries, literary canons, and
writing of grammar books are embedded within specific historical and
social formation, and reproduce a *pedagogical linguistic community* to
mobilize and institutionalize the linguistic identities. I suggest that these
practices produce particular forms of linguistic consciousness that often
times result in the formation of a pedagogical community, which inter-
rogates in numerous violent ways the given linguistic social order, its
practices, identities, and modes of representation. Similarly, the grammars, dictionaries, and books are written and prescribed by the state
which appoints an army of lexicographers, grammarians, folklorists, and
philologists to standardize, classify, and codify particular languages and
their literatures. New literary histories are written and modes of literary
representation such as translation and writing are re-established to
reproduce languages and their linguistic communities. These linguistic-
pedagogical practices can be seen through specific sites such as setting up
the exclusive schools for imparting education in a particular language
(Irish as opposed to English), writing of the school textbooks with ethical and moral narratives about particular languages (Habsburg monar-
chy) and creation of dictionaries, grammar books, scripts, and societies
(Hungarian academies, Danish language union and Academia Francaise).

LANGUAGE AS IDENTITY

The three forms of practices—enumeration, print, and pedagogy—
affected particular modes of linguistic community identity production as
well as construction and consolidation of the nation-formation in different parts of South Asia. I now return to language as identity—my third
mode of analysis in this chapter. Language as discourse and practice is
intimately related to the question of language as an identity. The question
of linguistic identity has been viewed at multiple levels overlapping with
identities of race, religion, caste, culture, territory, history, and gender. It
is not possible to take into account this vast field of language as identity
in this paper. Elsewhere, I have explored the relationship between language and identity by analysing the gendered evocations as well as representations through narratives of feminization and moralization of
language conflict between Hindi and Urdu in the first half of the

20th century colonial north India (Sarangi 2009, pp. 287–304). Similar kinds of identity discourses have centred around the violent outbursts of antagonism between Tamil and Sinhalese (Sri Lanka), Urdu and Bangla (Bangladesh), Urdu and Sindhi, Saraiki, Baluchi or Pashto (Pakistan), and Tamil and Hindi, and Hindi and Urdu (India) languages in different parts of 20th century South Asia. It is significant to note here as to how the discourse of representation and identification of linguistic differences used narratives of femininity and morality to determine the purity of *language cast as woman*. Such kinds of narratives posited gender equivalence between language and woman by ascribing feminized identity to both of them. A close reading of these narratives illustrates how the multiple discursive and institutionalized forms of gendered linguistic identity unfold. The question of gendered linguistic identity characterizes language as a verbal sign-system that can be extended to the non-verbal sign-systems including the social, political, and cultural spheres (Rossi-Landi 1990; Burke 1987; Burke and Roy 1991).

I suggest the narrativity and dialogicality rendered in the forms of violent exclusivity and ethno-genocidal activity are part of linguistic representation and mediation of the community identity. Narrativization is a form of linguistic identity made possible through selective uses of linguistic symbols and rhetoric. These narratives use language as political object and resource to create linguistic-social differentiation and cultural-political mobilization. Languages become communicative resources used for specific 'political negotiation and persuasion through rhetorical devices, symbolic expressions and performatory speeches, which deliberately select, manipulate or hide meaning and communication' (Grillo 1989, p. 240).

Balibar suggests that language and race together naturalize the individual's historical identity because 'the language community can be more united and self constituted through its mode of discursive communication or a set of linguistic practices' (Balibar 1996, p. 99). A linguistically constructed identity, Balibar argues, is both pre-determinate and open yet not ethnic because

no individual chooses his or her mother tongue or can change it at will…linguistic identity bears a collective ethnic memory at the cost of an individual forgetting of 'origins', because it is always in the element of language that individuals are interpellated as subjects, for every interpellation is of the order of discourse…linguistic identity immediately naturalizes new acquisitions…language community is a community in the present. (Balibar 1996, p. 101)

***

What I have tried to argue above is that by analysing the interaction between language as discourse, practice, and identity as mutually constitutive and reproducible, the category of language can be considered a form of social collectivity. To analyse language as a social collectivity is to signal a point of departure from the methodological approaches that treat language merely as a primordial, instrumental or an objectivist category of analysis. I suggest that social collectivity is, at times, mediated through a process of collectivization and a historically constructed representation in a much hostile manner. What is important, however, in these processes is to see how the social collectivities are politically mobilized, historically processed, and gradually produced as categories of representation taking on the forms of language, kinship, ethnicity, region, or nation.

The category of linguistic nationalism demands particular attention since it has often been used violently for creating boundaries of the nation-states (for example, India, Pakistan, and Bangladesh in South Asia). History shows us that the similar kinds of linguistic-cultural conflicts have appeared world over as being part of larger ethnic conflict in cases such as the standard Mandarin versus Tibetan in case of China or Taiwanese in Taiwan, English versus Afrikaans in South Africa, English and Spanish in USA, English and French in Canada, Arabic or French in Algeria, or Russian versus non-Russian languages in several Central Asian Republics after the disintegration of the former USSR. As Aamir Mufti has rightly suggested that the 'Hindi-Urdu conflict and its attendant myth of two distinct languages continues to be the site for the ongoing partition of South Asian society along religious lines' (Mufti 2010, pp. 63–68). The partition historiography in South Asia has drawn very little attention to the forms of violence manifesting due to the migration, loss, and death of languages, and their communities in their struggle for recovery and survival from the trauma of partition. The stories of rehabilitation and resettlement have to be linked within the narratives of linguistic violence in the everyday lives of refugees who had to learn and live by learning the new languages of the newly created states and nations. They had to navigate in a very subtle way through the vicious circles of religio-linguistic barriers of community identities since the majority of communities turned into unwanted minorities over night. Thus, the territories and borders of these new nation-states disturbed the perennial bonds of linguistic and religious affinities and their cultural locatedness. In the search for the purification of their languages in the new homelands after rescuing them from the worst forms of human violence perpetrated, these language communities began to construct philological, ethnological, and socio-cultural discourses, practices, and identities of the im/purity of the rival languages not without the exercise of distinct forms of violence against them. The idea of community honour and respectable identity found its expression in their linguistic commitments and devotion to their *Matri-Bhasha* (mother tongues) and therefore did not spare even violent efforts to save them. I propose that the question of linguistic–religious violence and the cultural identity in colonial South Asia can be analysed through a plurality of communicative realms, in symbolic, subjective, objective, real, and abstract domains of linguistic and cultural-political discourses, practices, and identities. The study of this kind requires a certain kind of methodological collectivism or pluralism to ascertain the sites and modes of violence and their perpetrators who enact and engage with religio-linguistic and cultural identities as being performative and processual. Violence of this kind leads to linguistic-cultural hierarchies and inequalities which subsequently lead to their communities' exclusion from both material and symbolic markets and denial of certain human capabilities in making choices and decisions about economic, political, cultural, and social life-world, and of authentic cultural self. This has to do with the freedom to choose or reject particular languages and their formal/informal learning on the part of the citizens in the new nation-states. Thus, the forms of violence that linguistic nationalism exhibits are most inhuman in nature exercised over physical and mental beings of human life making it in/communicable and thus unworthy of participating and living the life in its verses of freedom and dignity. Depriving communities of their languages is equal to depriving them from means of communication and culture making them vulnerable to economic and social decay and death. The polysemic text of violence inherent in the contours of linguistic nationalism writes its narratives and accounts through all three dominant modes of language as discourse, practice, and identity, and reproduces the violence of being and becoming a linguistic-cultural being of a certain kind.

ACKNOWLEDGEMENT

It is a revised version of the paper presented at the International Seminar on Religion, Violence, and Language held at the Indian Institute of Advanced Study, Shimla on April 9–11, 2012. I would like to thank Dr Saitya Brata Das for inviting me to this conference, and giving me an opportunity to share my ideas at this conference. I would also like to thank fellow participants for their valuable suggestions on this chapter. However, I solely remain responsible for any errors or omissions in it.

Notes

1. A number of scholars have contributed to this vast and significant field of study which has expanded our understanding of the regional histories and their social-cultural bases of community identity and politics during the era of nationalism in different parts of the country.

2. Lisa Mitchell (2009, pp. 213–18) shows this in case of the Telegu language in colonial India.

3. Humboldt argued that German educational system needed to be reformed to coincide with the linguistic structure of the society. He therefore constructed the category of *Bildung* which would 'replace the old form of aristocracy based on the estate and genealogy with one based on the cultivation of spirit and bound with the idea of emancipation and citizenship.' A German word *Bildung* referred to the totality of means used by humans in their efforts to improve life and thus consists of those qualities and virtues which are required for the preservation of race and its people who should inhabit a certain style of culture and morals. *Bildung*, in Humboldt's view, would define and demarcate linguistic-cultural communities as homogeneous communities (Grossman 1997, pp. 23–47).

4. The ideology of linguistic nationalism in colonial India did have Herderian vision of a nationality based on language. The nationalists did not aim at marginalizing or substituting one language by another. In their view, languages presented distinct worldviews and social epistemologies. Language for them, as for Herder, embodied the culture, consciousness and mentality of people and nation. However, it is important to note that these nationalists were themselves multi-lingual and multi-regional, and spoke different languages on different occasions (Ergang 1931; Morton 1989; Berlin 1976).

5. Gal and Irvine (1995) argue how the ideological uses of a language impact the institutions of family, schools, courts, and nation-states. They suggest how particular linguistic ideologies provide 'rationalization, coherence, order, and boundaries maintained through maps, grammars, and monographs.'

6. Gramsci argues that grammar as a historical document is embedded and produced within specific socio-cultural context of capitalistic historical

formation. The struggle for national language, in his view, is fought in the educational system, newspapers, theater, films, public meetings, religious meetings, local dialects, speeches, and conversations (see 'Language, Linguistics and Folklore', Gramsci et al. 1985).

7. In my understanding and conceptualization of language as practice, I have been greatly influenced by the Marxist category of labour interpreted most accurately and forcefully in Moishe Postone's writings (Postone 1993).

8. Charles Taylor argues that language 'expresses and constitutes the self' through certain communicative practices (Taylor 1985).

References

Anderson, Benedict, *Imagined Communities: Reflections on the Origin and Spread of Nationalism* (London: Verso, 1991).

Ayres, Alyssa, *Speaking Like a State: Language and Nation in Pakistan* (Cambridge, UK: Cambridge University Press, 2009).

Bakhtin, M.M., *The Dialogical Imagination: Four Essays* (Austin: University of Texas Press, 1981).

Balibar, E., 'The Nation-Form' in Suny, Ronald (ed.), *Becoming National: A Reader* (New York: Oxford University Press, 1996).

Benjamin, Walter, 'On Language as Such and on the Language of Man' in Demetz, Peter (ed.), *Walter Benjamin, Reflections: Essays, Aphorisms, Autobiographical Writings*, (New York: Shocken Books, 1986).

Berlin, Isaiah, *Vico and Herder: Two Studies in the History of Ideas* (New York: Vintage, 1976).

Bourdieu and Wacquant, *An Invitation to Reflexive Sociology* (Chicago: University of Chicago Press, 1992).

Bourdieu, P., *Language and Symbolic Power* (Cambridge: Harvard University Press, 1991).

———, 'The Economics of Linguistic Exchange' in *Social Science Information*, 16 (1977).

Burke, Peter, *The Social History of Language* (Harvard: Cambridge University Press, 1987).

Burke, Peter and Porter Roy (ed.) *Language, Self and Society: A Social History of Language* (London: Polity Press, 1991).

Duranti, Alessandro, *Linguistic Anthropology* (Cambridge: Cambridge University Press, 1997).

Ergang, Robert R., *Herder and the Foundations of German Nationalism* (New York: Columbia University Press, 1931).

Fabian, Johannes, *Language and Colonial Power: The Appropriation of Swahili in the Former Belgian Congo 1880–1938* (Cambridge: Harvard University Press, 1986).

Fichte, 'Nation Form' in Etienne Balibar (ed.), *Masses, Classes, Ideas: Studies on Politics and Philosophy Before and After Marx* (London: Routledge, 1994).

Gal, Susan and Irvine, Judith, 'The Boundaries of Languages and Disciplines: How Ideologies Construct Difference' *Social Research* (Winter, 1995): 967–1001.

Gramsci, Antonio, Forgas, David and Smith, G.N., (ed.) *Antonio Gramsci: Selections from Cultural Writings* (Cambridge: Harvard University Press, 1985).

Grillo, Ralph (ed.) *Social Anthropology and the Politics of Language* (London: Routledge, 1989).

Grossman, Jeffrey., 'Wilhelm Von Humboldt's Linguistic Ideology: The Problem of Pluralism and Absolute Difference of National Character or Where do the Jews fit in?' *German Studies Review*, Vol. 20:1 (February 1997). pp. 23–47.

Marx, Karl, 'German Ideology' in Robert C. Tucker (ed.) *The Marx-Engels Reader* (New York: Norton, 1972).

Marx, Karl and Engels, Frederich. *The Marx-Engels Reader* (New York: Norton, 1972).

Mir, Farina, *The Social Space of Language: Vernacular Culture in the British Colonial Punjab* (CA: University of California Press, 2010).

Mitchell, Lisa, *Language, Emotion and Politics in South India: The Making of a Mother Tongue* (Bloomington, IN: Indiana University Press, 2009).

Morton, Michael, *Herder and the Poetics of Thought: Unity and Diversity in Diligence in Several Languages* (Philadelphia: The Pennsylvania University Press, 1989).

Mufti Aamir R, 'Orientalism and the Language of Hindustan', *Critical Quarterly*, Vol 52, No 3. 2010, pp. 63–8.

Pollock, Sheldon, *Literary Cultures in History: Reconstructions from South Asia* (New Delhi: Oxford University Press, 2004).

Postone, Moishe, *Time, Labor and Social Domination: A Reinterpretation of Marx's Critical Theory* (Cambridge: Cambridge University Press, 1993).

Rossi-Landi, F., *Marxism and Ideology* (London: Clarendon Press, 1990).

Sarangi, Asha, 'Languages as Women: The Feminisation of Linguistic Discourses in Colonial North India', *Gender and History*, Vol 21, No 2, August 2009

Taylor, Charles, *Human Agency and Language: Philosophical Papers*, Vol. 1 (Cambridge: Cambridge University Press, 1985).

Turner, Terence, 'Representing, Resisting, Rethinking: Historical Transformations of Kayapo Culture and Anthropological Consciousness', in George W. Stocking (ed.), *Colonial Situations: Essays on the Contextualization of Ethnographic Knowledge* (Madison: University of Wisconsin Press, 1991).

Voloshinov, V.N., *Marxism and the Philosophy of Language*, translated by Ladislav Matejka and I.R. Titunik (Cambridge: Harvard University Press, 1986).

Zizek, Slavoj. *Violence: Six Sideways Reflections* (London: Profile Books, 2009).

13 The Violence of Linguistic Cosmopolitanism

Selma K. Sonntag

Cosmopolitanism, ever since Kant, has promised to offer peace over violence in human interactions with the Stranger. It promises to erase the primordial violence that has doomed humankind since the Tower of Babel. In the current era of globalization, where interactions with the Other have multiplied through the compression of time and space, the appeal of cosmopolitanism is its promise to end the violence of parochialism and of parochialism's political form, nationalism. Contemporary cosmopolitanism's negation of primordial violence has become a universal narrative of salvation, transcending political and ideological divides. On one side of the divide, neo-liberals, celebrating free-market globalization as the end of history, point to the journalist Thomas Friedman's McDonald's theory of peace: countries that have globalized economically and, by extension, culturally—countries that have, tongue-in-cheek, McDonald's fast food outlets—don't go to war against each other. Friedman (1999; 2006) is perhaps the best known spokesman for neo-liberal cosmopolitanism, seeing it as an accompaniment of globalization, a force to end violence. Yet Friedman's critics, who despair at the violence of neo-liberal global capitalism itself, also find salvation in cosmopolitanism. Many of them post-modern theorists, these 'critical cosmopolitans' (Robbins 1998, p. 8) tend to see cosmopolitanism as 'a philosophical project ... follow[ing] the Kantian tradition in thinking of cosmopolitanism as the emergence of norms that ought to govern relations among individuals in a global civil society' (Benhabib 2006, p. 20). It is a normative project of globalization-from-below, carried out by cosmopolitan individuals coming together in global civil society. As such, critical cosmopolitanism seeks to dispel the violence of a Westphalian, capitalist system (see, e.g., Pollock et al., 2000).

These two contemporary, and frequently opposing, cosmopolitanisms are grounded in projects outside of the state, outside of statist politics, and governmentality: one embraces the global marketplace as the succour to end violence; the other hopes for a global society of civility as the antidote to violence.[1] Both posit cosmopolitanism as different from, untainted by, and the alternative to the nation-state and its attendant violence in its political and/or economic form—as 'unmarked by particularity and politics' (Honig 2006, p. 116). The normative quest of contemporary cosmopolitanism is meant to solve hostility between states in its neo-liberal Friedmanite variation or within states according to critical cosmopolitanism, by separating the solution to violence (market, civil society) from the alleged source of violence (state nationalism and/or capitalism). By expunging the source of violence from the solution to violence, I argue, cosmopolitanism fails in its normative quest. By assuming that 'hospitality' (i.e., cosmopolitanism) is ontologically separable from the 'hostility' (violence) inherent in the political economy of nationalism, these contemporary cosmopolitanisms cannot, despite their claims, nullify the possibility of violence. As Bonnie Honig (2006, p. 105–6) puts it, in employing a Derridian critique, 'neo-Kantian cosmopolitanism' is problematic because it 'insistently identifies *hostility* with one singular principle—[…] state nationalism—and *hospitality* with another that is distinct and apart—Enlightenment universalism' (Honig 2006, p. 105–6,; emphasis in original).

I will make my argument by focusing on linguistic cosmopolitanism. Language plays multiple roles in cosmopolitanism. As a medium of human social interaction, it is principally through language that the cosmopolitan 'engages the Other,' enabling the cosmopolitan's 'intellectual and aesthetic stance of openness toward divergent cultural experiences' (Hannerz 1990, p. 239). In the past, artificial languages such as Esperanto were developed for this cosmopolitan purpose. But language is also a marker of identity. In this sense, then, language provides a window to the Other's culture, enabling the cosmopolitan to understand and empathize with the Other. While the Other may be originally, culturally, and linguistically different from the cosmopolitan Self, the assumption is that cosmopolitanism belies essentializing and ossifying those differences (Appiah 1994, p. 163). Hence while a language may be a marker of particular identity, it is only superficially so—language is inherently creative, socially constructed, and ultimately politically neutral if a cosmopolitan way of being is embraced. The cosmopolitan worries that language which does not perform this Habermasian communication—i.e., language that entraps individuals in a parochial, communal (including nationalist) identity—can provide an *a priori* excuse for violence. I will argue that this cosmopolitan understanding of language is problematic: it cannot and does not achieve cosmopolitanism's normative quest to nullify linguistic violence. The problem stems from cosmopolitans assuming that the communicative function of language is ontologically separable from its affective function, i.e., that the communicative 'hospitality' of language is different from—and can be a solution for—the 'hostility' or violence of linguistic identity. I will suggest that the Indian case offers a more nuanced understanding of linguistic cosmopolitanism, given its situated linguistic diversity in the context of a democratic postcolonial state. Critical to my account of linguistic cosmopolitanism in India is what Partha Chatterjee (2004) calls the 'politics of the governed.'

LINGUISTIC COSMOPOLITANISM

The dichotomy of language as a medium of communication and language as a marker of identity is well entrenched in Western philosophy. Peter Ives (forthcoming) traces it back to the Lockean versus Herderian, or liberal versus romanticist, view of language. Linguistic cosmopolitanism seeks to reconcile these two understandings of language. But it fails to do so because, while cosmopolitanism recognizes that language can be a marker of a particular identity, it nonetheless denies the validity of any political claims based on linguistic identity. The justification for this denial is an abhorrence of the violence associated with primordial linguistic identity. Yet this denial prioritizes the communicative (universal) function of language over language as an identity marker (the particular). Hence, in its attempts to expunge the primordial violence of affective linguistic identity, linguistic cosmopolitanism engages in the 'violence of assimilation' (Baker 2009, p. 109). To make this argument about the violence of linguistic cosmopolitanism, we need to explore more fully the linguistic dimension of cosmopolitanism.

In one sense, linguistic cosmopolitanism defines itself as multilingualism, either on an individual or societal level. In this sense, linguistic cosmopolitanism is a celebration of cultural and linguistic diversity. A cosmopolitan individual (the Cosmopolitan Self) and cosmopolitan spaces (New York, London, Toronto) are marked by multiculturalism and multilingualism. As Naomi Hodgson (2009, p. 181–3) has pointed out, multicultural democratic societies are assumed to be cosmopolitan. An open civil society in which multiple languages are in use supposes at minimum an exposure to the Other, a 'getting used to each other,' a predecessor to the more cosmopolitan 'level of sympathetic engagement' by the multilingual Cosmopolitan Self (Jalais 2010, p. 200).

This rather facile, celebratory view of multilingualism as inherently cosmopolitan is complicated by a more critical cosmopolitanism. Multilingualism in U.S. society, for example, has triggered fear rather than celebration (Cohen 2001, chapters 6 &7). American multilingualism is the product of what Pollock et al. (2000, p. 582) call 'minoritarian cosmopolitans,' the disenfranchised immigrants. For these cosmopolitans, engagement or interaction with the Other is often steeped in violence. The most salient image of this violence is of deportations, beatings, and humiliations. In the U.S., economic pressure, the push-and-pull of the market, ensures that only recent immigrants are polyglots: immigrants all learn English for instrumental reasons—to the extent that their mother-tongues are lost by the third generation. While neo-liberal cosmopolitans celebrate the triumph of the market in this case, critical cosmopolitans bemoan that the immigrant as multilingual cosmopolitan is rendered the monolingual marginalized. Critical cosmopolitans argue it is the political economy of the modern nation-state that enables this violence of marginalization, side-lining in their analysis the linguistic aspects of the violence of assimilation.

The linguistic project of the nation-state, so well documented and described by historians of nationalism such as Gellner, Hobsbawm, and Anderson, inculpated the violence of assimilation. It precluded and destroyed for the most part multilingualism in the national context. The national project, at least in the West, entailed a national language, a Herderian one-language-equals-one-state. While the nation-building process itself was violent (see Sarangi's chapter in this volume for more detail), linguistic uniformity facilitated solidarity as a foundation for the emergence of a liberal democratic state. Democratic consensus was/is maintained through solidarity, the 'fraternité' of the French revolution. In its modern (i.e., post-WWII) European variant, national democratic consensus underpinned a redistributive political economy, a social democracy model that mitigated the violence of capitalism. The medium of democratic consensus was a common (national) language. Here the function of a common language is purely instrumental: A liberal democratic state 'may support a common language to the degree that this language is instrumental to achieving justified public purposes' (Stilz 2009, p. 258). Yet a common language is an effective instrument for social democratic purposes because it also creates and maintains affective solidarity, needed for a redistributive political economy (see Barbier 2012). In a globalized world, in which states are increasingly marked by multilingualism and multiculturalism, many fear that this affective solidarity needed for a consensus on redistributive policies is being undermined. Hence the linguistic cosmopolitan project of (re)creating solidarity through democratic communication in an enlarged, more inclusive forum of global civil society. However, as Baker (2009, p. 109) notes, there is no guarantee that this process of building global civil society will be any less violent than the nation-state building process was, precisely because 'the concept of global civil society shares the same fundamental problem as state sovereignty, namely that it is better at articulating global identity than difference because it reproduces in different form statist attempts to describe a universal structure of particularity.' In linguistic terms, this suggests that linguistic cosmopolitanism, by prioritizing the communicative function of language and subsuming the affective (which Derrida would claim, according to Baker (2009) and Honig (2006), is problematic if not impossible), ends up re-enacting the violence of assimilation inherent in the national project.

The dual functionality of language—its affective, Herderian function and its liberal, instrumental function—produced, in general and in ideal form in the context of nationalism, monolingual societies. For linguistic cosmopolitans, the affective base of language, language as identity, while allowing for sympathetic engagement with the Other, feeds the parochial violence of the nation-state, i.e., the violence and hostility of monolingual nationalism that cosmopolitanism promises to erase. Cosmopolitans try to escape this paradox by latching on to the instrumental work of a common language, embracing a normative project of a neutral, de-nationalized language. For neo-liberal cosmopolitanism,

English has become the language of the global marketplace. For critical cosmopolitans, who welcome the emergence of a global civil society to offset powerful global economic actors, overcoming the democratic deficit inherent in globalization is the imperative normative project of the day (see, e.g., Held 1995). For them, the cosmopolitan project is to create democratic institutions at the global level 'which enable the voice of individuals to be heard in global affairs' (Archibugi 2003, p. 8). A common language performs this enabling. Daniele Archibugi (2005), a cosmopolitan democrat who seriously addresses the language question inherent in global democratic deliberation, promotes Esperanto as a cosmopolitan-type solution. Peter Ives (2009, p. 520) maintains that Archibugi's 'use of Esperanto as a metaphor for how cosmopolitanism must address [the] language problem' of global democracy is in effect 'none other than an advocacy of global English for cosmopolitan democracy.'

In this linguistic cosmopolitan vision, English predominates because English is valued as a tool, and not as a marker of a particular identity. English as a language is changing, many sociolinguists argue, and shedding its exclusive association with and ownership by Anglophone nations. English as a tool of international communication is different from the English language as a marker of identity for Anglophones. It is becoming, many claim, a neutral language for purposes of international or global communication (see, e.g., House 2003; Jenkins 2007). As such, Juliane House (2003) argues, English as a lingua franca is not a threat to linguistic diversity.[2] For Braj Kachru, the doyen of the 'World Englishes' approach, the increasing number of English(es), from Nigerian to Indian to Canadian, is an indication of multilingualism at the global level (see, e.g., Kachru 1992).

LINGUISTIC COSMOPOLITANISM IN INDIA

How do these notions of linguistic cosmopolitanism play out in India? India seems to have an inherent affinity for linguistic cosmopolitanism, based on the simplistic definition of cosmopolitanism as cultural/linguistic diversity. In this case of linguistic cosmopolitanism as multilingualism, if linguistic cosmopolitanism mitigates or nullifies violence, then India should be relatively free of linguistic violence. Indeed, a number of scholars have made this claim for at least independent India (e.g., Brass 2010, p. 213; Guha 2007, p. 208). Yet at independence, India embarked on a nation-building project. Does the promise of linguistic cosmopolitanism to erase primordial violence incited by nationalism and/or parochialism hold in India? I will first address linguistic nationalism in India to provide a historical context for examining current claims of linguistic cosmopolitanism.

Hindi Nationalism

Tharakeshwar (2011, p. 190) comments that whereas '[n]ationalism in Europe is predominantly based on language ... in the Indian subcontinent, we witness different communities getting envisaged/imagined on the basis of various other issues/factors.' As noted above, a common language is seen as the basis not only for national identity in the European context, but also for solidarity and democratic consensus. If language does not play that role in India, what does? Some would point to religion. But religion in India is not necessarily monolithic or dogmatic. For Mahatma Gandhi, an inclusive spirituality based on Hinduism could provide the symbiosis, the sense of community in India's villages, needed for non-violent redistribution of material goods (limited in both necessity and actuality though such goods were in Gandhi's vision) and social harmony in an independent India. Some would argue that the Gandhian basis of solidarity was marginalized in the post-colonial period. Instead, especially in recent decades, a more violent Hindutva has been promoted as the basis of solidarity. Gandhi recognized that one of the more violent aspects of Hindu nationalism manifested itself linguistically. At least in north India, Hindu nationalism was equated with Hindi nationalism (see, e.g., Rai 2000). Gandhi inveighed against an exclusionary Sanskritized, 'pakka' Hindi as the national language, arguing for the more inclusionary, colloquial Hindustani. For what was being excluded from Hindi was Urdu, increasingly assigned the label of a Muslim language.

In many ways, then, the politics of Hindi at the time of independence resembled the linguistic nationalism of much of 19th century Europe. In both cases, landed elites made common cause with cultural traditionalists and revivalists. But Hindi nationalism differed from linguistic nationalism in Europe in one important sense: the linguistic diversity of India. This diversity was more than dialectal (as was the case, arguably, in European nation-states); it was a diversity of languages from vastly different language families (primarily Indo-Aryan and Dravidian), many of which had rich literary traditions.

India's linguistic diversity factored into what Granville Austin (1966, chap. 12) has called a 'half-hearted compromise' and Krishna Kumar (1991) has called 'a foul contract' at the time of India's independence. The framers of India's constitution agreed to Hindi (and not Hindustani) becoming the official, but not the national, language of India, with English having 'associate' official language status. The compromise or contract was, in essence, between the traditional landed elite cum cultural nationalists and the Nehruvian English-speaking urban professionals, marginalizing the Gandhian alternative (a pro-Hindustani, anti-English alternative) in the process. It was Tamil speakers from south India who ensured that English was retained as an associate official language by violently protesting against the parochialism of Hindi masquerading as the linguistic basis for national solidarity. To a large extent, the debate over Hindi nationalism has been eclipsed by the debate over English in India.

English in India

Cosmopolitan notions of language are continually referenced in the debate over English in India. India's economic liberalization since 1991 has meant that neo-liberal cosmopolitan views on language have dominated this debate. However, given India's linguistic diversity, a tradition of 'rooted' cosmopolitanism, with conceptual links to what we identified as critical cosmopolitanism above, has inflected the debate as well. In examining a recent controversy in Karnataka over the medium of instruction in schools, I illustrate how both the pro-Kannada and pro-English sides of the controversy invoke linguistic cosmopolitanism.[3]

The Kannada-versus-English controversy was sparked in 2006, when the Karnataka state government invoked a 1994 directive stipulating the state official language, Kannada, as medium of instruction at the primary school level. The government action was directed against English-medium schools, resulting in over 2,000 schools, most in Bangalore (now Bengaluru), the 'Silicon Valley' of India and Karnataka's state capital, being 'derecognized.' The schools fought back, arguing that as private entities they were exempt from the state's policy. In the summer of 2008, the High Court of the State of Karnataka handed down a verdict favouring the English-medium schools. The state government appealed to the Supreme Court, where the case lingered, given the protracted legal drama: requests for stays have been denied, contempts of court have been issued, and hearings have been adjourned. In the meantime, the Karnataka state government itself has gotten into the business of establishing English-medium schools.

Supporters of the English-medium schools tap into the neo-liberal cosmopolitan discourse. They associate cosmopolitanism with globalization, and Bangalore with both. A facet of this globalization, particularly visible in Bangalore, is linguistic: English facilitates global integration, enabling middle-class Indians with English-language skills to identify with a cosmopolitan life-style. English is viewed as a neutral tool or skill, to be readily accessed as India enters into the global economy. While Kannada is acknowledged to have a rich literary history, flourishing in pre-colonial times, it is valued for its history and tradition, in a particular time and locale.

Nandan Nilekani, the co-founder of Infosys, one of India's premier IT (informational technology) and BPO (business process outsourcing) companies, and a good friend of Thomas Friedman, champions the pro-English cause in his 2008 book, *Imagining India*. According to Nilekani, English in India today is 'a symbol … of an economy come of age' (2008, p. 78). English is a global, cosmopolitan language: 'the language of international business[,] … science and research' (Nilekani 2008, p. 92). It is also a skill, a 'key,' or 'passport' critical for 'upward mobility' (Nilekani 2008, p. 91, 89, 88). In contrast, Nilekani (2008, p. 91) depicts supporters of Kannada in the controversy as 'chauvinistic' and ideologically and politically motivated, implying that ideology and politics are parochial and hence a potential source of violence.

Part of Nilekani's accusation of the politically hostile nature of pro-Kannada forces is the claim that they are denying access to English to those who have historically been the victims of violence in Indian society, in particular Dalits. Indeed, Dalit activists have been strong advocates of English-medium schools in Karnataka (Raghu 2007; Srinivasaraju 2008, p. 51). The well-known Dalit academician and activist, Kancha Ilaiah, from the neighbouring state of Andhra Pradesh, has presented the Dalit case for English:

Over time, English has become the common language of the global science and technology market and the overall economy. As Government schools do not teach in English medium, those who study in them are denied the opportunities given to their richer counterparts in English medium schools. Students in regional language schools cannot therefore think of achieving anything in the globalised economy. (Ilaiah 2007)

Ilaiah's invocation of English as the 'common language' of a global community marks his discourse as cosmopolitan. His claim that 'the divide between the English medium schools and the regional [local] language schools is a caste-class divide' (Ilaiah 2007) identifies his voice, not surprisingly, as a minoritarian or critical cosmopolitan. The Dalit solution is to overcome the caste-class divide by the marginalized taking possession of the tool of exclusion, English. As the president of a Dalit association in Karnataka, the Karnataka Dalit Sangharsh Samiti, puts it: 'The middle class and the rich can afford to send their children to private schools. For the poor, the only option is government schools. Then why should the poor be denied an opportunity to learn English?' (quoted in Raghu 2007). English is seen as empowering the powerless and a necessary tool for upward mobility.

This empowerment of and upward mobility for the individual allegedly happens through the global marketplace. Hence the Dalit solution to the violence of caste and class dovetails with the neo-liberal solution, making this linguistic cosmopolitan narrative particularly persuasive in the Indian context. According to this narrative, English liberates the individual from parochial, caste-based identity—and from the violence inherent in that identity. This market-based, neo-liberal cosmopolitanism does not transform social hierarchies in which those identities are embedded. Accordingly, individuals can remain entrapped in a parochial, communal identity, reacting violently to the increasingly globalized, cosmopolitan world around them—these are Nilekani's Kannada chauvinists. Similarly, Dalit leaders accuse Kannada supporters who oppose English in state schools of being 'regressive and biased' (Raghu 2007). Dalit leaders seem to have bought into the pretence of the market (i.e., English) as distinct from and a solution to—rather than reflective of—the violence of marginalization. This false dichotomy, characteristic of cosmopolitanism as we saw above, fuels a promise of erasing this violence that cannot be kept.

In contrast to neo-liberal linguistic cosmopolitanism espoused by the pro-English forces in the Karnataka controversy, another version of linguistic cosmopolitanism is evoked by at least some of the pro-Kannada activists. This alternative cosmopolitanism tends to be wary of any claims of neutrality of the state or market and, hence, of language being a neutral tool. Its linguistic ideology eschews the instrumental for the affective primacy of language. India's multilingualism is the cosmopolitan context that needs to be preserved. The main champions of this cosmopolitanism are writers and literati with an aesthetic appreciation of language. Usually identified as local—and hence parochial—language advocates, their challenge is to prove their cosmopolitan credentials.

Exemplary of this other linguistic cosmopolitanism, the journalist and translator Sugata Srinivasaraju (2008) titles his book (in English), *Keeping faith with the mother tongue*. For Srinivasaraju, this faith is linked to a commitment to linguistic diversity, which informs his reflections on 'the anxieties of a local culture' (the subtitle of his book). Drawing inspiration from the Kannadiga literary critic and colleague of critical cosmopolitans (Pollock & Breckenridge 2000), D.R. Nagaraj, Srinivasaraju (2008, p. 42) imagines '*Karnatakatva* [Karnataka culturalism] as one of the authentic forms of protest against global monoculture that is developing as a result of growing capitalism.' However, in his imagining, it is not a reactionary, parochial response to the violence of neo-liberal globalization. Instead Srinivasaraju (2008, p. 16) 'argues for an active networking of global minority tongues.' It is a cosmopolitan message that resonates beyond the parochialness of Kannada speakers. For Srinivasaraju (2008, p. 22), local language identities can 'magically create common pursuits' just as often as they can 'deter and destroy them.' Srinivasaraju suggests that language as affective identity is a universal rather than a particularist and xenophobic human attribute.

Srinivasaraju's imagining of Karnatakatva as the basis for this different linguistic cosmopolitanism has historical precedent. K.S. Dakshina Murthy (2006, p. 1834) notes how Karnataka had a linguistic 'cosmopolitan structure' compared to the more nationalist Andhra Pradesh and Tamil Nadu. Tharakeshwar (2011, p. 193–4) describes the conception of Karnatakatva espoused by Alur Venkatarao, a Karnataka leader during the anti-colonial struggle. For Venkatarao, Karnatakatva was the center circle of three non-hierarchical concentric circles, the other two being India and the world. Venkatarao describes Karnatakatva as 'a lens through which we look at India and the world' (Tharakeshwar 2011, p. 193). Tharakeshwar argues that this outlook of Venkatarao—what we might define as 'rooted' cosmopolitanism—was not inimical to Indian nationalism.

A contemporary literatus equivalent of Venkatarao would be the acclaimed Kannada writer, U.R. Ananthamurthy, author of *Samskara*. Clearly an advocate of Kannada in the current controversy, Ananthamurthy is not against English per se, but worries about English becoming an end in itself. In Derridian terms, we could say that Ananthamurthy worries about the 'perverse effects' of unlimited hospitality—the loss of home itself' (Baker 2009, p. 122, referencing Derrida). This 'risk of dispossession' (Honig 2006, p. 106)—in this case, the loss of affective identity with Kannada—is itself a hostility or violence. For 'without a home[,] we cannot practice hospitality at all' (Baker 2009, p. 122). Ananthamurthy is hospitable to English: he proposes an engagement of students with spoken English. This engagement is a way of being in the world, an espousal of a linguistic cosmopolitanism. But student literacy and analytical skills should be in the mother tongue or Kannada.[4] Like Venkatarao, we may consider Ananthamurty's cosmopolitanism as a rooted or *namak-halaal*—a 'nation-oriented' or 'compatriot'—cosmopolitanism, different from the post-modern/post-colonial cosmopolitanism of Indian writers who write in English (Jani 2010, p. 17, 21).

THE POLITICS OF THE GOVERNED

Pranav Jani (2010, p. 8) argues that both namak-halaal and postnational cosmopolitanism 'seek to develop a critical consciousness'—i.e., are more attuned to critical cosmopolitanism than to neo-liberal cosmopolitanism—but only namak-halaal, or rooted, cosmopolitans recognize 'the need for solidarity whereas postnational ones question its possibility.' For the postmodern cosmopolitan, 'History and Power are portrayed as so overwhelming and transcendent that only the solitary, migrant, protagonist/storyteller/writer can have agency' (Jani 2010, p. 8). Hence, postnational linguistic cosmopolitanism is an individualized cosmopolitanism that feeds back into the liberalism of individual choice in language, allying itself with the linguistic cosmopolitanism that underlies Dalit claims for access to English language skills. In postnational cosmopolitanism, language is more of an individually attained skill than a critical political endeavour. By failing to reconcile the instrumental and affective claims of language, this critical cosmopolitanism is rendered apolitical, unable to validate political claims based on linguistic identity.[5]

Do Jani's namak-halaal cosmopolitans, by relying on a national ethos (and, as we saw in the case of India, this often is a Hindutva-tinged ethos), risk primordial violence as the price to pay for a politics of solidarity? A reversion to primordial violence has dogged the pro-Kannada side of the Karnataka controversy (see, e.g., Nair 2009). Yet this potential of violence does not necessarily stem from nationalism (to which, as we saw above, contemporary cosmopolitanisms, of either the neo-liberal or critical variety, pose as the antidote). According to Partha Chatterjee (2004), in the postnational state, politics is no longer necessarily a national project. Drawing on Foucault, Chatterjee argues that 'political society [is] ... a site of negotiation and contestation opened up by the activities of governmental agencies aimed at population groups' (Chatterjee 2004, p. 74). Hence, although often only national communities are 'conferred legitimacy within the domain of the modern state,' today 'the activities of governmental functions produce numerous classes of actual populations that come together to act politically' (Chatterjee 2004, p. 75). This is Chatterjee's 'politics of the governed.' For Chatterjee (2004, p. 57), a 'crucial part of the politics of the governed [is] to give the empirical form of a population group the moral attributes of a community' (Chatterjee 2004, p. 57). Accordingly, 'there are many imaginative possibilities for transforming an empirically assembled population group into the morally constituted form of a community' and 'it is both unrealistic and irresponsible to condemn all such political transformations as divisive and dangerous' (Chatterjee 2004, p. 75).

If the population target can garner the 'moral content of community,' then it can 'effectively make its claim in political society' (Chatterjee 2004, p. 75). Kannada speakers are an officially enumerated population group, as are other regional-language speakers in India, according to the 1956 linguistic Reorganization of States Act and the Eighth Schedule of the Indian Constitution listing official languages. More recently, in late 2008, Kannada was given 'classical language status'—a further central governmental linguistic categorization/grouping that carries a high degree of prestige. These political enumerations reflect India's linguistic diversity, i.e., its 'inherent' linguistic cosmopolitanism. They are policy instruments of linguistic governmentality, providing the political space for investing Kannada speakers with the 'moral content of a community' (see also Nair 2009, p. 378). Imbuing that moral content with a commitment to hospitality—that is, politically transforming it into a cosmopolitan community—does not expunge linguistic violence, but instead subjects the possibility of violence to the politics of the governed.

Nair (2009, p. 381) references D.R. Nagaraj to point out that governmental enumeration of Kannada speakers has led to a demographic fear-mongering on the part of at least some Kannada activists. The victims of this mongering have been Tamils and other linguistic minorities, particularly immigrant minorities, in the state. A politics-of-the-governed linguistic cosmopolitanism must start with recognizing and engaging the internal linguistic heterogeneity within Karnataka, rather than framing the struggle as one between Kannada and English. Bangalore is a linguistically cosmopolitan city, not just because of the IT and BPO sector, but also because of the informal, unskilled labour market of sweatshops and construction work. In a field visit in August 2008 to a private Kannada-medium primary school in Bangalore, run by charity, I was struck by the linguistic diversity of the students. These students had a variety of mother tongues: Tamil, Marathi, Telugu, Hindi, Malayalam, etc. Their parents are the lowest-of-the-low, the Dalit immigrants, many working in the garment sweatshops tucked away in the slums. It is essential to not repeat for these children the experience of the Dalit academic and pro-English activist Kancha Ilaiah: 'Textbook Telugu was Brahmin Telugu, where we were used to a production based communicative Telugu. In a word, our alienation from the Telugu textbook was more or less the same as it was from the English textbook in terms of language and content' (quoted in Mukherjee, 2008, p. 4).

A 'politics of the governed' would mean recognizing and celebrating the cosmopolitan character of—the linguistic diversity inherent in—a Kannada-medium school and, in a more general sense, of a cosmopolitan city such as Bangalore. Until Kannada speakers can garner the 'moral content of community,' they cannot 'effectively make its claim in political society' (Chatterjee 2004, p. 75). Cosmopolitan norms are 'morally constructive' (Benhabib 2006, p. 72), not against the state but rather structured by the state. In India that structure is language-based, yielding the potential for linguistic hospitality/cosmopolitanism but always risking the possibility of linguistic hostility or violence.

***

Linguistic cosmopolitanism as a normative non-political project is incapable of offering an alternative to the primordial violence which it seeks to expunge. This inability stems from a lack of reconciliation between affective and instrumental functions of language, rendering most versions of linguistic cosmopolitanism dependent upon an apolitical, individualized, neutralized understanding of language. What is needed is a more political cosmopolitanism: a cosmopolitanism which continually questions politically the conditions of cosmopolitanism and hence the moral content of the home from which the world is engaged. It requires a politics of the governed. Such cosmopolitanism questions violence, knowing it cannot expunge it. In terms of linguistic cosmopolitanism, the Indian case helps us understand and contain linguistic violence without the false pretense of ridding the world of it.

Notes

1. This liberal reasoning seems to have been the basis for the Karnataka High Court decision in the summer of 2008 against the state government mandating Kannada as the medium of instruction in what are essentially *private* schools. The court's decision repeatedly referred to the freedom of parents to make choices for their children, i.e., the freedom of the individual and, by extension, the market based on individual choices ('No Coercion on Medium of Instruction', *Times of India*, 2008).

2. It is important to note that 'critical sociolinguistics' launches a variety of critiques against the English-as-a-lingua-franca camp. It is impossible here to diverge into a discussion of these critiques. See Sonntag (2010) for a thorough discussion.

3. I have offered a similar analysis of language politics in Karnataka in a forthcoming article. See Sonntag, forthcoming.

4. U.R. Ananthamurthy, personal communication (Bangalore, 3 August 2008).

5. An example of adopting an instrumental rather than political ideology of language comes from a student hunger strike in March 2012 at Jawaharlal Nehru University in New Delhi. One of the demands the student activists made was 'elimination of the language barrier' through translating texts and study materials from English into Hindi and other major languages of India. In an informal interview I conducted with one of the hunger strikers, the student activist defined the problem in terms of access to social science texts currently

available only in English. The activist offered absolutely no political critique of the linguistic production of knowledge, despite being from a radical leftist student group.

References

Appiah, Kwame Anthony, 'Identity, Authenticity, Survival: Multicultural Societies and Social Reproduction,' in Gutmann, Amy (ed), *Multiculturalism: Examining the Politics of Recognition* (Princeton: Princeton University Press, 1994), pp. 149–163.

Archibugi, Daniele, 'Cosmopolitical Democracy' in Archibugi, D. (ed), *Debating Cosmopolitics* (London: Verso, 2003), pp. 1–15.

———, 'The Language of Democracy: Vernacular or Esperanto? A Comparison between the Multiculturalist and Cosmopolitan Perspectives,' *Political Studies*, vol. 53, (2005), pp. 537–55.

Austin, Granville, *The Indian Constitution: Cornerstone of a Nation* (Bombay: Oxford University Press, 1966).

Baker, Gideon, 'Cosmopolitanism as Hospitality: Revisiting Identity and Difference in Cosmopolitanism,' *Alternatives: Global, Local, Political*, vol. 24 (2009), pp. 107–128.

Barbier, Jean-Claude, 'Languages, Political Cultures and Solidarity in Europe,' Online Working Paper No. 01, Recode (Responding to complex Diversity in Europe and Canada) Working Paper Series, 2012 (www.recode.fi; www.esf.org/recode).

Benhabib, Seyla, *Another Cosmopolitanism* (New York: Oxford UniversityPress, 2006).

Brass, Paul R, 'Elite Interests, Popular Passions, and Social Power in the Language Politis of India' in Sarangi, Asha (ed), *Language and Politics India* (New Delhi: Oxford University Press, 2010), pp. 183–217.

Chatterjee, Partha, *The Politics of the Governed* (New York: Columbia University Press, 2004).

Cohen, Edward S., *The Politics of Globalization in the United States* (Washington, D.C.: Georgetown University Press, 2001).

Dakshina Murthy, K.S., 'Rajkumar and Kannada Nationalism,' *Economic & Political Weekly*, vol. 41, no. 19 (May 13–19, 2006), pp. 1834–5.

Friedman, Thomas L., *The World is Flat: A Brief History of the Twenty-First Century* (New York: Farrar, Straus, and Giroux, 2006).

———, *The Lexus and the Olive Tree* (New York: Farrar, Straus and Giroux, 1999).

Guha, Ramachandra, *India After Gandhi* (New York: Ecco, 2007).

Hannerz, Ulf, 'Cosmopolitans and locals in world culture,' in Featherstone, Mike (ed), *Global Culture* (London: Sage Publications, 1990), pp. 237–51.

Held, David, *Democracy and the Global Order: From the Modern State to Cosmopolitan Governance* (Stanford: Stanford University Press, 1995).

Hodgson, Naomi, 'Educational research, governmentality and the construction of the cosmopolitan citizen,' *Ethics and Education*, Vol. 4, No. 2 (2009), pp. 177–87.

Honig, Bonnie, 'Comments: Law and Politics in the New Europe,' in Benhabib, Seyla (ed), *Another Cosmopolitanism* (New York: Oxford University Press, 2006), pp. 102–27.

House, Juliane, 'English as a Lingua Franca: A Threat to Multilingualism?,' *Journal of Sociolinguistics*, vol. 7, no 4 (2003), pp. 556–78.

Ilaiah, Kancha, 'English Empowers,' excerpted from What Kind Of Education Do Dalit-Bahujan Children Need? [Originally published in *Tehelka*, May 5, 2007, vol. 4, issue 17, pg 13], *Dalit Freedom Network* (May 2, 2007), http://www.dalitnetwork.org/go?/dfn/blog/C117/ [Accessed June 2, 2009].

Ives, Peter, 'Language and Collective Identity: Theorising Complexity,' in Skenderovic, Damir & Späti, Christina (eds), *Language and Identity Politics* (Oxford: Berghahn Books, forthcoming).

———, 'Cosmopolitanism and Global English: Language Politics in Globalisation Debates,' *Political Studies*, 58 (2009), pp. 516–35.

Jalais, Annu, *Forest of Tigers: People, Politics and Environment in the Sundarbans* (New Delhi: Routledge, 2010).

Jani, Pranav, *Decentering Rushdie: Cosmopolitanism and the Indian Novel in English* (Hyderabad: Orient Blackswan, 2010).

Jenkins, *English as a Lingua Franca: Attitude and Identity* (Oxford: Oxford University Press, 2007).

Kachru, Braj B., *The Other Tongue: English across Cultures* (Urbana: University of Illinois Press, 1992).

Kumar, Krishna, 'Foul Contract,' *Seminar* 377, (January 1991), pp. 43–6.

Mukherjee, Meenakshi, *Elusive Terrain: Culture and Literary Memory* (New Delhi: OUP, 2008).

Nair, Janaki, 'Language and the Right to the City,' in Sarangi, Asha (ed), *Language and Politics in India*, (New Delhi: OUP, 2009), pp. 368–415.

Nilekani, Nandan, *Imagining India: The Idea of a Renewed Nation* (New York: Penguin, 2008).

'No coercion on medium of instruction, rules HC,' *The Times of India* (Bangalore: 3 July 2008), p. 1.

Pollock, Sheldon, Homi K. Bhabha, Carol Breckenridge & Dipesh Chakravarty, 'Cosmopolitanisms,' in Breckenridge, Carol (ed), *Public Culture*, vol. 12, no. 3 (Fall 2000), pp. 557–89.

Pollock, Shledon and Carol Breckenridge, 'In Honor of D.R. Nagaraj,' in Breckenridge, Carol, (ed), *Public Culture*, Vol. 12, No. 3 (Fall 2000), p. xiv.

Rai, Alok, *Hindi Nationalism* (Hyderabad: Orient Longman, 2000).

Raghu, K. 'Economy and Politics: Neglected English gets a leg-up in Karnataka' (June 2007). http://www.livemint.com/2007/06/12003014/Neglected-English-gets-a-legu.html [From: owner-lgpolicy-list@ccat.sas.upenn.edu on behalf of Harold Schiffman [hfsclpp@gmail.com]; sent: Wednesday, June 13, 2007 7:00 AM].

Robbins, Bruce, 'Introduction Part I: Actually Existing Cosmopolitanism,' in Cheah, Pheng & Robbins, Bruce (eds), *Cosmopolitics* (Minneapolis: University of Minnesota Press, 1998), pp. 1–19.

Satchidanandan, K., 'Indian Literature: Singular or Plural,' invited lecture at CIIL (Central Institute of Indian Languages), Mysore, Karnataka, 16 July 2008.

Sonntag, Selma K., 'La diversité linguistique et la mondialisation: Les limites des théories liberales,' *Politique et Sociétés*, vol. 29, no. 1 (2010), pp. 15–43.

————, 'Narratives of Globalization in Language Politics in India,' in Ricento, Thomas (ed), *Language Policy and Political Economy: English in a Global Context* (Oxford: Oxford University Press, forthcoming).

Srinivasaraju, Sugata, *Keeping Faith with the Mother Tongue: The Anxieties of a Local Culture* (Bangalore: Navakarnataka, 2008).

Stilz, Anna, 'Civic Nationalism and Language Policy,' *Philosophy and Public Affairs*, vol. 37, no. 3 (Summer 2009), pp. 257–92.

Tharakeshwar, V.B., 'Competing Imaginations: Language and Anti-colonial Nationalism in India', in Sarangi, A. & Pai, S., (eds), *Interrogating Reorganisation of States: Culture, Identity and Politics in India* (New Delhi: Routledge, 2011), pp. 190–208.

14 Carving Out a Region Beyond Religious Violence in Partition Narratives

Prachi Gurjarpadhye

The inheritance of loss that the partition of the Indian subcontinent into India and Pakistan in 1947 entailed, has deepened rather than faded across the span of three generations that separates us from the event. Our collective imagination has sought to revert repeatedly to the trauma of Partition throughout these sixty and odd years. A continuing legacy of communal politics in the Indian subcontinent is perhaps the single most compelling reason why it is so. In a way, the partition has been a collective psychosis and it is as if for over sixty years now, a number of writers and scholars have felt the need to reconnect with the experience of the Partition to analyse what exactly went wrong then and why it keeps going wrong periodically in our social-psychological life.

I will use a slight detour here. In his essay 'Photographs of Agony' John Berger (1991, pp. 41–4) makes an interesting observation about how war photographs in newspapers are received by the readers. He points out that the moments of agony captured in such photographs do not merely bring into our lives a representation of reality that supposedly arouses concern. In fact, contrary to our expectations and assumptions, the very nature of this mode of representation prevents it from having the impact it is supposed to have. The fact that the photographs are 'utterly discontinuous with normal time' (Berger 1991, p. 43) makes the reader's experience of that moment of agony qualitatively very different from that of the people who witnessed it in real time as part of the event and is bound to be a compromised experience. This discontinuity makes the readers receive those images, especially when they appear in publications that otherwise continue to support the ideologies behind the war, with a sense of their own moral inadequacy which, when experienced, is as shocking as that of the perpetrators of that violence. Berger says the reader either:

> ...shrugs off this sense of inadequacy as being only too familiar, or else he thinks of performing a kind of penance–of which the purest example would be to make a contribution to OXFAM or to UNICEF.
>
> In both cases, the issue of the war which has caused that moment is effectively depoliticised. The picture becomes evidence of the general human condition. It accuses nobody and everybody (Berger 1991, p. 44).

The processes of such depoliticization and erasure at the level of sign, especially the degeneration into an overstretched, universalized narrative in which nobody and everybody is implicated are not at all unique to war photography but can be seen at work in all modes of representation in different measure. Indeed, in the postmodern hyper-real world of today, we experience the same disconnect when we witness those events in real time on TV or even as they happen in front of us on the street.

Berger's perceptive observation, however, can be an interesting entry point to use when one looks at the representation of religious violence in the Partition narratives. A predominant ploy used in these narratives to achieve the same kind of rupture in the flow of time that Berger notes, is to surround the narrative with a discourse of madness; to suggest that there is no rational and cogent explanation possible of what happened in the aftermath of the partition. People had lost their ability to think and feel and it was an unfortunate aberration and nothing more than that (Saint 2010, pp. 245–6).

A wide range of creative works in English, Hindi, Urdu, Punjabi, Sindhi, Bangla, and so on, translations of these works into other languages and a sustained scholarly-critical discussion of these texts cumulatively bring to us a fairly complex reading of the representational dynamics of the Partition. This chapter begins with a proposition to re-chart the saturated field of the critical discussions of the partition narratives with a simple question: what role does the critical intellect play in the imaginative engagement with violence that indeed got characterized time and again as 'madness'? Do creative writers also draw on the resources of the Reason when they give shape to this collective trauma?

I have selected three texts: one from each of the three generations that followed the event of Partition, to work out a tentative answer: the short stories of Manto, written between 1947 and 1955 (which is when he died); the novel *Tamas* witten in 1973 when the memories of Rawalpindi during the partition were triggered in Sahni's mind by his visit to the riot-hit area of Bhiwandi in 1970 and the film *Khamosh Pani* made by the Sindhi Pakistani filmmaker Sabiha Sumar in 2003, but set in 1979 Pakistan when General Zia had initiated a process of Islamization in Pakistan. The texts that I have selected for analysis here are to be seen as only arbitrarily selected samples, and since I am neither a partition scholar, and nor can I say I have read extensively on partition, my intention here is limited to simply drawing attention to an aspect of fictive partition narratives that seems to have been underappreciated so far. While memory and post-memory are undoubtedly very important categories to deploy when one is grappling with the need to understand how the religious violence of the days of the partition is assimilated by a culture through creative expression, I have approached that problem here by tracing the presence of a critical gaze in these exercises. An analytical intervention seeking to offer a reconstruction of the processes that led up to the massive religious violence witnessed during the partition is an important strand of the body of creative works dealing with the partition and here I shall try to explore the strategies that were used in such works to escape the predicament of depoliticization by default.

Creative writers of great calibre have deployed a number of distinctly identifiable techniques to bypass this problem of the discontinuity of their narrative with normal time and to urge the readers to commit to a progressive politics in a non-superficial way. The best creative representation of the partition seems to achieve this task by finding ways of drawing the reader into the continuity of time that surrounded episodes of violence, into the event and into the moral and political lapses, embedded in the flowing time, from which the violence emanated. In a very significant contrast to many other fictional representations of the partition, such texts do not dwell on the arbitrariness of the incidents that escalated into a conflagration nor do they take recourse to plain unmediated description. Rather, they seem to carefully construct a model of the social processes that culminate into religious violence. It is as if, they seem to say, if we are to avoid repeating history, let's closely pay attention to knowing what exactly happened. It is very remarkable that none of these texts flinch from fixing the sources of communalism, they seem keen on stating firmly their findings so as to almost clinically establish a diagnosis of events that others seemed to think were nebulous.

I am going to try to show here that this critical mode of representing, re-constructing the partition in such creative works has offered us a more nuanced reading of the event than was possible within the available dominant epistemological frameworks at the time of the partition. Creative treatment of religious violence in these texts is 'creative' not so much because it uses fiction but because it seeks to reinvent categories of thought and moral frameworks of judgment that seemed to have simply collapsed.

A not-so arbitrary coincidence perhaps, is that all three writers of these texts straddle two worlds, all three have parts of their personal histories on both sides of the border and it doesn't take them much effort to see clearly with their two eyes what others seem to see with a split vision, so to say.

I would also like to press the point that the progressively broadening range of formal expression that we can see in these three selections, starting with the cryptic short stories of Manto that work like quick, blinding flashes, going on to a sustained canvass of the novel in *Tamas* and finally growing into the richly layered semiotic text that cinema can be in *Khamosh Pani*, is also paralleled by a progression from the comic to the tragic and finally to the *shanta rasa* or silence that transcends all modes of expression. I am tempted to argue, at least tentatively, that there is a continuity between the insights of Manto's short stories and a more richly unfolding narrative of *Khamosh Pani*. With each successive text more thought, more analysis, more detailed study has gone into the creative work. I shall try to show that across three generations a critical, (psycho)analytical treatment of religious violence has evolved, grown increasingly refined and nuanced, and has developed a rich acumen of creative form to bring home those analyses.

MANTO: CARVING OUT A CRITICAL REGION BEYOND

In order to bring out this specific aspect in Manto's writing I'll take up 'Toba Tek Singh', 'Khol Do' (trans. as 'the Return') and 'Thanda Gosht' (trans. as 'Colder than Ice', Manto, 1997), three best known stories of

Manto, on partition—stories that have already been analysed by several scholars in many ways for other purposes. All three stories are structured in such a way, with layered points of view, that the reader is ultimately taken to an epistemological plane from where the interconnections between violence and a complex emotional logic that fuels it or feeds into it and is impacted by it becomes clear to the reader. It allows the reader a critical vantage point from where to appreciate, render comprehensible the mystery of religious violence.

I need to dwell here briefly on the point that more than the extremely nuanced forms of witnessing that Manto deploys in his stories we need to perhaps better appreciate his insistence on extending them into an act of judging. Veena Das and Ashis Nandy have analysed with great appreciation the range of techniques used by Manto to give shape to the experience of collective violence that is essentially beyond what can be represented (Das 1986, p. 190–4). Tarun Saint too, has sensitively identified literary devices in Manto's short stories such as the 'atypical witness figures…that allow glimpses into the nature of extreme situations to which different responses might be possible' or 'fragmentary witnessing…that allows recognition of fallibility.' (Saint 2010, p. 245–6) I would like to suggest that the readings of Das and Nandy as well as of Saint, refined as they are, do not quite do justice to the fact that Manto also sought to be judgmental, albeit, to improvise upon Manto's own claim to greatness[1], judgmental in a way only God would be. I would like to argue that his exceptional empathy and imagination also eventually lead the readers on towards a critical framework from which to make sense of what is being represented and that his narrative structures betray that urge to be partisan.

Manto seems to deliberately encourage the reader to take a clear critical stand by orchestrating the narrative frameworks, especially points of view, in his stories in such a way so as to enable the reader to have heard the witnesses and then by taking him to a point from where he/she cannot avoid the responsibility to pass a judgment. If a judgment imposes an interpretive framework on the data, testimonies, submissions made, in Manto's story-telling one can distinctly feel this intention of imposing an interpretive framework onto the material presented to the reader. Manto nudges the reader—who is also a reader of the powerful grand narratives of the day and who carries the discursive texts of

nationalism, jingoism, religiosity, and so on within himself/herself—
Manto nudges him towards sifting through these available texts/dis-
courses—towards discounting them as grossly inadequate and to pass
fresh judgments on the events around. Manto deliberately carves out
locations in his stories from where a clearer, non-deluded, non-evasive,
and judicious assessment of history as it unfolded would be possible.

While 'Khol Do' and 'Thanda Gosht' are about direct physical violence, 'Toba Tek Singh' deals with internal violation of identity. Bishan
Singh, the protagonist of 'Toba Tek Singh' dies on a 'bit of earth that has
no name' (Manto, 1997, p. 10). Another lunatic in the same story
declares from the top of a tree, 'I wish to live neither in India nor in
Pakistan. I wish to live in this tree.' (Manto 1997, p. 3) Thematically of
course these are metaphors for a maddening quest for a space beyond
the oppressive choices life forces upon you. Narratologically, however,
something more is happening within the structure of the narrative. We
note that as the reader, one doesn't quite identify with these two characters and the structure of the narrative makes little effort to invoke one's
sympathy for them—indeed Manto seems to stand among the sane,
normal people and narrate the story in the only language they understand when talking about mad people, the language of the comic.
Curiously, however, as readers, we find we cannot laugh with him. We
find a third space opening up for us, from where the humour of the sane
world and the desperation of the lunatic world both seem equally
remote. The narrative of 'Toba Tek Singh' seems to work by opening up
this third space for the reader beyond the categories of sanity and insanity, so to say.

It is not enough to say that Bishan Singh is a witness, or that the
narrator who recounts the story without any interpretation, in the casual
tone of a bystander, is a witness. It is more important within the structure of the story that the reader has to examine the witnesses and pass a
judgment. In 'Toba Tek Singh', the verdict is of the absurdity of the
logic of partition and its summary rejection as the only sane response to
partition. With an insight as keen as that of Kafka or Samuel Becket into
the human psyche Manto puts a nonsensical line in Bishan Singh's
mouth: '*Uper the gur gur the annexe the mung the dal of Guruji da
Khalsa...*' (Manto 1997, p. 7). Bishan Singh's perspective from where
the sanity of the world outside the asylum appears like insanity is also a
perspective not accessible through cogent language. By attributing the

senseless words to the character of Bishan Singh, Manto seems to suggest that there is a gulf between the readers from the so-called sane world and the wisdom of Bishan Singh that no language can bear you across. As if we now do not have the language to be able to think wisdom. Manto's critique therefore, cannot be simplistically reduced to a humanistic critique of the partition.

In *Siyah Hashiye* (1948), too one comes across several stories that deploy this well-honed technique of placing the reader in a point-of-view position that transcends all the other points of view within the narrative. Readers of Manto will recognize that most of his stories are carefully structured to gradually lead the reader to such a frame. He seems to have found it a specially suited device to talk about the imponderable when writing about Partition violence.

To briefly outline the technique, using terms of narratology, one could say that this standard narrative technique, a trope, uses the point of view of the outsider to off-set the dominant points of view that the readers will identify with most naturally and which also continue to dominate the surface level of the text. The outsider could be a lunatic, an invalid, a convert, a prostitute, a transgender, and so on. The point of view of such an outsider is left hanging out, as possibly invalid, indeed is sometimes actively discounted by the other points of view within the narrative as suspect, absurd, wrong, ridiculous, or evil and the reader is kept suspended between the two planes of perspectives. The narrative however, in its course, unambiguously undermines the dominant points of view without ever really validating the outsider's point of view and this creates a sense of un-ease in the narrative. Simply by disallowing the reader the comfort of having common-sense, of knowing the regular from the odd, the right from the wrong, the valid from the invalid, and the pure from the impure, the narrative sets up for the reader an imperative to take up a critical position. The closure of the narrative ultimately rests on the reader arriving at a higher, third plane of perspective from which a rethinking of important categories of thought available to the reader becomes imperative. The witnesses and their testimonies—while they indeed are fallible, Manto never fails in placing the reader in a point of view position that has to be critical in a very sophisticated way, that has to discount crude frames of reference—of morality, of the notions of purity, nationality, etc. in order to arrive at a judgment. But judge he must.

To put it in a nutshell, this narrative technique brings out the blind spots, the fault-lines of the mainstream discourses of nationalism and religion to put the reader in direct touch, as it were, with the complexity of lived day-to-day reality and to force upon him/her a newer, more nuanced epistemology.

'Khol Do' is among several other stories of Manto's that make a similarly deft use of perspectives that reveal the gaps between reality and the partial knowledge available to the characters, leaving it to the reader to own up to reality. In 'Khol Do' along with the storyline there also develops a horrifying vision of the trusting blindness of filial love. As Sakina opens the *salwar*, the reader is torn between the blind vision of the father, the delusion of his happiness at finding her alive, and the clinical vision of the doctor who is horrified to see the starkness of facts. The knowledge that is revealed to the reader, however, is more blinding, more stark because the reader sees what none of the characters in the story sees: that the predatory world of political reality is just at the back-door, a step away from the civilized, humane spheres of the domestic or the professional world.

Sakina, in 'Khol Do' is merely an object, an inert site on which the men have played out their desires. Many depictions of the violated body of a woman in Manto leave us with a debilitating realization of the complete negation of their being that has taken place. Yet, Manto's empathy is not reserved only for the victim. There is no permanent damnation status in Manto's world. In 'Thanda Gosht' Manto boldly places the reader behind the eyes of a rapist. Boldly, the story opens a psychological dimension that would seem inaccessible. Here, as in many other stories, Manto traces the links between violence and an interior world of the mind. The micro-scoping of violence on a large scale to the site of individual sexuality is a particularly fascinating aspect of Manto's work. The anatomy of violence that Manto presents deliberately links the large-scale political realities to the micro-world of the individual's sexuality and desire.

In showing us the rapist as a lover who futilely tries to make love, Manto takes us into the psychological abyss that is left after one has seen oneself as less than human. Ishwar Singh's loss of his manhood is really his loss of the ability to love as a human being. His 'failure to perform' is a result of the dying of desire as he has known it in his meaningful and passionate relationship with Kulwant before the ghastly incident in his life. That ability to desire and to make love has died down in him as he has witnessed a bestial lust within himself that is capable of invading a corpse. The only way he can find redemption is now in confession and in death. As a human being he has died already. It is in his confession before his death that he reclaims his humanity. Kulwant Kaur's rage at being betrayed, her insistence that Ishwar Singh owes her an answer even as he lay dying and the finality of the punishment that she gives him are not to be taken at the literal level. I think Manto presents Kulwant as a symbolic representation of the moral critical intellect, that is exacting, demanding, uncompromising—from where all meaning-making of human existence springs and to which Ishwar Singh finally surrenders.

I argue that Manto, ironically, a writer who was sued for obscenity, builds an exacting moral framework through his stories—a framework that can do better than assign the phenomenon of partition violence to 'madness'. It is a framework that seeks to pass a judgment. In 'Khol Do', the verdict is of assigning guilt to hypocrisy, lust and exploitation within 'us', within the community rather than to the 'Other'. In 'Thanda Gosht' the verdict is of the need to see violence as emanating from the bestiality within us—and ultimately our being answerable to the humanity within us—as there being no escape from the moment of seeing our own guilt, confessing, and facing our own death.

Manto's stories eschew sentiment, adopt a harsh, embittered cynical tone, at times, of black humour. It is remarkable that Mantoesque style is emblazoned by a searing sense of humour. It is indeed laughter that can restore sanity to a world in which humaneness itself had come apart. Manto had the boldness to take his contemporary audience beyond the land of trauma, beyond the borders of unspeakable grief and tragedy. He sought to skip the age-old remedy of time that allows a slow healing process of reconciling oneself to loss and of understanding one's mistakes by churning out stories that would force a society to begin to come to terms with its own repressions, by beginning to 'know' itself.

To my mind, Manto's greatness is in giving form to the processes of self-analysis when it seemed too soon to do it. Political discourse, historical, and scholarly discourse of this generation fell woefully short of such a task but the humble short story could fill that vacuum and fulfil that need. An articulate barrister such as Gandhi could do no better than hang the spectre of his own death—Gandhi practically converted his person into a symbol of sanity and humanity—to make people 'see', to make them 'understand'.[2] It was amazing that at such a time, Manto sits by the wayside and unleashes powerful tornadoes on a society that had ceased to think, that had lost the ability to think. His writing is designed to force people to stop in their tracks and to make them re-think all their categories. He knew better than offering solutions—he knew he cannot live anybody's life for him and he did not spare his generation. He made them ask the right questions so that they could arrive at their own answers and begin to see sense. Manto's stories seem to administer little doses of sanity and create possibilities of sanity through their critical gaze.

TAMAS: A DYSTOPIA, OFFSET BY A UTOPIA

While laughter and a wry cynicism point to that region of critical thought beyond in Manto's short stories, in Bhishm Sahni's *Tamas* (Sahni, 2011) the shooting pain of the earlier era morphs into a dull sustained ache for which the tragic novel offers a form. *Tamas* too has its share of humour with its function of sarcasm, irony, etc, but it does not gloss over the sharpness and the depth of the pain. It seems to allow it to spread evenly across a wide canvass.

It needs to be said that *Tamas* is a flawed text in many ways. It does not have the sharpness of Manto. Several flaws such as its Dickensian theatricality, excessive coincidences, improbability of episodes such as the one in which Milkhi is ruthlessly kicked from behind by Shahnawaz certainly bring down the artistic merit of the text. Murad Ali the shadow-like villain floating around mysteriously whose motives are never known fails to give a convincing shape to the interpretation of evil. A particu-larly marring feature is the romanticization of the life of the poor: women who are perfectly womanly, wives who are epitomes of understanding and empathy, who would not eat before the husbands feature with regu-larity throughout the novel. Moreover, the poorer the people the more perfect seem to be their marriages. Nathu's relationship with his wife and Banto's relationship with Harnam Singh typify this trait in Sahni. Upper class marriages are, however, generally flawed because of disempowered and frustrated wives and ideologically misled husbands. The list of the drawbacks of the text can go on but in general, it does flesh out the themes that Manto had articulated in the previous generation.

Indeed *Tamas* could be seen as a synthesized re-working of Manto. Several characters and episodes in *Tamas* are reminiscent of Manto. The tremendous impact that religious imagination has on people, the defeat of a naïve idealism, the thrall under which the colonizers held the natives, the vulnerability of the weak, and the cowardice of the perpetrators of the violence, the interconnections between class-location and ideological positioning, between gender and violence, practicalities involved in having to deal with the mammoth scale of the violence—everything that Manto evokes is taken up and woven into the rich quilt of *Tamas*.

If we were to list the positive qualities that *Tamas* adds to the representation of partition, aspects which Manto could not bring to his writing we will have to acknowledge that the sheer ethnographic detail makes the socialist realism of *Tamas* engaging. The inconsistencies, paradoxes, moral, and emotional compromises of day-to-day life and the knottiness of all these gradually builds before us an image of a complex social fabric with all its grainy reality. Nuances of caste practices, superstitions, or community beliefs, individual trajectories in personal histories, local variations of the business-politics nexus, the age-old plain ethos of individual localities and communities, and the thickly organic life of their members—everything goes into the making of the canvass of *Tamas*. The rich graininess, thickness of the narrative of *Tamas* serves to re-create the sense of a flowing time with myriad possibilities. *Tamas* does not sound teleological in spite of its artificiality because of this detailing.

I would like to take up for analysis one episode in the novel where the narrative succeeds in drawing the reader into its live moment. It is the episode in which the Sikh refugee couple Banto and Harnam Singh take refuge in the house of Ehsan Ali, who is away at the moment looting their shop and burning down their house (Sahni 2011, pp. 227–43). Sahni's strategy is to not just present a dialogic interplay of perspectives but also, more interestingly, to show the extent of the common ground that actually sustains the humaneness of the interaction that takes place in this scene. It is a rich scene. Taking place in the house of a Muslim, on the Muslim turf, we still sense how thickly their lives are interwoven and how many codes they share. They share the linguistic, regional and social codes that make communication between them symbolically much deeper than would be possible in a rarified model where these specificities would not be taken account of. The dialogues in Punjabi, gestures such as Banto sitting down on the ground beside

Rajo as she made the cow-dung cakes, the offering of the buttermilk and its acceptance, at the level of phatic communication, underline the commonality. Especially when we read the text in Hindi the richness of the organic life that sustains the humanitarianism comes home to us very strongly.

A very interesting feature of *Tamas* is its charting of class-consciousness as an alternative and more real paradigm. Class-identity is that unacknowledged dimension beyond the dimension of religion and ethnicity that influences the inflections of violence. Shahnavaz's generous, expansive treatment of the Hindu members of his own social class changes when he is dealing with the servant class. A different value system seems to come into play in dealing with each social class. Servants are not only exploited, they are sacrificed actively and their lives are less important than property. They are entrusted with the task of guarding houses and property at grave risk to their own person and no effort is expended to save their lives when they do land in trouble. All servants are faithful, though, and helpless victims of this class logic. Despite the bourgeois romanticism that afflicts Sahni's portrayal of class dynamics, it is a valuable contribution to the representation of social dynamics that contribute to religious violence.

Another significant feature in *Tamas* is a positive depiction of religion. Religion is not just mass-hysteria. It is also a tool of meaning-making. For Banto-Harnam and for Rajo, it is their private, individual interpretations of religion that seem to give them that dignity, sanity, strength to sustain others that is eroded so quickly on the larger public sphere. The secularism of *Tamas* is not the politically cautious secularism that avoids all religious symbolism. It is a secularism that derives from a progressive interpretation of religion and offers a possible model.

Religion is not the only source from which courage can be drawn. Any ideology, when faithfully followed, seems to offer that courage of conviction. Bakshiji the Congressman's action of bravely intervening to remove the dead pig from the steps of the mosque, Devdatt, the Communist's equally brave efforts to mobilize the forces of peace in troubled times, Jeeto's sensitivity in offering refuge to Harnam and Banto, Jernail's uncompromising commitment to Gandhian ideals are instances in *Tamas* of desirable models of behaviour and faith in humanitarianism. These are the islands of peace that unfortunately cannot take the rest of the society with them but they do seem to offer the reader a concrete anchor in a narrative that otherwise is about the pitch dark night of a political dystopia.

KHAMOSH PANI: REJECTION AS REDEMPTION

The film *Khamosh Paani* made by Sabiha Sumar (Sumar, 2003) gives another shape to this metaphor of a higher plane, a new moral space that opens to the viewer. The protagonist of the film is Ayesha who has lived as a Muslim convert in the village of Charkhi in Pakistan from where her father and other male members of her Sikh family escaped to India at the time of partition, after forcing their women to commit suicide in the village well to protect their honour. Veero, then a young girl refuses to jump into the well, escapes from her own men to fall into the hands of the 'enemy', from among whom, ironically, a young man marries her and with whom as Ayesha after conversion, she has a son who is now eighteen. After all these years her brother comes as a Sikh pilgrim to look for her, traces her, and asks her to come back home with him because her old father is on his deathbed and wants to see her once so that he can die in peace. Veero-Ayesha is shaken but very clear when without any hesitation she asks her brother to return without her to India. She makes a firm choice, 'Now this is my life, this is my house.'

What is remarkable is that it is a clearly thought out choice that comes easily to her not so much because she is loyal to her present social setting but because she has correctly put her finger on her erasure by her supposedly 'real' family and 'real' religion. She has a rational question for her brother:

'For what? Does he want to complete what did not happen at that time? Is he not yet happy after killing mother and Jeeto? The old man wants to die in peace. Back then he wanted to kill me for his own peace.... Now, what will happen if he sees me alive? Alive, and a Muslim! What heaven is left for *me*? Sikh or Muslim?... For so many years you have been happy after killing me. But I was alive. I made my own life without you all. Now this is my life, and this is my house.'

As one can imagine this little incident in Ayesha's life, however, does not remain a secret in the village of Charkhi. Soon people hear about it and the village youngsters are up in arms against men who come in the

garb of pilgrims and accost their women. Ayesha herself suddenly
becomes suspect, her loyalties are questioned and to associate with her
seems undesirable in the claustrophobic social world of the village, even
to people closest to her. The woman who fetches water for her every day
from the village well so that Ayesha can avoid the painful memories of
her past suddenly stops her services. Her close friend and neighbour,
Meena, with whom she shares a rich relationship of sharing housework,
doing the daily chores together, sharing the good and bad events of the
family, including resolving her tiffs with her husband, asks her not to
come for her daughter's wedding. Soon the carefully built world of
Ayesha comes apart. The worst blow, however, yet again, comes not
from outsiders but from one of her own blood, this time her son, Salim.
And yet again, the blow comes in the form of the dictates of religion—
religion, as men understand it.

The film's perceptive reading of a patriarchal social structure that
dehumanizes women by reducing them to either menial labourers and
to pieces of property is persistently carried over into an assessment of
patriarchy's allied institution of religion as well. *Khamosh Pani* draws
very strong links between the culture of masculinity and politicized religion. Religion acquires the same menacing colours of patriarchal social
structures that work to humiliate, intimidate, and subjugate women,
especially when it is deployed to whip up cheap popular sentiments by
the male political establishment. The film is set in 1979 when Zia Ul
Haq's regime was spreading Islamist fervour among the people of
Pakistan. Her son, Salim, a young inexperienced, dreamy and emotional
lad, gets swept off his feet in no time by the promise of glory in the great
cause of Jihad. In his own personal quest for a masculine identity, an
identity that is independent of the two demanding and strong-minded
women who seem to dominate his world: his mother and his girlfriend
Zubeida, Salim turns to a group of male friends who introduce him to
the adventures of public life, going to the city, participating in political
activism, making speeches which people listen to with rapt attention,
playing with pistols, all these things fill the great vacuum of his life. He
feels important, grown up, wiser, and stronger—like a regular man of
the world who can put his women in their place.

Ayesha's story comes full circle when Salim begins to assert himself
as the man of the house. He feels he doesn't have to answer her questions

about where he has been or what he has been up to, let alone listen to Ayesha's directives about whom to befriend and whom not to befriend. Soon he begins to decide whether Ayesha can send food to the camp of the Sikh pilgrims or not. It is a shame for him when he discovers that his mother's brother is a Sikh and that she is not a 'true' Muslim, after all. In order to rescue his promising career as a man of politics, Salim asks his mother to publicly declare that she has got nothing to do with the *kafir*s, with men from the enemy country who have come to spy on their women.

Ayesha, once again refuses to bend. She cannot go to India where her men whose religion taught them to kill her to save their honour reside, and she cannot live in Pakistan where her son, whose religion wants her to bend to an aggressive form of cultural politics, resides. Ayesha this time chooses the village well. The silent waters of the village well envelop her rebellion, now permanently silenced.

Yet, for the viewers the film opens up a new ground from which to judge the events of Ayesha's life. Two very brief scenes from the film do it eloquently. In one scene Zubeida, grown tired of the immaturity of Salim has gone her own way. She moves to a city and lives as an independent single woman who is building a life for herself. On her way to work or college, one day, she happens to catch some TV footage in a shop, in which Salim, now a politician, is making a speech about the age-old true traditions of Islam that need to be reinforced in modern Pakistan. Zubeida smiles pitifully and moves on. The film ends with that gesture as a verdict.

The other scene is an interesting composition where the reader witnesses the hostile expressions on the faces of Salim's fundamentalist friends as they overhear a conversation between Ayesha and a few small girls who come to study the Koran at her place in the evening. The conversation is like this:

1st girl: 'Aunty will all go to heaven?'

2nd Girl: 'Fool, heaven is only for the Muslim.'

Ayesha: 'No dear, whoever will do good deeds, he will go to heaven. God knows what is in our heart and he forgives whomever he wants.'

The scene in which Ayesha jumps into the well is a fleeting scene, bereft of all drama, shot in a long shot and preceded by another brief

234 THE WEIGHT OF VIOLENCE

shot that shows her praying on her mat peacefully as a devout Muslim. Ayesha's religion is the true Islam, an Islam that does what every religion is supposed to do: it salvages human dignity and offers refuge and succour. I think the film makes a point about the strength that religion gives to Ayesha. Her suicide is not presented as her defeat. It is her willed and deliberate rejection of a world that is beyond redemption. Throughout the film Ayesha exudes a quiet strength and her Islam is indeed her ally in her lone battle.

The entire suicide sequence is shot in semi-darkness, emphasizing the silence of the night and of perhaps the early dawn when the suicide is committed. Indeed the prominent impression that the film leaves us with is of silence, of being silenced. In retrospect one begins to strongly feel the presence of silence throughout the film. It is silence with which women seem to deal with the aggression they meet with in their daily life. At very critical points they seem powerless, unable to argue their point, unable to put into words what they can see and understand so clearly and what the viewers can so clearly see and understand through their intense eyes. Even when they do state what they think clearly, out of sheer desperation, they do it all too briefly. They are unable to repeat, insist, argue. In more than one instance, the men they talk to, use physical aggression to intimidate them and to shut them up.

This enforced silence, a denial of speech, of language to women and the final silence that Ayesha embraces of the water in the well, is really the theme of the film. The most intense moments in the film are without words. Ayesha's story is not told as an individual's plight. The film keeps pointing to the larger malaise that breeds this silence. By locating the reader behind the eyes of these silent women, the film opens a critical field for the viewer from where an unambiguous politics can be unravelled. As a creative text this film is not talking about the chaotic madness of religious violence. It is offering the reader a clearly etched logical sequence in which gendered patterns of aggression and violence in personal lives increase manifold and develop into the raging flames of communal violence.

John Berger's acute observation (1991) about the depoliticization of texts about violence is in fact an insurmountable challenge for authors that seek to represent that which has taken place outside the very realm of meaning. In Manto's story-telling, in a comparatively dreamy *Tamas*, and in a suave twenty-first century text such as *Khamosh Pani*, there is a fascinating resistance to such depolitization and what is truly surprising is that they all do it without drifting too far off from realism.

At the beginning of the chapter I had used the word shanta rasa in connection with *Khamosh Pani*. It may seem a bit too far-fetched that such a term from Sanskrit aesthetics, a term that refers to the ninth rasa envisioned by Abhinavgupta as representing the highest aesthetic experience should be applied to a film that offers a radical critique of society. It may seem that such an application may take away from the radicality of the film and in fact subject it to the very same depoliticization that it is trying to escape. I would like to draw your attention, here, to the sense of complete reconciliation and spiritual peace with which Ayesha embraces the end of her life. If she ends her own life, she ends it without any bitterness and having fought it out with all her strength. If she does not accept any easy compromises, it speaks for the intense moral dignity and sovereignty that she appropriates for herself when the entire world has closed in upon her. In her last act of praying, one feels sure, she is praying neither for revenge nor for forgiveness. A world in which such prayers would obtain is not for her. She chooses to leave it all behind as if to enter another state of being, a new life. Ayesha leaves—not for the land of forgiveness, not for the land of reconciliation—but for that notional land of redemption that, in fact, all narratives that talk about violence dream of.

Notes

1. Manto wrote his own epitaph: 'Here lies Saadat Hasan Manto. With him lie buried all the arts and mysteries of short story writing. Under tons of earth he lies, wondering if he is a greater short story writer than God' (Manto, 1987, p. 10).

2. Scholars have often associated Gandhi's death with his active though ineffectual questioning of the political logic that led to communal violence and Partiton: see Saint (2010, p. 11) and Mahajan (2012).

References

Berger, John, 'Photographs of Agony', in *About Looking* (New York: Vintage, 1991).

Das, Veena and Ashis Nandy, 'Violence, Victimhood and the Language of Silence', in Veena Das (ed), *The Word and the World* (New Delhi: Sage, 1986).

Mahajan, Sucheta, 'Why Gandhi Accepted the Decision to Partition India', in Kaushik Roy (ed), *Partition of India: Why 1947? Debates in Indian History and Society* (New Delhi: Oxford University Press, 2012).

Manto, Saadat Hasan, *Mottled Dawn: Fifty Sketches and Stories of Partition*, trans. Khalid Hasan (New Delhi: Penguin, 1997).

Manto, Saadat Hasan, *Kingdom's End and Other Stories*, trans. Khalid Hasan (New Delhi: Penguin, 1987).

Sahni, Bhisham, *Tamas* (New Delhi: Rajkamal Prakashan, 2011).

Saint, Tarun K., *Witnessing Partition: Memory, History, Fiction* (NewDelhi: Routledge, 2010).

Sumar, Sabiha, dir., writers Sabiha Sumar, Paromita Vora, *Silent Waters: Khamosh Pani*, 2003.

15 Conflict as a Site for Perpetuation of Traditional Values

Veena Sharma

We are not a people of yesterday.... against all the destruction some yet remained among us unforgetful of origins, dreaming secret dreams, seeing secret visions, hearing secret voices of our purpose.
—Ayi Kwei Armah, *Two Thousand Seasons* (1973)

Accepted as an inevitable part of life, conflict played, and continues to play, an important role in the transmission and perpetuation of cultural and ethical values in African Traditional Religion (ATR). Conflict, as such, was an eruption that was even desirable. Besides, we can say that, in post—colonial Africa conflict and its resolution has proved to be a site for the instatement of history and culture as the African negotiates the damage caused by the denial of history and culture to the African by the European—a cultural and intellectual violence that was necessary for the justification of the colonial project. Conflict in post-colonial Africa has thus, become a site for revisiting and critically evaluating the past to 'develop new conceptual paradigms' (Kigongo 2011, p. 2) and, we might add, for proposing an alternative humanitarian framework, which may be seen as Africa's contribution to world civilization. Ali Mazrui states:

The present world culture is Eurocentric, the next world culture is unlikely to be Afrocentric, even if that were desirable. The best solution is therefore a more culturally balanced world civilization. That is the burden of the next generation, not to provide an alternative hegemony, but to provide a new balance. (Mazrui 2002, p. 26)

Africa, as the mother of the human species may fulfil this role by drawing on its past. This need to draw from the past is what has caused the popularity and importance of the Akan (Ghanaian) symbol *Sankofa*, which means 'go back and get it'—referring to retrieving values from tradition. It often stands alongside the other symbol *Nwe Mu Dua* which signifies critical evaluation.

Critical evaluation becomes more urgent in view of what Kaphagawani and Malherbe label as 'the C^4 factor': the Contemporary Confluence of Cultures on the Continent' (2003, p. 222). This post colonial situation in which different cultures are juxtaposed has a double edged impact—one, that it threatens the distinct identity of a particular culture, but, second, it can also enable the discarding of 'outworn practices and ideas, taking what...[it] need[s] from other cultures to adapt to changing circumstances' (Kaphagawani and Malherbe 2003).

Before taking up the issue of conflict as a site for instatement of traditional values the essay clarifies, in the first segment, what is meant by the term ATR. In the second segment it elaborates on the ethics and morality implicit in it. In the third segment it deals with how this world-view comes to be propagated in conflict situations. The fourth segment shows how these values are used for healing the scars of violence caused by conflict situations and also for proposing an alternative framework for negotiating violence and conflict. The essay shows how a number of countries across Africa have drawn upon and are continuing to draw upon similar values, in differing situations, to bring back a semblance of peace and harmony into their societies.

AFRICAN TRADITIONAL RELIGION (ATR)

The term 'African' (rather than the name of a particular country in Africa) has been used, even by Africans themselves, to express phenomena that arise from and relate to the Continent. Even the origins of the movement for equality and independence started with the construction of a Pan-African identity calling for the liberation of 'Africa'. The movement did not make distinctions between countries or nations as geographic or political entities. It addressed the Continent of Africa and the African people. As such there must be certain elements or characteristics that give credence to the word 'African'. Is it colour or race? Is it the common history of colonization—a 'gift of Europe' as Ali Mazrui called it (Mazrui, 2002, p. 37)—that almost the whole continent suffered? Is it culture? Or is it some spiritual or metaphysical beliefs? What is it that connects Africa, particularly Africa south of the Sahara? What is Africa and Africainity?

Kwame Nkrumah the first President of Ghana, a great promoter of the Pan-African identity wrote that in spite of the great differences between Africans from different parts of the Continent the forces that united them were greater. He wrote:

In meeting fellow Africans from all parts of the continent I am constantly impressed by how much we have in common. It is not just our colonial past, or the fact that we have aims in common, it is something which goes far deeper. I can best describe it as a sense of one-ness in that we are *Africans*. (Nkrumah, 1964, p. 132)

Despite his impassioned plea for and a belief in an African identity Nkrumah did not identify what he meant by that 'something...deeper.' Ali Mazrui proposes that one of the factors that unites Africans may be European cartography that by determining the boundaries of Africa made Africans look upon themselves as one in relation to the Europeans (Mazrui 2002, p. 38–9). At a symposium in Wellesley College, Julius Nyerere of Tanzania, had emphasized that 'the sentiment of Africa,' the sense of fellowship between Africans, was 'something which came from outside' (quoted in Mazrui 2002, p. 46). Though 'bequeathed without grace or design,' this sense of identity was a reality nonetheless. While the colonial history may refer to the Continent as a whole (including North Africa) our present purpose is to deal with Africa South of Sahara only.

Notwithstanding the colonial impact—which nevertheless brought changes greater than Africa had undergone in millennia—there is something more that by and large connects sub-Saharan Africans. Many reasons are extended for this. The cross-Continental migration due to the 'population explosion' caused by better varieties of food and due to better tools and weapons after the coming in of the iron-age during the middle of the first millennium B.C., affected an intermingling of peoples across 'western and central Sahara,... and the regions of the Niger River' right down to the southern tip of Africa (Davidson 1964, pp. 12–3). This movement brought about a 'diversity that is nonetheless rooted in a profound and ancient unity...Pan-African unity [as such] is a political ambition of modern times, but its roots go far back into the past.' (Davidson 1964, p. 13).

While different migrant groups evolved their different socio-economic patterns and rituals according to the geographic and climatic
situations at hand, there yet remains, at a fundamental level, a world
view that connects Africa. Kwame Gyekye writes:

> I believe that in many areas of thought we can discern features of the traditional
> life and thought of the African peoples sufficiently common to constitute a
> legitimate and reasonable basis for the construction (or reconstruction) of a
> philosophical system that may properly be called African–African not in the
> sense that every African adheres to it, but in the sense that that philosophical
> system arises from, and hence is essentially related to, African life and thought
> (Gyekye 1995, pp. 187–212.)

Mogobe Ramose bases this oneness in the concept of *Ubuntu* which
he sees as the wellspring of both ontology and epistemology in Sub-
Saharan African philosophies (Ramose 2003, p. 230). The concept
popularized by South Africa as it was seen to be the basis of the Truth
and Reconciliation Commission in post apartheid era, is discussed later.

Some essential features that underlie most Sub-Saharan African religious and metaphysical concepts may be listed as (1) the belief in one
god that is both transcendent and immanent. (2) This God is worshipped
through a number of tutelary deities as He permeates all that exists and
there is no cult of directly worshipping this Supreme God. (3) Everything
in this world view is 'inspirited' by virtue of its being imbued with a force
which arises from one singular source and for that reason enables one
thing to be connected to and act on another (Minkus 1980, p. 182). (4)
Belief in God and spiritual beings implies a moral order, a 'conduct that
respects the order established by God and watched over by divinities and
the ancestors. At the centre of traditional African morality is human life.'
(Onah n.d., p. 4) Life is the greatest gift of God and it is sacred.

AFRICAN ETHICS AND MORALITY

The ethical values prized by Africans are encapsulated in the ultimate
goal upheld by ATR. The ultimate objective upheld by the African
world-view is explicated in its conception of the metaphysical origin of
the human person. Conceived in religious/spiritual terms the human
being is not viewed through theoretical, conceptual categories only, but
is visualized through the prism of concrete day to day situations in
which he enacts and unfolds his life. An Akan proverb, which states
'when a person descends from heaven he descends into a human town'

(*onipa firi soro besi a, obesi onipa kuro*) (Gyekye 1995, p. 155; Danquah 1968, p. 193, no. 2380) stresses the idea of a pre-existing 'human town', created by God, and the consequent social nature of the person. As an already existing reality whose nature and origin is known only to God, the universe is seen to be without beginning or end, as it continues to exist as long as God exists, which is forever. The maxim *Gye Nyame*, meaning 'except God', i.e., none except God, knows its reality, crystallizes and confirms this belief.

The human, as a part of the great spiritual process of creation and, by the very nature of his origin and composition, remains actively involved in keeping up the integrity, order and social harmony, as also the well being and cohesion of the community at both the social and cosmological levels, i.e., between humans and humans, and humans and ancestors, and the spirits[1] (Opoku 1978, p. 7). The individual, thus, does not remain a unitary, disparate, or alienated entity but irrevocably becomes a part of this organically connected universe in which there is a high degree of interdependence between the different elements. This entry into a situation of 'natural relationality' places certain duties on the person. A code of conduct that conforms to certain norms for the upkeep of the universe becomes a necessity, as descent into a human town 'immediately plunges him/her into a moral universe, making morality an essentially social and trans-individual phenomenon focused on the well being of *others*' (Gbadegesin 1998, p. 332). Morality here is, thus, 'weighted by obligations and duties' (*Stanford Encyclopaedia*) as he is involved in obligations and responsibility for the perpetuation and welfare of clan right from the beginning (Gbadegesin 1998, p. 332). Ronald Green stresses the same point when he contends that 'Africans live in a morally saturated religious universe. Theirs' is a world in which all really significant interpersonal relationships...have moral content and are governed by moral considerations.' (Green 1983, p. 5). Referring to the sociality of the African person, James Kigongo states,

African ethics places considerable value on conformity of the individual to the social group in order to preserve the unity of human relationship.... The support of others was more important than one's capacity to achieve one's existential ends–hence the value of corporate existence... (Kigongo 2011, p. 3)

Just as, he states, 'the individual had to look after the well-being of others' so too, 'the others had to look after the well-being of the individual, i.e., the responsibility of many for one' (Kigongo 2011 , p. 3).

John Mbiti has stated that it is only in terms of other people that the individual is conscious of his own being. 'I am because we are, and since we are, therefore I am.' He goes on to state that this is 'a morality of "conduct" rather than a morality of being' (Quoted in Kigongo 2011, p. 3), which means that one's relationships and conduct in the social sphere dictate one's sense of morality. This is contrasted to a morality in which 'the individual's sense of self, autonomy, or being...does not place much value on...social relationships.' The stress here is on the 'social self' (Kigongo 2011, p. 3).

The Akan (Ghana) word for the human person, *Onipa*, is made up of two words—*oni* meaning human and *pa* meaning goodness. Goodness is encapsulated within the understanding of the human person. It 'embodies ethical presuppositions' (*Stanford Encyclopaedia*) that refer to an ideal that the person is expected to aspire for. It conveys a possibility of 'becoming', of transforming himself into a moral being, a human person. Participation in communal life and discharge of obligations defined by one's station in the community enables an individual to attain personhood, the ultimate aim of life (Pobee 1976, p. 8). The descriptive connotation posited by the word *oni*, on the other hand, gives an irrevocable, unalterable, existential status to the person, a status that cannot be taken away. Both connotations of the person are given due weightage.

So when a person is seen to be falling short of the ideal, or behaviour, or displaying a conduct that is contrary to social, communal good, (*Stanford Encyclopaedia*) the existential status of the person, as a human creature, is not denied. He continues to command rights and privileges by dint of his status as a human being. This is because one of the constituent elements of the human 'comes *directly* from God'. The human, as Kwasi Wiredu states, is 'a speck of the divine substance. This is the life principle. [Hence the proverb]... all human beings are the children of God; none is a child of the earth' (Wiredu 2003, p. 289). A human being *ought* to be helped because he is part of the same organic whole and arises from the same source as oneself and because every being makes up the whole (*Stanford Encyclopaedia*).

Similarly, in Yoruba metaphysics the word *iwa* stands for both existence and character. 'Existence is primary... [while] character is derivative, based as it is, on human ideas of morality. Each creature of *Olodumare* is thought of as having its beauty... by the fact of its existence, and it is not to be undermined by human evaluation,' writes Gbadegesin (1998, p. 139). He goes on to state that the:

Yoruba expression '*Iwa l'ewa*' depicts their understanding of existence itself as constituting beauty, while the cognate expression '*Iwa rere l'eso eniyan*' (Good character–good existence–is the adornment of a human being) depicts the significance attached to good character.... [E]xistence in virtue of its source in the deity, is good and to be appreciated...Existence itself is beautiful. But however beautiful a thing is, there is always room for improvement...' (Gbadegesin 1998, p. 139)

Gbadegesin goes on to quote a proverb which states 'we do not throw a child to the tiger just because he/she is bad.'

In a similar context Mogobe Ramose deconstructs the word *Ubuntu*.

Ubuntu is actually two words in one. It consists of the prefix *ubu-* and the stem-*ntu*. *Ubu-*evokes the idea of be-ing in general. It is enfolded be-ing before it manifests itself in the concrete form or mode of ex-istence of a particular entity. At the ontological level there is no strict and literal separation between *ubu-* and -*ntu*. [they are] not two radically separate and irreconcilably opposed realities. (Ramose 2003, p. 230)

Stressing the normative and ethical aspects of *Ubuntu*, Ramose goes on to state that the word is both a gerund and a 'gerundive' because one, 'is enjoined, yes, commanded as it were, to actually *become* a human being. What is decisive then is to prove oneself to be the embodiment of *ubu-ntu* because the fundamental ethical, social, and legal judgement of human worth and conduct is based upon *ubu-ntu*' (Ramose 2003, p. 230).

One may, thus, say that onipa, iwe, and ubuntu—concepts arising in different parts of Africa—connote the same metaphysical and ethical reality.

The communitarian outlook of the social whole that arises in an organically unified universe created by God, enjoins a person to live harmoniously and enhance the solidarity of the group. An act is wrong if it fails to develop the community. 'What is right is what connects people together; what separates people is wrong' 'The right builds up society; the wrong tears it down.' (McVeigh) Bishop Desmond Tutu states: 'Harmony, friendliness, community are the great goods. Social harmony is for us the *summum bonum*—the greatest good. Anything that subverts or undermines this sought after good is to be avoided...' (Quoted in Metz 2007).

Highlighting the contextual nature of this morality, while contrasting the concept of *Ubuntu* with Western ethics as a basis for constructing a universal morality, Thaddeus Metz writes, 'Focussing on relationship, as opposed to just personal self-development, presents an interesting contrast to what is dominant in Western ethics and in any event better coheres with firm moral judgements about when, how and why to help others' (Metz 2007, p. 324). African ethics is communitarian as against individualistic.

Interestingly, the communitarian framework gives a higher status to the individual as a human being than perhaps would be the case in some other systems of morality. Reconciliation of individual interests for the welfare of the larger whole is an important element of African ethics. This conception enjoins that opinions of all humans be accommodated. African village life is known for long drawn out discussions for arriving upon a consensus. Ideas of majority and minority have little place in a framework in which all individuals must be carried along. Discussions go on till those who do not share the opinion of the many agree to give up theirs in the interest of harmony.

Drawing from the fundamental tenets of Ubuntu philosophy Metz, through a *negative formulation*, lays down what for Africans would be *uncontroversially immoral*. We refer to some of those which suit our present purpose:

1.   To make policy decisions in the face of dissent, as opposed to seeking consensus (Metz 2007, p. 324). Every voice is given a hearing, as opinions of all humans need to be accommodated. The idea is 'to harmonise...warring interests through systematic adjustment and adaptation' (Wiredu 2003, p. 309). While individual opinions are valued and they may differ, yet in the interest of the larger whole personal opinions are held back in the interest of harmony of the whole—eventually the dissenting voice agrees to disagree.

2.   To make retribution a fundamental and central aim of criminal justice, as opposed to seeking reconciliation (Metz 2007, p. 325). Driberg confirms the same when, talking about the concepts of restitution and reparation in traditional jurisprudence, he says that African law is based on a maintenance of the equilibrium, that it is a code of positive rules rather than of negative prohibitions. Justice in ATR is restorative rather than punitive or vindictive, expecting a good result of some kind

for all rather than just punishing a singular individual. Penalty would be directed only towards a readjustment of the status quo—the harmony of the group. That is why, Driberg says, under native law a thief so often goes unpunished. If theft is committed, material equilibrium has been impaired; but if restitution is made there is nothing more to be done (Driberg 1934, p. 233). It is reconciliation and not retribution that is the fundamental and central aim of criminal justice (Metz 2007, p. 326). A crime of murder, for instance, could lead to the creation of a bond of marriage between the victim's family and that of the accused—by the giving of one person from the offending group, in addition to the perpetrator being punished both inside and outside his social circles.

Corporate morality also exhorts that wealth does not belong to the individual alone, it calls for being shared with others, so that no one remains needy. But an important point to be noted here is that the sharing as also moral and legal injunctions apply only within the clan or the extended family. Another Akan artistic symbol which shows the lizard and the crocodile having the same stomach, so that if one eats, the other also should get a morsel, highlights this fact as the monitor lizard and crocodile are regarded as being of the same clan. Reaffirming this fact Driberg states that:

African traditional law does not recognize non-tribalists. To achieve tribal status every tribesman has to submit to certain rites and ceremonies which entitle him to the privileges of the tribe. One who is not a member of the tribe and has not undergone those ceremonies... has not the status which would give him legal recognition.' (Driberg 1934, p. 230)

To get recognition by the law they must belong to the same 'cultural inheritance'. As such, the conception of a law that extends beyond the community is lacking in African traditional law. John Mbiti also sees traditional African religions having the drawback of remaining 'tribal and nationalistic' (Mbiti 1971, p. 99).

Conflict and propagation of Traditional Values

Conflicts in indigenous African societies were, and are, often generated by violations of religious or metaphysical norms that tend to create a dissonance between the human and the spiritual which in turn causes social dis-harmony. They arise from a transgression of the moral or metaphysical order causing structural violence to the social whole. As such, peace in African tradition is conceived 'not in relation to conflict and war, but in relation to order, harmony and equilibrium.' It is not, Godfrey Onah writes, 'an abstract poetic concept, but rather a down-to-earth and practical concept... Peace is, thus, both a religious and a moral value' (Onah n.d., p. 5).

When this world runs its normal and satisfying course, Africans may or may not engage in religious activity. But if this course is disturbed, as it invariably is, Africans seek an explanation in terms of their morally comprehensible spiritual beliefs (Green 1983 p. 6). It is in times of conflict that Africans look back to tradition in order to find solutions, as strategies are built into the traditional system for conflict resolution.

Since traditional African metaphysics and religion are not postulated systematically as a 'series of coherent and logically related propositions,' they are propagated through 'pragmatically worked out system...[of] the day-to-day living of the people' (Ackah 1988, p. 20). In such situations it is the proverbs, linguistic formulations, symbols, religious rituals, and practices, and the statements of wise persons that have an impact on the 'shaping and controlling human behaviour, individual and social; in co-ordinating the systems of law and morality; and in providing the sanction for social organization and co-operative enterprise' (Clarke 1930, p. 434).

Kasongo writes that in the traditional African society, the absence of Westerntype of library justified the development of storytelling techniques that circulate the large number of myths, legends, and oral history that characterizes the process of education and socialization. These, most of the time, are used as public policy or rule of wisdom in resolving social conflicts (Kasongo 2010, p. 316).

Similarly with regard to the role of Tswana legal maxims I. Schapera states, that:

in Tswana law we must remember that in pre-European days the Tswana were a non-literate people. Consequently the only way in which legal rules could be formulated was orally; and in order to be passed on the wording necessarily had to be both brief and unambiguous. Moreover, it is usually only through hearing them quoted as occasion arises that people become familiar with them; and such occasions were of course most likely to occur in the course of a trial, or when men sitting round the *kgotla* fire subsequently talked over the issues that had been raised. Hence, as Tswana also say, *Ngwana wamosimanem olao ootsaya kgotleng*, 'A boy derives his (knowledge of the) law from the council-place'. (Schapera 1966, p. 132)

Proverbs, which contain the grammar of African morality, do not arise without a problem to suggest one. Christensen, while studying the Fante proverbs, cites the example of one elder who explained this difficulty by quoting another proverb which says 'there is no proverb without the situation'. Their ability to remember proverbs seemed to be greater during conversation or in a contest than when discussing them in abstraction, or just theoretically (Christensen 1958, p. 232). Proverbs, he states, resort to indirection rather than reprimand. (Christsensen 1958, p. 234) He cites the example of a person charged with maintaining decorum at a Fante court. When tempers rose he could restore order by use of a proverb. He would announce, 'Some must inform the sea to stop being rough so that the coconut branches may stop rustling,'—an example of how the African prefers indirection to a direct reprimand. It is this elegance of speech that created another maxim which state 'proverbs are the palm oil with which words are eaten.'

The Fante, when discussing custom and tradition, constantly emphasize a statement by quoting an appropriate maxim. They become aids for engendering the ideal norms of behaviour, and may be taken as the verbalization of customary law (Christsensen 1958, p. 242). In Tiv culture, proverbs are employed in a variety of situations: to control activities without the use of force, as devices for shaming, for getting out of difficult situations without losing face, as a means of praise, in prophetic utterances, and as general explanations for that sphere of environment which is beyond comprehension, especially illness or 'acts of God'. The injection of the parable into an unpleasant situation immediately signals to the opponent and onlookers that an end is sought to the dispute. It is used as a non-cowardly reminder that things have reached an impasse and must be resolved (Bergsma 1970, p. 155).

Anyone who knows more proverbs is at an advantage. The Anang among the Ibo, as John Messenger says, have been given their name by their neighbours, as the term denoting 'ability to speak wittily yet meaningfully upon any occasion,' and not a little of Anang eloquence, admired by Africans and Europeans alike, stems from their skilful use of maxims (Messenger 1959, p. 64).

VIOLENCE, HEALING AND ETHICAL VALUES

In the post-colonial situation conflict has become the site for reinstate-
ment of the violated values and history of the African and for the projection of an alternative, reconciliatory, and inclusive, mode of resolving
the imbalances and injustices caused by the colonizer.

Helena Cobban undertook a study of three countries—Rwanda,
Mozambique, and South Africa—during the period of 1990s. All of
them 'bore extremely deep scars from the preceding violence; and in
each...the national leadership chose a very distinct set of policies in
order to deal with... those painful legacies from the past' she writes.
(Cobban 2005, p. 1126). In Rwanda she found that the new government on coming into power initially adopted a policy of *criminal pros-
ecutions* that accorded with their own desires and those of the leading
actors in the U.N. By 1997–98 they found that they had 130,000
people mainly of breadwinning age, each with six or seven dependents,
out of a population of 7 or 8 million, incarcerated in crowded stinking
prisons affecting the economy most adversely. So, in 1998 the govt
'decided to move most of these cases out of the regular system and send
them to a revitalized form of a traditional community-based hearing
mechanism called *gacaca*' (Cobban 2005, p. 1127). Rwanda was one of
the countries where the traditional system of governance and maintenance of order had become almost extinct due to the policies adopted by
the colonial powers and due to the extermination of millions of people.
Yet that system was thought to be more beneficial for the maintenance
of human dignity and for the practical reasons of keeping up the economy in a better shape.

In Mozambique the seventeen year long civil war, incited by the
erstwhile ruling powers and the apartheid regimes in South Africa and
Rhodesia, was brought to an end in October 1992 (Cobban 2005, p.
1129). But, in Mozambique, she writes, there was the 'survival of many,
many very significant indigenous cultural resources, including indigenous religion' (Cobban 2005, p. 1133). The Portuguese in Mozambique
'did not push their influence very far inland. They did not push huge
populations of Portuguese...settlers onto the land there...for most of
their time...they...left the indigenous people alone' (Cobban 2005). As
in other parts of Africa in Mozambique too, the concept of the 'self' 'is
intimately bound up in the web of relationships that that self has with
extended family, with the homestead, with the ancestors who are buried

there, and with the spirit world in which these ancestors belong'
(Cobban 2005, p. 1133). The Mozambicans had many robust indigenous cultural resources on which they were able to draw. Those played a
crucial role in helping them withstand the rigours and privations of
those wars. The traditional healers still had many practices, spells, rituals, medicines, and other interventions that they could use to heal both
individual spirits that had been wounded by war as also the social rifts
that had been caused by the war (Cobban 2005).

As such, former child soldiers who had been forced by military
commanders to commit atrocities against their own home village:

Were taken back into the village communities and speedily have their community membership reinstated… after going through the necessary rituals that
aimed at spiritual cleansing of the individual and affecting his reconnection
with the ancestors and the rest of his rightful world. (Cobban 2005, p. 1134)

Cobban did not find the people there burdened with a feeling of
vengeance. Many of her interviewees said that 'according to their world
view 'violence' is an anti-human force that can sometimes hold people
in its grip and from which the person or persons have to be rescued if
they are to be restored to their full status of humanity' (Cobban 2005,
p. 1135). This resonates with the idea of the possibility of transformation of the human from a mere existential creature to a human person.

In South Africa during 1990–94, some 25 million people were:

struggling to find a way to emerge from the forty-plus years of apartheid and the
preceding four centuries of brutal colonial violence…. one of the most conten-
tious issues throughout… was the question of what to do about individuals who
had planned and perpetrated the horrors of apartheid and how to deal with
their beneficiaries. (Cobban 2005, p. 1127)

Several forces in the international community and within SA 'called
for the perpetrators of the crime of apartheid to be tried and punished *a
la* Nuremberg.' Finally it was decided, for many reasons (which undoubtedly also had political and economic ramifications and content), that
some form of amnesty would be available 'in the interests of national
reconciliation' (Cobban 2005, p. 1128). The Truth and Reconciliation
Commission required that those who applied for amnesty satisfy the
commission.

About all the rights-abusing actions they had been a part of during the apartheid era. The deal was amnesty for truth-telling… The…high level public
acknowledging of the 'truth' about what happened to the victims of the

apartheid-era atrocities was seen... as a constructive act that could contribute to national reconciliation in a number of ways.

The act helped to:

1. restore the humanity and dignity of those who had been horribly tortured;
2. provide concrete details about the location of the bodies murdered victims that had been buried or dumped in secret places. The retrieval of the bodies and their tradition-ordained reburial could help put their wandering and tortured spirits finally to rest; and
3. establish an incontestable historical record of just how the perversions of thought (including religious thought) had allowed the rulers to visit such lengthy and brutal train of suffering on their fellow-men. (Cobban 2005, pp. 1128–9)

Cobban refers to the Anglican Archbishop Desmond Tutu, who would open the sessions with a prayer and by lighting candles. She narrates how, though belonging to a Christian religious order Bishop Tutu.

Considerably enriched and broadened the 'theological' underpinnings of the TRC's work by making frequent references to the indigenously African concept of *ubuntu*—... which Tutu defines as the ideal that a 'person is human inasmuch as he or she recognizes the humanity of others.' (Cobban 2005, p. 1131)

Here we find a pragmatic stretching of the concept of ubuntu to include non-tribals to suit the situation and in the interest of harmony and reconciliation of the existing whole. This extension of the traditional world view to include outsiders (which initially tended to exclude them) may be contrasted to the restrictive interpretation of Aristotle by the European colonisers which as Mogobe Ramose states, came to be used to justify 'conquest and slavery on the other side of the meridian line' (Ramose 2003, p. 607). He writes,

Before the start of the voyages of discovery, Aristotle's definition of man as a rational animal was deeply rooted in the European culture. When the voyagers met other human-like animals, they refused to attribute rationality to them. Aristotle's definition was given a restrictive interpretation. (Ramose 2003)

The stretching of traditional values to include others who now constituted the new nation and formed a part of the social whole is where a critical re-evaluation of African tradition has proved to be Africa's contribution to world civilization.

Cobban quotes Chris Hedges as arguing that 'War is a force that gives us meaning.' As against this she argues that what gives meaning to 'the lives of people living through traumatic times in not 'war' but religion... different forms of religion can help restore meaning and dignity to human lives' (Cobban 2005, p. 1138). Here we may add that the trauma perpetuated by the ruling powers has often sought to gain the backing of religion, especially religions that sought to prove themselves to be the only civilized ones. But the pragmatism of the Africans has enabled them to revive and extend their traditional religious practices to heal the scars inflicted by that violence and also to include the perpetrators of that violence into the fold of peaceful reconciliation.

While the Fanonion concept of violence was necessary for the overthrow of the colonizer since as he writes in *The Wretched of the Earth* that 'decolonization can only be a violent phenomenon... because the colonial project can only be erased from its deep roots by counter violence... because colonialism itself is violent' (Kiros 2006, p. 221). Yet this philosophically insightful last book of Frantz Fanon ends with a call for a radical humanism which is required for the building of a new nation which, he writes, 'is of necessity accompanied by the discovery and encouragement of universalizing values' (Fanon, quoted in Kiros 2006, p. 223).

The experiment carried out in South Africa shows just that kind of search for 'universalizing values' which aimed at healing both the perpetrator and the victim of violence. While the route of violence may have been necessary to free the country of apartheid yet the new independent country needed the healing spirit that in this case was drawn from the traditional religion to set the country on a new humanitarian course as also show a new way of dealing with violence. The leadership of the new South Africa displayed strength and ingenuity for drawing from tradition. It was Nelson Mandela's

resolute decision to negotiate the terms of the new non-racial democratic South Africa with the apartheid regime (headed by F.W. de Klerk) rather than choose the winner-takes-all, violent revolutionary route, [that] made him, together with de Klerk, a... candidate for the Nobel Peace Prize (More 2006, p. 212).

The ethical values drawn from tradition, and used with an open mind, are proving to be Africa's contribution to world civilization.

Note

1. 'It is the living person who makes the inhabitant of the spirit world long for the mashed yam,' says a proverb stressing the point of interdependence between humans and ancestors. This also connotes that it is the humans that create and sustain the spirits of the dead, which in turn are symbols of the solidarity and perpetuation of the clan.

References

Ackah, C.A., *Akan Ethics* (Accra: Ghana University Press 1988).

Armah, Ayi Kwei, *Two Thousand Seasons* (Maelezo: Dar es Salaam, 1973).

Bascom, William R., 'Verbal Art,' *The Journal of American Folklore*, Vol. 68, No. 269 (Jul–Sep, 1955), pp. 245–52.

Bergsma, Harold M., 'Tiv Proverbs as a Means of Social Control,' *Africa: Journal of the International African Institute*, Vol. 40, No. 2 (Apr, 1970), pp. 151–63.

Christensen, James Boyd, 'The Role of Proverbs in Fante Culture', *Africa: Journal of the International African Institute*, Vol. 28, No. 3 (Jul, 1958), pp. 232–43.

Clarke, Edith, 'The Sociological Significance of Ancestor—Worship in Ashanti,' *Africa: Journal of the International African Institute*, Vo. 3, No. 4, Oct. 1930.

Cobban, Helena, 'Religion and Violence,' *Journal of the Amercian Academy of Religion*, December 2005, Vol 73, No. 4, pp. 1121–39.

Danquah, J. B., *The Akan Doctrine of God: a Fragment of Gold Coast Ethics and Religion* (Frank Cass, London. 1968).

Davidson, Basil, *The African Past: Chronicles from Antiquity to Modern Times* (Longmans, 1964,), p. 11.

Driberg, J.H., 'The African Conception of Law,' *Journal of Comparative Legislation and International Law,* Third Series, Vol. 16, No. 4 (1934), pp. 230–45.

Gbadegesin, Segun, 'Yoruba Philosophy: Individuality, Community, and the Moral Order', in Eze Emmanuel Chukwudi (ed), *African Philosophy, an Anthology* (Blackwell Publishers, 1998).

Green, Ronald M., 'Religion and Morality in the African Traditional Setting,' *Journal of Religion in Africa*, vol. 14, Fasc. 1 (1983).

Gyekye, Kwame, 'Person and Community in African Thought', in Eze, Emmanuel Chukwudi (ed), *African Philosophy: An Anthology* (Blackwell Pulishers U.K., 1998).

Gyekye, Kwame, *An Essay on African Philosophical Thought: The Akan Conceptual Scheme* (Philadelphia: Temple University Press Revised Edition, 1995).

Kaphagawani, Didier N. and Malherbe, Jeanette G., 'African Epistemology,' *The African Philosophy Reader*, Second Edition, Coetzee, P.H., and Roux A.P.J. (New York: Routledge, 2003).

Kasongo, Alphonse, Impact of Globalization on Traditional African Religion and Cultural Conflict, *Journal of Alternative Perspectives in the Social Sciences*, Vol 2, No 1, (2010), pp. 309–22.

Kigongo, James K., 'The Relevance of African Ethics to Contemporary African Society', www.crvp.org/book/Series 02/II——8/Chapter——II.htm, accessed 20.9.2011.

Kiros, Teodros, 'Frantz Fanon (1925–1961),' *A Companion to African Philosophy*, in Kwasi Wiredu (ed), Advisory editors: William E. Abraham, Abiola Irele, and Ifeanyi A. Menkit, (Blackwell Publishing, 2006).

Mazrui, Ali A., *Africanity Redefined: Collected Essays of Ali A.Mazrui*, Vol. 1 (Eritrea: Africa World Press, 2002).

Mbiti, John S., *African Religions and Philosophy* (London: Heinemann [1969], 1971).

Messenger Jr., John C., 'The Role of Proverbs in a Nigerian Judicial System,' *Southwestern Journal of Anthropology*, Vol. 15, No. 1 (Spring, 1959), pp. 64–73.

Metz, Thaddeus, 'Toward an African Moral Theory,' *The Journal of Political Philosophy*, Vol. 15, No. 3 (2007).

Minkus, Helaine, K., 'The Concept of Spirit in Akwapim Akan Philosophy', *Africa: Journal of the International African Institute*, vol. 50, No. 2 (1980).

More, Mabogo P., 'Philosophy in South Africa Under and After Apartheid,' in Kwasi Wiredu (ed), Advisory editors: William E. Abraham, Abiola Irele, and Ifeanyi A. Menkiti *A Companion to African Philosophy* (Blackwell Publishing, 2006).

Nkrumah, Kwame, *Africa Must Unite* (Frederick A. Praeger, reprint, 1964).

Onah, Godfrey, 'The Meaning of Peace in African Traditional Religion and Culture,' Pontifical Urban University, Rome, n.d.

Opoku, Kofi Asare, *Hearing and Keeping: Akan Proverbs* (Accra: Asempa Publishers, Christian Council of Ghana, 1997).

———, *West African Traditional Religion* (Accra: FEP International Pvt. Ltd., 1978).

Pobee, John, 'Aspects of African Traditional Religion,' *Sociological Analysis*, Vol. 37, No.1, (Spring, 1976).

Ramose, Mogobe, 'The Philosophy of Ubuntu and Ubuntu as Philosophy,' in Coetzee P.H. and Roux A.P.J (eds), *The African Philosophy Reader*, Second Edition (New York: Routledge, New York, 2003).

Schapera, I., 'Tswana Legal Maxims,' *Africa: Journal of the International African Institute*, Vol. 36, No. 2 (Apr., 1966), pp. 121–34.

Stanford Encyclopaedia of Philosophy, African Ethics (First Published Thu Sep 9, 2010) www.plato.stanford.edu

Wiredu, Kwesi, 'The Moral Foundations of an African Culture,' *The African Philosophy Reader*, Second Edition, Coetzee, P.H., and Roux A.P.J. (New York: Routledge, 2003).

Index

Editors and Contributors

Gérard Bensussan is one of the most contemporary important philosophers in France. He teaches at University of Strasbourg, France. He is the author of *La Philosophie Allemande dans la Pensée Juive, Franz Rosenzweig: Existence et Philosophie, and Le Temps Messianique: Temps Historique et Temps Vécu.*

Maria João Cantinho was born in Lisbon. She studied philosophy in Lisbon, at the University Nova of Lisbon. She has a PhD in contemporary philosophy, from the University Nova of Lisbon and University Marc Bloch in Strasbourg. Currently she is Professor at IADE (Institute of Visual Arts, Design and Marketing) at Lisbon, Portugal.

Soumyabrata Choudhury is a former fellow at Indian Institute of Advanced Study, Shimla. Currently he teaches at the School of Arts and Aesthetics, Jawaharlal Nehru University, New Delhi. His research interest lies in contemporary critical thought, political theology and contemporary French philosophy.

Clayton Crockett is Associate Professor and Director of Religious Studies at the University of Central Arkansas. He is the author of four books, including *Radical Political Theology: Religion and Politics after Liberalism*, and most recently, *Deleuze Beyond Badiou: Ontology, Multiplicity and Event*, both published by Columbia University Press. He is a co-editor, along with Slavoj Zizek, Creston Davis, and Jeffrey W. Robbins, of the book series In*surrections: Critical Studies in Religion, Politics and Culture,* for Columbia University Press.

Saitya Brata Das was a fellow at Indian Institute of Advanced Study, Shimla from 2009 to 2011. Currently he is Assistant Professor at Centre for English Studies, Jawaharlal Nehru University, New Delhi. He is associated with the UFR Philosophie, Université de Strasbourg, France, and with *Maison des Sciences de L'Homme*, Paris, where he was post doctorate fellow during the academic year 2006–2007. His first book titled *The Promise of Time: Towards a Phenomenology of Promise* has been published from Indian Institute of Advanced Study, India.

John Frow is Professor of English Literature and an ARC Professorial Fellow at the University of Sydney. He is the author of *Cultural Studies and Cultural Value* (1995), *Time and Commodity Culture* (1997), *Accounting for Tastes* (with Tony Bennett and Michael Emmison, 1999), *Genre* (2006; second edition 2015), a collection of essays, *On Literature in Cultural Studies* (2013), and *Character and Person* (2014). He co-edited *Australian Cultural Studies: A Reader* (1993) with Meaghan Morris, and with Tony Bennett *The Sage Handbook of Cultural Analysis* (2008).

Mike Grimshaw is Associate Professor, Sociology, University of Canterbury, New Zealand. Perhaps best described as a secular theologian and critical theorist, he has written widely on religion/theology as hermeneutics expressed and experienced as 'the necessary problem' in the project of modernity. Put simply, his approach starts from a view of religion/theology as 'the claim of an alternative' that takes various forms and expressions, including culture, society and politics. He is one of the editors of the series *Radical Theologies* (Palgrave Macmillan)

Prachi Gurjarpadhye has formerly been a Fellow of the Indian Institute of Advanced Study, Shimla. Her monograph titled *Bringing Modernity Home: Marathi Literary Theory in the Nineteenth Century,* was published in 2014; it draws on the methodologies of the two disciplines of comparative literature and culture studies and seeks to locate the emergence of literary theory in Marathi in the context of the cultural processes of colonization. Prachi's doctoral thesis on a comparative analysis of Western and Marathi literary theory was accepted by Mumbai University in 2004. She teaches English at Jai Hind College, Mumbai.

Aïcha Liviana Messina is Associate Professor of Philosophy at Universidad Diego Portales (Chile). She has studied philosophy and literature in Paris and Strasbourg. She's the author of *Poser me va si bien* (P.O.L, 2005) and of a recent essay on Marx called *L'amour. Les manuscrits de 1844.* She has mainly published on Blanchot, Derrida, Kafka, Lévinas, and Nietzsche.

Andrea Potestà is Professor of Philosophy at the Pontificia Universidad Católica de Chile in Santiago, Chile. He has received a PhD in Philosophy from the University of Parma (Italy) and from the University of Strasbourg (France). He has taught at the University of Strasbourg (France), University of Metz (France), and University of Chile (Chile). He is the author of a book in Italian on Kant (*La "Pragmatica" di Kant*, Milano: Franco Angeli, 2004), a book in French on Plato (*Voyages à Syracuse*, Paris: Phocide/Portique, 2009), and several articles on Heidegger and Derrida.

Asha Sarangi is Associate Professor at the Centre for Political Studies, Jawaharlal Nehru University, New Delhi, India. The main areas of her interest are political and cultural economy of development in modern India, state politics in India, and identity and politics in South Asia. She has most recently edited a volume (with Sudha Pai) titled *Interrogating Reorganisation of States: Culture, Identity and Politics in India* (Routledge, 2011). Her other publication is an edited volume, *Language and Politics in India*, published by Oxford University Press, 2009.

Veena Sharma is a former Fellow of the Indian Institute of Advanced Study where she worked on comparing two spiritual traditions–the Advaita Vedantic tradition from India and the Akan from West Africa. Currently she is the Secretary of the Research Committee on Leisure (RC 13) of the International Sociological Association (ISA). Her latest book (co-ed.) *Leisure and Tourism: Cultural Paradigms* was brought out by Rawat Publishers, Jaipur, 2012. Between 1999 and 2005 she was Editor of *Africa Quarterly* brought out by the Indian Council for Cultural Relations (ICCR) and of *Africa Review*, a journal of the African Studies Association of India, respectively.

Rustam Singh has held various research and editorial positions. He is the author of *'Weeping' and Other Essays on Being and Writing* (2011) and *A Story of Political Ideas for Young Readers, Volume 1: Socrates, Plato, Aristotle, Machiavelli* (2010). He has published three collections of poems in Hindi: the most recent collection was brought out by HarperCollins India in 2009. He has translated into Hindi a collection of poems by the Norwegian poet Olav Hauge (2008) and two plays by Henrik Ibsen (2006). His poems have been translated into English, Telugu, Swedish, and Norwegian.

Selma K. Sonntag is a political scientist at Humboldt State University (California, USA). Her recent publications include 'Linguistic Diversity and Globalization: The Limits of Liberal Theories' in *Politique et Sociétés*, and 'The Changing Global-Local Linguistic Landscape in India' in *English Language Education in South Asia*. Dr. Sonntag has received two Fulbright awards: in 2007 as Research Chair in Globalization and Cultural Studies at McMaster University's Institute of Globalization and the Human Condition (Canada), and in 1993–94 for research in India and Nepal. In spring 2012, she was a Visiting Scholar at the Jawaharlal Nehru Institute of Advanced Studies (New Delhi).

Jason M. Wirth teaches philosophy at Seattle University, USA. He is the author of *Conspiracy of Life: Meditations on Schelling and his Time* and translator of Schelling's *Ages of the World*.